WEAPONS OF
MASS
DESTRUCTION

'The attached detailed report concerns the possibility of construct-
ing a 'super-bomb' which utilizes the energy stored in atomic nuclei
as a source of energy. The energy liberated in the explosion of such
a super-bomb is about the same as that produced by the explosion of
1,000 tons of dynamite. This energy is liberated in a small volume,
in which it will, for an instant, produce a temperature comparable to
that in the interior of the sun. The blast from such an explosion
would destroy life in a wide area. The size of this area is difficult to
estimate, but it will probably cover the centre of a big city.

'In addition, some part of the energy set free by the bomb goes to
produce radioactive substances, and these will emit very powerful
and dangerous radiations ...'

THE FRISCH–PEIERLS MEMORANDUM
'On the properties of a radioactive super-bomb', March, 1940.

'Within four months, we shall in all probability have completed the
most terrible weapon ever known in human history, one bomb of
which could destroy a whole city.'

U.S. SECRETARY OF WAR HENRY L STIMSON
in a memorandum to President Truman, informing him of the
atomic bomb's existence, April 25, 1945.

'A few people laughed, a few people cried. Most people were silent.
There floated through my mind, a line from the *Bhagavad-Gita* ... "I
am become death: the destroyer of worlds."'

J. ROBERT OPPENHEIMER, 'father of the atomic bomb',
recalling the first nuclear test explosion, TRINITY, July 16, 1945

'We have got to have this thing over here, whatever it costs. We have
got to have a bloody Union Jack on top of it ... '

BRITISH FOREIGN SECRETARY ERNEST BEVIN,
1946 on the pressing need for a British atomic bomb.

'HAVE JUST COME FROM WRECKAGE OF B-47 WHICH PLOUGHED INTO AN IGLOO IN LAKENHEATH. THE B-47 TORE APART THE IGLOO AND KNOCKED ABOUT 3 MARK SIXES. AIR-CRAFT THEN EXPLODED SHOWERING BURNING FUEL OVERALL. CREW PERISHED.... PRELIMINARY EXAM BY BOMB DISPOSAL OFFICER SAYS A MIRACLE THAT ONE MARK SIX WITH EXPOSED DETONATORS SHEARED DIDN'T GO ...'

> TOP SECRET/OPERATIONAL IMMEDIATE telegram
> from U.S.A.F. GEN JAMES WALSH to Gen. Curtis LeMay,
> Commander-in-chief, Strategic Air Command, after a near
> nuclear weapons accident at Lakenheath, England, July 27, 1956.

'Of all the challenges facing the [U.S.] Department of Defense in the future, none is greater or more complex than the threat posed by weapons of mass destruction.'

> PENTAGON DEFENSE REFORM INITIATIVE REPORT,
> November, 1997

WEAPONS OF MASS DESTRUCTION

The No-Nonsense Guide to Nuclear, Chemical and Biological Weapons Today

ROBERT HUTCHINSON

Weidenfeld & Nicolson

LONDON

Weidenfeld & Nicolson

The Orion Publishing Group Ltd
Orion House
5 Upper Saint Martin's Lane
London WC2H 9EA

British Library Cataloguing-in-Publication Data
A catalogue record for this book is available from
the British Library

ISBN 0-297-83091-0

Distributed in the United States by
Sterling Publishing Co. Inc.
387 Park Avenue South
New York, NY 10016-8810

Printed and bound in Great Britain by
Clays Ltd, St Ives plc

To my beloved wife, Sally

ACKNOWLEDGEMENTS

My grateful thanks are due to a very large number of kind people who have helped in the compilation and writing of this book. In particular, I have a deep obligation to many friends and colleagues in the intelligence and military communities and defence industry around the world for information supplied over the years. For obvious reasons, most would not care to be identified. Open government is alive and well in the United States, but remains only in embryo form in Britain. No doubt there remain many in Whitehall who are determined to see it still-born. That, of course, makes the quest for information more challenging and enjoyable.

The ever courteous and helpful staff at the Public Record Office made the nightmare task of sifting hundreds of documents to find that missing nugget of information considerably easier. It is a constant source of surprise to see what is there now in the public domain and the delight of discovery is always a moment to savour. I am delighted to acknowledge the dogged investigative powers of two former colleagues, Peter Hennessy, once of *The Times*, of London and now Attlee Professor of Contemporary History at Queen Mary College, University of London, and Steve Zaloga, one of the foremost experts on Soviet and now Russian missiles, for their unwitting trail-blazing on my behalf.

Amongst many others, my thanks are also due to Julian Hoad for valuable technical advice in the area of biological weapons and a very old friend, Christopher F. Foss, for his cheerful and willing assistance. Ian Drury, at Weidenfeld & Nicolson, has been a source of constant encouragement and help. Last, but by no means least, my very heartfelt thanks go to my wife Sally, who had to endure, uncomplainingly, long months of my obsessive compilation and writing about the human race's insane drive for self-destruction and willingly provided more assistance than she could ever know. Conversation should now become more cheerful.

CONTENTS

WEAPONS OF MASS DESTRUCTION

INTRODUCTION

I AM A CHILD of the Cold War. Although I was born immediately after the Second World War, the grim detritus of conflict remained all around for years afterwards: derelict bomb sites, anti-aircraft gun emplacements, air-raid shelters. Like millions of others, I grew up beneath the shadows of the terrible mushroom clouds of Hiroshima and Nagasaki; watched anxiously the race to develop and deploy atomic and thermonuclear, or hydrogen, bombs and worried over the environmental impact of the atmospheric weapons tests, culminating in the giant 50 megaton TSAR BOMBA explosion in October 1961 at the Soviet Union's Novaya Zemlya site, a large island in the Barents Sea, 600 miles north of the Arctic Circle.

Finally, of course, there was the nuclear brinkmanship of the Cuban missile crisis in 1962 and the palpable sense of popular relief when the Soviet ships transporting more missiles were turned back on Moscow's orders.

Later, as a journalist writing about defence issues, firstly for the Press Association, the UK national news agency, and latterly for Jane's Information Group, the international purveyor of impartial and authoritative military data, I saw the Cold War close-up at first hand. Two very personal examples, at macro and micro level, illustrate what the Cold War meant on the ground.

In the late 1970s, I was allowed to spend a little time inside the Fylingdales Ballistic Missile Early Warning Site on the North Yorkshire moors, one of the chain of radar stations used by the North American Air Defence Command (NORAD) to warn of impending Armageddon. The radars, hidden inside huge, incongruous white golf ball radar domes, tracked space debris and watched for missile launches from the east, 24 hours a day. The radar arrays moved constantly in unnerving, noisy, jerky movements seemingly animate, like questing hounds, despite all their metal and circuitry.

Inside the command centre, four RAF officers manned the screens, checking what the radars picked up against constantly updated catalogues of known objects in space. Prominently on the wall above them were two display boards that summed up the nightmare of the Cold War. One was headed 'Number of attacking missiles', the other, 'Minutes/seconds to impact'. Those status or tote boards were mirrored in command bunkers across the NATO commands. The watch commander kindly offered to demonstrate what would happen if nuclear deterrence — by then the policy of mutually assured destruction, aptly abbreviated to MAD — had failed and the major nations of the world faced imminent oblivion. After warning NORAD, 8,000 miles away, buried beneath Cheyenne Mountain in Colorado, that this *was* a training exercise, Fylingdales' computers simulated an attack — a 'bolt from the blue' first strike by Soviet SS-11 'Sego' intercontinental ballistic missiles (ICBMs) from the silo fields in the steppes and birch forests of the western Soviet Union. Western intelligence knew that each one was armed with three 350-kiloton (kT) nuclear warheads, independently targeted.

As the klaxons sounded and the RAF team analysed the data indicating the supposed attack, the display board on the wall showed 110 incoming missiles — in strategic terms, a small attack — but the minutes and seconds of life ticked away with mechanical precision. Unstoppable. Implacable. It was hard to keep a grip on reality. Particularly, as one of the officers wryly pointed out, at least one of the missiles had Fylingdales as its target.

Throughout, the RAF officers, like many thousands of their American, Russian, French, and Chinese counterparts, worked assiduously and professionally, in the full knowledge that one day, if diplomacy failed, if there had been a desperate mistake, if a lunatic was seated behind the anonymous desk of power, they had no chance of survival. Indeed, if this was real, they had only minutes to live. It was a chilling and sobering experience.

At the sharp end, I remember the tactical nuclear weapons, with the controls to increase or decrease their yields, jocularly known by the United States Air Force as 'dial a death.'

There was surprise in the West, after the collapse of Communism, when it was confirmed the Soviet armed forces would have had no compunction in immediately using nuclear or chemical weapons in their drive to the Channel Ports in World War Three.

I recall one Russian nuclear planner telling me the Soviets had a plan to detonate tactical nuclear warheads on Denmark immediately after the start of hostilities. 'Why Denmark?' I asked. 'Because,' he said, in a stunning display of Slavic irony, 'they are a nuclear-free zone.' The objective was to demonstrate to NATO the Soviet Union's power and might and raise concerns about the destruction that would be soon heaped upon the European allies. Denmark was clearly expendable, as far as Moscow was concerned.

This was all very strategic. At the micro level, the Cold War manifested itself 24 hours a day just a few yards from where I live, in a small remote village in the country, south of London. My next-door neighbour's home was connected to the UK Warning and Monitoring Organisation (UKMO), the government agency ultimately responsible for informing the public of nuclear weapon bursts and the subsequent spread of radioactive fall-out across the nation. His dedicated telephone line produced a dull tone every few minutes to demonstrate the system was working – the very heartbeat of the Cold War. In the event of an alert, the UKMO would change the pulse into a scream, warning of imminent nuclear attack. Because of the remoteness of our community, well away from sirens or police stations where warning maroons or rockets would be fired, my doughty and public-spirited neighbour would rush out into the square with a hand-cranked siren to inform the village of impending armageddon. What this rural community would do in such circumstances can only be a matter of speculation.

As the elected chairman of the local parish council, the lowest tier of local government in England, I was surprised to learn of my wide sweeping powers in the event of a nuclear attack on Britain. I was very much on the bottom rung of the UK's by then creaky administrative machine to cope with nuclear war. At the top, were the politicians and the senior civil servants in their heavily protected bunker, codenamed TURNSTILE, under the Cotswolds, near Corsham, with a frightening array of powerful weaponry at their disposal – the Royal Navy's missile firing submarines, at least one of which is always patrolling the ocean deeps, ready to unleash Britain's awesome retaliation.

The rules said I had to designate my wartime headquarters – with a

carefully thought out view of such a grim future, I chose the cellars of
the local public house – but discovered afterwards that this only enti-
tled us to priority restoration of a telephone line by British Telecom.
No doubt they would charge special rates. Occasionally, I received
dour confidential documents detailing wartime plans from the Home
Office. These instructed me in the mass burial of the dead ('if possible,
keep records of identifications') and how to set up catering ('construction of field kitchens') for the hungry in the community. I was
told that I was authorised to use 'minimum force' ('we recommend
the use of pickaxe handles') to maintain law and order and to prevent
looting. It all seemed very grim and rather lonely. We would clearly be
on our own to survive.

This all seemed far removed from the rarefied world of government
bunkers or airborne national command posts issuing orders to submarines or silo fields to loose off their missiles in a terrible rain of
destruction. But if, using World War Two parlance, the 'balloon had
gone up,' and nuclear war was visited on this unhappy planet, no one
would have escaped its awful consequences.

This book charts the human race's insane efforts to destroy itself.
The desire to kill dates back to the dawn of man's presence on Earth
and whether we like it or not, it's part of our genes. Scratch our
civilised surface and it remains beneath today. Although some of the
weapon concepts, such as chemical or biological agents, go back a
long way, it was only in the 20th century that we learnt to harness
technology to enable us to kill on a mass scale.

What constitutes a weapon of mass destruction? We are all only too
aware of the horrors of present-day nuclear, biological or chemical
warfare, with their capability to destroy or kill, to create casualty
numbers verging on the astronomic in scale. Despite the end of the
Cold War, those threats remain – in fact, they are worse today because
these weapons may be in the hands of those who have not learnt the
lessons of deterrence, or mutual assured destruction, or ignore the
finesse of diplomacy. The mushroom cloud, the odourless, colourless
vapour of nerve gas or the unseen but nonetheless deadly biological
weapon remains with us, despite countless pages of international
treaties banning them or reducing their numbers.

But the world has moved on in its definition of what is a weapon of
total devastation. Who would have envisaged a civilian airliner, packed
with passengers and high-octane fuel as a potential weapon of carnage

and desolation before the events of September 11, 2001 in New York and Washington? And today, with the growth of international communications and computer technology, a cyber attack on a nation's financial institutions with the subsequent damage to its economy may well be reckoned a weapon of mass destruction.

We remain vulnerable, scaringly so. A report from eminent politicians, statesmen and military leaders commissioned by the US Council of Foreign Relations in October 2002 warned that the USA remains open to a terrorist attack on its nuclear power plants and oil refineries. Only a tiny fraction of the ships and containers entering the 361 commercial ports in America are inspected. How easy would it be for a terrorist group to hide a nuclear device or a chemical or biological weapon inside the blank metal faces of a freight container? Just over 40% of all shipping containers flow through only two ports – Los Angeles and Long Beach, California – and the cost to the US economy of the detonation of a weapon of mass destruction there would 'bring the global container industry to its knees,' says the report.

Even though the Bush Administration has spent hundreds of millions of dollars after September 11 to build the USA's defences against terrorist attack, their mighty nation remains vulnerable to biological attack – particularly through the food chain. Although the American public health system has received $1 billion, much of it being used for plans by individual States to respond to such an incident, the area of protecting crops and livestock remains largely undefended. The Food and Drug Administration doubled the number of its food inspectors to 1,500 in 2002, but the US government remains 'woefully inadequate in this area' according to some experts.

The scourge of weapons of mass destruction will never be removed. All the verification in the world will not eradicate the potential threat of these horrendous weapons. Charles Duelfer, former deputy head of UNSCOM, the weapons inspection team which spent six years trying to discover the location of Iraqi chemical, biological and nuclear weapons, believes the mission is hopeless.

He told a Senate hearing in 2002 that this realisation came to him in 1995 during a late night meeting with Iraqi ministers in Baghdad. In Saddam's view, 'possession of weapons of mass destruction had saved the regime on two occasions.'

The first was during the 1980s first Gulf War with Iran when Iraqi forces halted human wave assaults of Iranian volunteers by firing chemical artillery munitions. UNSCOM was told that more than 100,000 chemical weapons had been fired during the decade-long war. The second time was during DESERT STORM, the Coalition attack on Iraq in 1991, when Saddam's forces were issued with chemical and biological weapons and told to use them if the enemy forces threatened Baghdad.

Subsequently, Washington was convinced that its threat of nuclear attack in response to the use of chemical or biological weapons deterred Saddam Hussein. But the Iraqi leader saw events differently. He believed the Coalition forces did not press on with their attack on Iraq after recapturing Kuwait because of the threat of *his* chemical weapons.

Even if the West destroyed all the weapons of mass destruction held by Iraq, the technology is *known* and could be reinstated within a matter of weeks. As the former British Defence Secretary Francis Pym stated bluntly: 'Nuclear weapons cannot be disinvented.' The same is true of chemical and biological weapons. Iraq *knows* how to build a nuclear weapon but lacks only sufficient fissile material to make one; indeed after the deposing of Saddam, a new Iraqi ruler may be unencumbered by UN sanctions and would find it easier to go down this path.

It may not only be an evil quest for regional power. The motivation to develop such weapons lies all around Iraq. Syria has developed chemical warheads, including nerve agents, for its extended-range Scud missiles. In the east, the traditional foe of Iran is said by western intelligence to be developing its own set of weapons of mass destruction and is certainly building the ballistic missiles to deliver them. Israel has at least 200 nuclear warheads of its own, perhaps more, together with long-range fighter-bombers or ballistic missiles to carry them. Some may reason that it is no surprise that Iraqis, of whatever political persuasion, developed their own deterrent.

This book makes grim reading.

The nervy but peaceful co-existence of the Cold War has given way to a new and dangerous era of uncertainty. But we cannot maintain our guard unless we fully understand the nature of the threat confronting us. As the Chinese general Sun Tzu Wu, born 544BC and author of the *Art of War*, wrote: 'Know thy enemy' – whoever they may be in the first decade of the 21st century. We should also know their weapons and their ability, as well as their motivation, to use them to harm us. I hope this book helps in that cause.

Robert Hutchinson
December 2002

CHAPTER 1
DR STRANGELOVE LIVES!

FICTION HAS AN UNNERVING HABIT of becoming fact. Remember Stanley Kubrick's 1963 film satire on an unintentional, catastrophic nuclear war between the USA and the Soviet Union, *Dr Strangelove*, with its cynical sub-title *How I Learned to Stop Worrying and Love the Bomb*? At the climax of the movie, the grim-faced Russian ambassador to Washington discloses that Moscow possesses a massive 'doomsday' weapon that would be triggered, automatically, by an American nuclear attack, wiping out all life on the planet by a huge cloud of radioactive fall-out spreading over its entire surface. The film ends sombrely, with news footage of atomic and hydrogen bomb tests, towering harbingers of immediate global oblivion.

In reality, the Russians *have* laboriously and expensively developed a similar last resort 'doomsday' system and deploy it to this day. But instead of being a thermonuclear weapon of mass destruction, it is an automatic launch mechanism, ensuring that if Moscow's top leadership is decapitated by an American 'bolt from the blue' nuclear attack, orders for a retaliatory strike will always get through to the missiles. A massive launch of Russian intercontinental ballistic missiles (ICBMs) would be triggered to avenge the destruction of Mother Russia, by obliterating the attacker. Therefore, the term 'doomsday' mechanism seems quite justified.

It's codenamed *Perimetr*, although some in Russia use the more macabre nickname 'the dead hand'.

Its existence was first revealed in the West by the foreign policies scholar Bruce G. Blair of Washington's Brookings Institute in 1993, based on Russian 'sources whose reliability and sincerity had long

been established to my satisfaction'. The West's intelligence community was initially very sceptical, believing Perimetr was mere Russian
disinformation, designed to hoodwink and mislead American strategic
planners. The agencies no longer doubt its existence – or its purpose.

Is the doomsday system really necessary, or is it symptomatic of
the last vestiges of Stalinist paranoia for the overriding need for
absolute state control? In part it is, but there are sound strategic reasons
for its development. Perimetr's origins date back to 1974 when the
Soviet leadership was preoccupied by growing fears that a surprise
US nuclear strike, employing submarine-launched missiles, could
effectively knock out its command and control system. Multiple
layers of redundancy in its authorisation procedures had therefore
to be constructed, in case one or other communications network
was destroyed. Internally, it was also concerned about preventing
accidental or unauthorised launches of nuclear weapons, so it required
true 'failsafe' systems. Coupled with embarking on the Perimetr
programme, they began building a duplicate national command
post, reportedly deep beneath a mountain, as an expensive insur-
ance policy against an enemy attack designed to destroy the Kremlin's
political leaders. With no one left alive to issue the launch authorisation codes, no Russian retaliatory strike could be mounted.
Bang (in every sense of the word) goes the concept of nuclear
deterrence.

It is one of the great ironies of the Cold War that, aside from these
all-pervading fears about vulnerability, it was the same leadership's
simultaneous major diplomatic offensive to destabilise, or indeed dismantle the NATO western alliance that accelerated the deployment
of the doomsday system to protect the integrity of the Soviet Union's
nuclear arsenal.

It is a long and complex story, not without piquancy. In 1976, the
SS-20 (NATO codename 'Saber') intermediate range road mobile
missile entered service with the Soviet rocket forces. Moscow called
the weapon *Pioner* and mounted it on all-terrain vehicles that could
lumber around the Russian countryside and launch the missiles at
short notice. The weapons were thus difficult, if not impossible, to
locate and destroy by existing NATO forces, then comprising land-
based US Air Force F-111 aircraft and the RAF's ageing Vulcan
bombers. These lacked the necessary range, without refuelling, to
reach the SS-20s' operational areas and the strike aircraft were anyway

confronted by the daunting challenge of having to overfly successive layers of improved Russian heavy air defences before they could approach anywhere near the threatening missiles. Not many would survive such a mission. It was almost certain that none could accomplish it successfully. There was no credible NATO response.

Twenty-nine separate locations in the USSR, west of the Ural mountains, were built to house the SS-20s, each one with as many as five operating bases, containing concrete shelters fitted with sliding roofs to allow last-resort, quick-reaction launches. The missile was armed with three independently targeted warheads, each one of 150 kiloton (kT) each – explosive power equivalent to 150,000 tons of TNT. A total of 405 were deployed by 1987. Their 3,000 mile-plus range and increased accuracy meant that almost any target in Western Europe was now within easy reach.

The Kremlin believed that the SS-20 was invulnerable to NATO attack. To its chagrin and frustration, NATO HQ in Brussels believed so too. It was only too obvious that well over 1,000 of the alliance's cities, military and naval bases and airfields in Europe were all now gravely threatened. The key element of NATO's war plan to repel a Soviet invasion – massive reinforcement by US troops and their military hardware – would be swiftly neutralised if the ports and airfields were knocked out by salvoes of 'Pioner' warheads. But there was no intermediate rung in NATO's ladder of deterrence between the strategic nuclear option and its less than adequate conventional forces. It was quickly apparent to those in the know that the balance of power in Europe had suddenly swung in Moscow's favour.

The strategic objective of the SS-20 deployment was all too clear to NATO politicians and planners. It contained unsubtle, intimidating messages to the West. In effect, the Soviets were taunting the Americans with some unspoken but tough questions.

Would Washington dare risk or even contemplate an all-out nuclear exchange if the Soviets used, or threatened to use a weapon that could not possibly reach targets in the USA? Would Washington *really* use strategic nuclear weapons – the only potential military answer to the SS-20 – in defence of its allies? Was Europe *really* worth that terrible risk to the American people and way of life? The Kremlin had driven a ponderous missile vehicle straight through the West's policy of 'flexible response' to nuclear threats. There *was* no flexible response to the SS-20. The Kremlin hoped that the stresses and strains that these implicit

questions raised inside the Western alliance would rock it to its foun-
dations, if not tear it apart.

It was a Cold War gambit worthy of the most cerebral and analytical
of Soviet chess grandmasters. Here was a cynical attempt to *decouple*
the European NATO partners from the American locomotive driving
the Western alliance. The SS-20 really was a 'NATO-busting weapon,'
both militarily and diplomatically.

Moscow congratulated itself on a stunning *coup de force*. Then matters,
as far as the Russians were concerned, began to go horribly wrong.

NATO response was surprisingly robust, for an alliance whose
acronym, according to some cynics in Europe, normally stands for 'No
Action, Talk Only.' To the Kremlin's astonishment, (and, frankly, many
inside NATO were similarly taken aback), the alliance eventually
agreed to deploy in Europe the American Griffin mobile ground-
launched cruise and Pershing II ballistic missiles, both nuclear-tipped,
beginning in 1983. The latter's terminal guidance system, based on
radar matching the terrain below its flight path with a satellite-gener-
ated map, provided unheard-of accuracy for its variable yield (five to
50 kT) warhead – with much less than 150 ft straddling a target.

The surprise in Moscow at NATO's reaction quickly changed to
vexation and alarm when it was suddenly realised, from reports from
their military intelligence agency, the GRU (*Glavnoye Razvedyvatelnoye Upravlenie*), that the extended range Pershing IIs could now hit
Moscow before the political leadership could be warned of an attack,
let alone order the counter-strike.

The American missile's forward deployment in Europe meant a
very short flight before it reached Russian targets, or, put another way,
much reduced warning times. Its pinpoint accuracy was enough to
decisively knock out the Soviet national command centre and its
earth-penetrating warhead would probably defeat all the concrete,
earth and steel protective hardening the Russians could possibly heap
on their command bunkers. Like the SS-20, Pershing II was mobile,
and so was largely immune from any Soviet military attempts to neutralise it. The Kremlin was very much hoist with its own petard.

It was not only a clever strategy that had crumbled into dust. It did
not take the Soviets long to wake up to a new strategic nightmare: by
deploying the Pershing II, Washington had unwittingly created the
first credible and effective nuclear first strike weapon against strategic
targets in Russia.

It was a realisation that terrified the Kremlin, already haunted by fears about the vulnerability of their nuclear command structure. Despite substantial modernisation of the 'Signal' communications system in 1976–82, it still took 20 minutes between receiving a warning of an attack and the orders to launch being executed by the Soviet missile forces. The old, familiar threat of American submarine-launched weapons now paled alongside that posed by the US Army's Pershing II with its average seven minutes' flight time, launched from who knows where.

In an attempt to snatch success from the jaws of failure, Moscow tried to block the NATO deployment by offering to freeze the number of nuclear-armed missiles in Europe. The true intent of Soviet President Leonid Brezhnev's offer was quickly bowled out in Western Europe, in that it would allow the SS-20 deployments to continue unaffected, whilst halting the basing of the US weapons. His offer came too late and offered too little and only served to harden resolve within those European nations that were hosting the new missiles. Despite much political soul-searching in continental Europe, the Griffin and Pershing II deployments went ahead.

No surprise then that NATO's new missile deployments eventually brought a worried Kremlin to the international negotiating table. The result was the Intermediate Nuclear Force (INF) treaty eliminating short and intermediate range nuclear missiles with ranges of between 310 and 3,400 miles in Europe, signed on December 7, 1987. By May 1991, all the 120 Pershing IIs and 322 Griffins by then deployed by NATO had been destroyed, sliced up into scrap metal shards under verifiable supervision – as had the 405 Russian SS-20s in the field and a further 245 held in store.

The Kremlin had suffered a nasty scare, but was happy to trade in the expensive SS-20s to buy time to make their nuclear command structures more robust. Concurrently, they had also removed a grievous threat to the integrity, or rather survivability, of their nuclear strike authorisation system. The swift change in policy was a good example of decisive Russian realism.

Amidst all the international hubbub over the SS-20 and unknown to the West, the Perimetr project had been quietly gathering momentum, its progress accelerated by fears over the new threat posed by the Pershing II. The order authorising full-scale development had been signed in Moscow in October 1974. The Soviet concept of an automatic launch authorisation system was based on three key factors or events, all of which have to happen before their ICBMs could be fired.

FIRST, the *Vyuga* nuclear command link to the Soviet political leadership must be cut, presumably by enemy action and the dedicated *Kazbek* communications system interrupted – indicating that the Moscow national command post had been destroyed and the political leadership killed.

SECOND, the General Staff had *previously* to approve a nuclear strike, by issuing the first portion of the ICBM launch authorisation codes from its command post at Chekhov, 60 miles south of Moscow. Those in charge of the system had to *stop it* proceeding further down the critical path to launch, if this criterion was not met.

THIRD, a complex network of ground sensors had to detect around 500 nuclear explosions at a number of specific Russian targets – ICBM silo fields, command posts, early warning radar stations – by monitoring of seismic shockwaves through the Earth's surface. Long-range infrared detection of nuclear airbursts at strategically important sites is also believed to form part of the sensor system.

This information would be instantaneously fed into a powerful computer system, believed to be held inside a special protective bunker under Yamantau mountain, in the Urals, which decides, purely on the basis of an algorithm, that Russia has been attacked and that the irretrievable catastrophe of nuclear war has occurred. The computer is programmed, on the basis of a database of earthquake effects, to discount natural phenomena in making its decision. The nuclear blasts have also clearly to be caused by a massive US attack: it is thought the system is *not* triggered by smaller bombardments as would be mounted by British, French, Israeli or Chinese strikes.

Perimetr therefore defines Armageddon in its truest sense: its authorisation to launch would be one of the last military orders to be issued before the holocaust of total nuclear war.

Instead of relying on normal communication lines used to launch the ICBMs, Perimetr employs special command missiles equipped with UHF radio transmitters to issue the final authorisation codes to the silo fields, initiating launches without the missile controllers turning any keys or pressing any buttons. In the doomsday scenario, they would be redundant. The missiles would just suddenly depart their silos.

Once all the three factors have come into play, Perimetr is activated, via a low- frequency radio antenna network, buried underground to protect it against damage caused by microwave emissions or electromagnetic pulses (EMPs), emitted during nuclear explosions. The command missiles' 20–50 minute flight time takes them over a number of ICBM silo fields, as the unlock and launch codes are relayed.

Within a year of the go-ahead for the project, missile design bureaus began work on developing the command missile. In January 1978, a modified version of the two-stage 15A15 SS-17 (codenamed 'Spanker' by NATO) ICBM was selected as the vehicle for the new 15B99 communications nose cone assembly that would replace the missile's normal four multiple, independently targeted, re-entry vehicles (MIRVs) with their variable-yield warheads. Another version, based on the Pioner rocket, had to be abandoned because of the INF Treaty's elimination of this missile.

The Perimetr launch missile, designated 15A11 and designed by the Yangel Design Bureau, (now called NPO Yuzhnoye) at Dnepropetrovsk, Ukraine, was first flight tested in December 1979. A further six development tests were staged in 1981–2. A launch to prove the system's operational capability was held on November 13, 1984 when a command missile was fired from Kapustin Yar which successfully launched an unarmed 15A14 SS-18 ('Satan') ICBM from its silo at Derzhavinsk, Kazakhstan. Two more launches were staged in 1983–4 to confirm the operational effectiveness, or integrity, of the system.

Perimetr entered service in January 1985 with launch silos at the SS-17 base at Vypolzovo (Yedrovo) in the Valday hills, 100 miles northwest of Moscow and at Kostromo, 150 miles north-east of the Soviet capital. Development, refining the system's effectiveness, continued.

A new version, called Perimetr-PTS, embodying a new command module, designated 15P011, entered service in December 1990, based on the silo-launched version of the new Russian ICBM, the SS-27 Topol-M, designed by the Moscow Institute for Thermotechnology. This rocket is solid-fuelled, giving it a faster reaction time than the earlier liquid-fuelled SS-17. It was tested in a 1988 launch.

Various modifications were considered by the military but rejected for this new version. Some thought was given to including the remote launching of Russia's submarine-based missiles by the upgraded Perimetr system, but this was ruled out because of the uncertain communications involved. The Russians also considered an option to boost the element of automated response by building in a mechanism that would always fire the Perimetr missiles after a set period had elapsed – unless a 'stop' message was received. This feature was also discarded because of fears of unauthorised or accidental launches if the countdown to firing somehow could not be halted.

Perimetr remains in service, with reports of a further modified version becoming operational in 1996. Russian officials maintain privately that far from being an automated path to nuclear war, Perimetr provides their leadership with a comforting step back from a hair-trigger launch of their nuclear forces. They say it creates confidence in the Russian nuclear command and control system as, if all else fails, there could *always* be a retaliatory strike, thus theoretically removing the temptation to launch the ICBMs early, when the network of warning radars report incoming missiles, rather than coolly waiting to evaluate the scale and severity of the attack. In the stress and tumult of decision-making while teetering on the brink of nuclear war, some may think that the notion of Perimetr bringing a calming reassurance that there remains one shot in the locker, is no more than conjectural.

Concurrent with the development of Perimetr, the Soviets continued with a programme to improve the survivability of their nuclear arsenal. New hardened ICBM silos were constructed, beginning at Tatischevo in 1976, to withstand air pressures of 190–220lbs per square centimetre, enabling them to withstand the enormous blast and shockwave of a nuclear airburst. Up to the early 1980s, the 'Signal-M' control system, via satellites, radio and landlines, hard-wired the missile silos to the national command authority so that ICBM launches could be directly controlled by the Soviet hierarchy. In addition, the new special Vyuga net used short wave and extremely long wave radio for General Staff communications to divisional command posts. Swift re-targeting of individual missiles – in 10–15 seconds – by the Soviet high command was accomplished by the introduction of the improved 'Signal-A' system in 1982. Each local command held various flight plans and targets in its computers and these could be remotely selected by the General Staff and downloaded into each missile's guidance system. On top of all this, the Kremlin instituted an expensive programme to build new long-range over-the-horizon (OTH) Duga radars, a network of advanced high-technology Volga radars and launched more capable satellites, all to provide safer and above all, earlier, warning of attack.

By the late 1980s, at long last, the Kremlin's long-standing paranoia about the vulnerability of Russia's strategic forces seemed to have gone away, eased by the sweet panacea of technology. Massive redundancy built into the system provided strong assurances that no matter what an adversary could throw at them, the retaliatory strike capability would survive, still under Moscow's rigid control.

Admittedly, there were some hiccups along the way. An OTH early warning radar station at Komsomolsk-na-Amure, Siberia, had to be closed down in 1990 after a disastrous fire. Then there was another OTH station, built at Pripyat in the Ukraine, right next door to a thriving nuclear power generation complex – at Chernobyl. This was closed in 1986 after the disastrous accident there. (Aficionados know these backscatter radars as 'Russian Woodpeckers' because of the rapid clicking of pulses that disrupt short wave radio transmissions.)

Overall, though, the Soviet strategic planners could congratulate themselves. At a very high price indeed, in roubles and scientific endeavour, the deterrence value of the inviolable policy of Mutual Assured Destruction* had been preserved.

The satisfaction was not to last. The collapse of the Soviet Union in 1991 and the break-up of its communist empire suddenly brought back the nightmare of vulnerability, with undreamt-of ramifications to the security of the Russian state.

The much-vaunted SPRN (*Sistema preduprezhdeniya o raketnom napademii*) network of nine missile early warning stations, 16 long-range radars and a network of launch detection satellites had provided 24-hour protective coverage of all Soviet territory – from every direction. In the aftermath of the Soviet regime, ten of the missile early warning radars located in non-Russian republics, (two still uncompleted), suddenly found themselves on foreign soil, after those nations' declarations of independence from Moscow. Some of the industries concerned with the support and maintenance of these radar stations were also now outside Russian political reach or influence. Almost overnight, the strategic picture, as seen from the Kremlin, looked very sick indeed. The all-seeing SPRN eyes had gone blind, at least in some directions.

---

* The nuclear doctrine of Mutual Assurance Destruction, or the aptly coined acronym 'MAD,' laid down that if you were *mad* enough to launch your nuclear weapons in a massive pre-emptive strike upon your enemy, you must expect complete obliteration in the retaliatory attack.

The new Russian leaders were understandably eager to act. The new loose grouping of former Soviet republics, the Commonwealth of Independent States, or CIS (one can imagine the agonising over *that* choice of name), signed an Agreement on Missile Warning and Space Monitoring Systems on July 6, 1992, giving some access to data. However, the CIS states turned down proposals by Moscow for the radar stations to be used in a dual role, providing early warning coverage both for the Russian Federation and for the host state. Of course, said the Kremlin, the stations *would* remain as Russian military bases.

Just who is likely to attack us? asked the CIS states. Thanks, but that's not for us. You can forget the military base idea too. We're independent states, freed of the shackles represented by the hammer and sickle flag.

Desperate to rebuild its nuclear early warning umbrella, the unhappy Moscow negotiators were forced down the gritty road of bilateral talks with each new state possessing an early warning radar station on its territory. Latvia, on the strategically important Western borders of the Russian Federation now found itself with two radar stations, plus an unfinished new Daryal-UM radar at Skrunda, 50 miles inland from the Baltic, looking north-west towards the North Atlantic and Barents Sea and the Western missile submarine operating areas there. Russia finally agreed with the Riga government in 1994 to lease the Skrunda site but the incomplete radar facility was dismantled in 1995. The lease expired in August 1998, and the two operational radars closed down that month. Both were torn down in 1999.

The Kremlin turned to the more compliant Republic of Belarus to fill, at least partially, the gap in ground-based radar cover caused by the loss of the Latvian facilities. The fall of the Soviet Union trapped a partially constructed Volga type radar station on its soil, at Gantsevichi, near Baranovichi. Belarus agreed to lease the site to Russia for 25 years and construction work restarted there, but constrained by having to hammer out new contracts for electronics equipment with the old supplier Dnepropetrovsk Machine Building Plant, which was now in the Ukraine, and of course, grave shortage of funds in the Moscow coffers. The radar completed testing in October 2000 but was only expected to become operational at the time of writing.

The Ukraine had three radars on its territory – two of the older Dnepr (or Hen House, to use the unflattering NATO codename) facilities at Beregovo in the Zakarpatskaya Oblast and at Nikolayev, and an unfinished Daryal-UM site at Mukachevo. After very protracted negotiations, the Ukraine agreed in February 1997 to lease the Beregovo and Nikolayev sites, at a cost of $4 million a year paid in spare parts in order to maintain the Ukrainian air force's ageing Soviet-vintage aircraft. Moscow would also cover all operating costs – but Ukrainian personnel would man the radar stations. Data is now being fed into the Russian early warning computers.

In Kazakstan, the two Dnepr radars at Balkhash tracking manmade objects in space, as well as providing early warning, remain operational, but disagreements remain over insistence that the area should be a Russian military base. Together with the Ukrainian sites, Balkhash provides much needed cover for the SW quadrant of the Russian Federation. The Daryal-U site at Balkhash remains unfinished and looks likely never to be completed.

Problems remain over status of the Daryal radar station at Gabala, Mingechuar, Azerbaijan, which became operational in 1985 and watches over the SE portion of the southern flank, including the Indian Ocean. The Azerbaijanis would not budge from the standpoint that the facility is *their* property and sought a five-year lease agreement rather than 20 years sought by the Kremlin. Eventually, they compromised on a lease until 2010, with $31 million paid by Russia for outstanding costs and a further $70 million until the agreement expires. However, the radar, now the property of the Azerbaijani government, reportedly operates only sporadically.

Russian president Vladimir Putin may well sit in Moscow and muse that 'Change and decay in all around I see,' to quote from the hymn *Abide with Me.* For those early warning radars happily still within Russian borders also faced their own problems – this time, of growing obsolescence and widespread lack of funding for development of new systems, or even maintenance. Putin may be comforted that latest thinking from his experts now points to greater reliance on satellites providing early warning rather than static ground-based radars.

But currently, here too Moscow faces grave problems, again mainly caused by shortages in cash. Originally nine *Oko* ('Eye') satellites had been planned and were operated in high elliptical 12-hour orbits around the Earth, watching westwards, high over Europe, for launches from the US ICBM fields and missile submarine operating areas in the oceans. The network could detect launches, calculate flight paths and predict the missiles' targets. Another network of eight second generation *Prognoz* ('Forecast') satellites, this time in geostationary orbit, (allowing each to remain in one place over the Earth's surface), was created in the late 1980s to watch over the US, China, the Pacific and Western Europe.

That was the plan. But by the end of 1997, 68% of Russian satellites had gone beyond their planned service lives and there was substantial 'down' time in coverage, due to mechanical failure, or them drifting out of orbital position. US estimates then suggested the satellites were operational for no more than 17 hours in every 24. With the launch of Cosmos 2388 from Plesetsk on April 1, only five out of the required nine Oko type satellites remained operational in elliptical orbit in mid-2002, and just one Prognoz remained in a 24-hour geostationary position – Cosmos 2379, launched from Baikonur on August 24, 2001. A second Prognoz was to be launched later in 2002. Fiscal constraints have restricted launches of more replacement satellites, even though seven have reportedly been built.

So, the current protective radar and satellite cover over the Russian Federation now has two yawning gaps in coverage. In the West, there is a 600-mile-wide corridor over France and northern Spain in which a submarine-launched missile attack from the North Atlantic could penetrate Russian early warning systems undetected. Similarly, a US ICBM strike could be deliberately programmed to exploit this corridor of opportunity, created by the loss of the Latvian radars. A second, more serious gap is in the east, 1,000 miles wide over Russia's Kamchatka peninsula. A Trident missile strike launched from a submarine in the Gulf of Alaska, in US territorial waters, could reach Moscow in around ten minutes, completely unseen on Russian radar screens. The first the Russians would know of it could be nuclear airbursts over their capital.

If this is the stuff of nightmares for Putin, there's worse to come. During the night of May 10, 2001, a fire, caused by a short circuit in a cable, in a building at Serpukhov 15, the early warning satellite control centre near the village of Kurilovo, in the Zhukovsky area of the Kaluga region, about 70 miles south-west of Moscow, knocked out all communications links with the then four remaining Oko satellites for four days, despite attempts to use another command station, Golichino 2., or the flight control centre at Koroljevo, near Moscow. Serpukhov 15 only came back on station on August 20, 2001.

Worryingly, Russian early warning systems, even working with a full complement of radar stations and satellites, are not infallible. A number of cases of false alarms have occurred, all with alarming potential consequences.

The Volga-type ground-based radar at Gantsevichi, Belarus, generated false images on its screens when it first became operational. The first *known* spurious alert was on September 26, 1983, when one of the Oko warning satellites on high elliptical orbits above the Earth wrongly detected what was believed to be a launch of American Minuteman II ICBMs from their hardened silos in the mid-West. Its infrared sensors, that detect light and heat, mistook the sun for the hot exhaust gases emitted from the motors of missiles leaving the Earth's atmosphere.

Happily, the alert was speedily found to be false. The subsequent investigation indicated that a software glitch within the satellite's computers created the false warning when the satellite moved from dazzling sunlight into the blackness of the Earth's shadow thrown in space by the sun.

Reportedly, Colonel Stanislav Petrov, who was in charge of Serpukhov 15 that day, refused to pass the alert higher up the command chain because he doubted the veracity of the warning. 'When people start a war, they don't start it with only five missiles. You can do little damage with five missiles,' he said afterwards.

A more serious and public incident followed around dawn on January 25, 1995, when the launch of a four-stage Black Brandt XII sounding or research rocket unintentionally triggered the creaking Russian nuclear defence command system by testing the SPRN missile attack warning system and found it wanting.

The Russian radar stations at Pechora, in Komi-Permyatsk, Olenegorsk, in the Murmansk region, and Skrunda, in Latvia, detected the innocent launch from Andøya Island, off the north-west coast of Norway, near Tromso. The computers believed it to be a Trident missile launched from an American submarine positioned off the North Cape, and issued an attack warning, possibly automated, which appeared on the *Krokus* special alert terminal inside the Russian command post near Moscow.

The Russian General Staff believed an explosion in the atmosphere of the single missile's eight W-88 475 kT nuclear warheads would be an attempt to blind or cripple Moscow's strategic communications through a series of massive electromagnetic pulses (EMPs). These destroy electronic components in much the same way, as do, on a smaller, localised scale, nature's electrical storms. They reasoned that such an assault on their national command and control system could be a prelude to a full-scale pre-emptive nuclear attack and immediately triggered the top-echelon *Kazbek* communications system (used to issue orders for nuclear attack). They simultaneously raised their strategic forces' level of alert. The Russian nuclear countdown had begun.

The then Russian president, Boris Yeltsin, Defence Minister Pavel Grachev and the Chief of the Armed Forces' General Staff, Army General Mikhail Kolesnikov were quickly alerted via their mobile versions of Kazbek terminals, the black *Chegets* (nicknamed *yaderniy chemodanchik*, or 'nuclear suitcases'), that accompanied them everywhere since 1983. They held a three-way emergency videoconference. One can only speculate as to their emotions and the tone and content of their conversation.

Eight agonising minutes elapsed before the same Russian radars determined that the sounding rocket's trajectory was, in reality, taking it safely to a splash point off the island of Spitzbergen in the Norwegian Sea, rather than to Russia and flashed news of the error. There remained, perhaps, just two minutes before a 'launch on warning' decision for the strategic forces to retaliate would have confronted the Russian leadership, a decision that has to be personally validated by the President, using his Cheget.

Presumably, the order to rescind the countdown followed confirmation from the Russian early warning Oko satellite system, then functioning fully, that a follow-up attack by American Minuteman III or Peacekeeper ICBMs had not materialised. The failsafe system worked that time; although the Moscow leadership would not have been certain that a Trident attack was not building from the Pacific or North Atlantic. They may have gambled that it wasn't.

It is believed this was the first and as yet only time the Russians had initiated the countdown to launch their nuclear forces in anger. Previously, it was doubted by some Western strategic planners that Moscow really would have initiated a counterstrike, using a launch on warning decision. Clearly, they might.

Of course, if Russian ICBMs *had* been launched, they would not necessarily have been armed. As part of the failsafe – an ironic word in these circumstances – precautions surrounding all nuclear weaponry, warheads are not armed until just before separation from their launch missiles and they begin to re-enter the Earth's atmosphere, en route to their targets. This is not just an eleventh-hour, eleventh-minute function designed to avert the apocalyptic horrors of a modern Armageddon – there's always an unspoken fear, amongst nuclear planners, of malfunction and an accidental warhead detonation as the missiles roar out of their silos in clouds of flame and smoke.

In addition, a national command authority has the closely guarded ability to order the missiles to self-destruct in flight, a necessary precaution in the event of accidental or unauthorised launch. The warheads would be harmlessly destroyed in the explosions. But imagine the reactions of the then US Strategic Air Command, deep in its command bunker, as Russian missile launches are detected and reported. Does the US Commander-in-Chief do *nothing* and waste precious minutes in the vain hope that the missiles remain unarmed or are destroyed as their trajectories take them ever nearer their targets? No, once any missiles are launched, by anyone, the nuclear war clock starts ticking inexorably onwards to the mass destruction of populations and nations. Only a miracle can stay its hands.

In 1995, that corrected coded message – '*NO ATTACK, REPEAT, NO ATTACK*' – flashed to the Russian General Staff national command post at Chekhov, represented a very narrow step back from the brink. What had gone wrong? How could it happen?

In these days of swift and sophisticated global signals intelligence (SIGINT), there was no disguising of the fact that Moscow's forces had escalated their nuclear alert status. In the international furore and recriminations that inevitably followed, it emerged that the Russian Foreign Ministry *had* received an official notification of the launch (which was merely routinely investigating nature's *aurora borealis* or 'northern lights' over the polar region), from the Norwegian government some time before it was scheduled. The Ministry apparently failed to pass on this warning to the nuclear command and control system.

Then there was the issue of the 65ft-long Black Brandt rocket itself, which flies to an altitude of up to 800 miles above the Earth. Its first stage is based on a 1950s-vintage 'Honest John' intermediate range ballistic missile, with high initial take-off speeds, closely resembling those of Trident. The radar signatures may be similar, particularly if the third-stage burnt out below the Russians' radar horizon. At least, that's what Moscow claimed afterwards, (although as the NASA Sounding

Rocket Program has between 20 and 30 launches a year, admittedly not all from this site, one would have imagined the Russians would be familiar with the flight characteristics). The importance of the incident, said Moscow rather sniffily, had been greatly exaggerated in the West.

Was the incident overblown? Would the Moscow leadership have decided to launch its missiles? Under the Strangelove-like nomenclature of nuclear strategy, a number of options or scenarios present themselves then, as now, to a political leadership forced into making that breathtaking, horrendous decision in a very few short minutes.

There's **Launch Under Attack** (LUA): You must decide to fire your weapons in an immediate and devastating counterstrike in the face of a confirmed and *overwhelming* missile attack building on your radar screens. **Launch on Attack Assessment** (LAA) entails deciding to launch all, or some, of your missiles after establishing the scale and magnitude of the incoming enemy strike. Similarly, **Launch Through Attack** (LTA) is not for the faint-hearted national leader. This process involves making the decision to retaliate, if it is apparent that the incoming waves of missiles will sequentially hit their targets. A cool-headed political leadership would sit back, absorb the impacts of the first missiles, assess the strategy and destruction revealed by these early strikes and then launch a calculated response through the follow-on salvoes of enemy missiles. **Launch On Impact** (LOI) trades survivability of some of your own missile forces with the sure knowledge of your enemy's intentions. You launch your counterstrike after nuclear detonations on or over your ICBM silos. You hope that some, at least, survive the bombardment. **Launch on Warning** (LOW) is always the most dangerous option to adopt. In the bizarre logic of nuclear strategy, this decision would only be taken to protect a land-based ICBM force – getting them out of their silos, or away from their mobile launchers before attacking missiles destroy them in a holocaust of blast, heat and EMPs. In US strategic thinking, LOW would probably be activated only if there are incontrovertible indications of an incoming massive attack. Certainly, a high state of readiness within the missile forces would be required for a LOW response.

In any event, submarine-launched missiles would be largely immune from pre-emptive strikes because of the difficulty of tracking the boats in the ocean deeps, and defeating (particularly in the Russians' case) the protective ring of nuclear-powered hunter-killer submarines, short of a huge nuclear assault on the high seas. It would be virtually impossible to be certain that you had taken out every enemy strategic missile submarine and totally neutralised that threat.

Indeed, Russia's leviathan missile boats, the 26,500 tons dived displacement 'Typhoon' or 'Akula' class submarines were designed to provide Moscow with a survivable post-pre-emptive strike capability. The boats, the largest submarines ever likely to be built, were designed to sit out US nuclear attacks safely under the Arctic polar ice cap. As the radioactive dust and rubble settled in the homeland, they would break through 12ft of pack ice and launch their 20 Makeyev SS-N-20 'Sturgeon' missiles, each one armed with 10 200 kT warheads, in retaliation. Two missiles can be fired every 15 seconds. Their range enables them to reach targets anywhere in the world. (But with the Typhoon's high cost of maintenance and complement of 175 crew demanding trained manpower that is not available, just two remain operational today.)

What was worrying about the 1995 Russian false alarm was the uncertain operational state of Moscow's strategic nuclear forces, which raises question marks over warning and strike capability. Worryingly, another false alarm may yet do so again, despite Russian attempts to reassure the West, through a series of large-scale exercises, codenamed REDUT, in 1996 and the following year, which tested the nuclear command and control system and launched unarmed ballistic and cruise missiles.

Long gone are the days of the Soviet Union with its impressive triad of fully operational nuclear forces – ICBMs, submarine-launched missiles and manned bombers. In 1995, because of budgetary constraints, poor maintenance and indifferent crew training, Russia's strategic missile submarines (in Royal Navy parlance, 'bombers'), could only mount a few operational patrols in the Barents Sea or the Pacific. The same is true today. Most of the various variants of 'Delta' class SSBNs were (and are) tied up alongside at their bases at Saida Guba in the Northern Fleet, and at Strelok in the Pacific. Some were (and remain, in the short-term) 1960s-vintage 'Delta Is,' armed with ageing Chelomey SS-N-8 'Sawfly' missiles with single 800 kT warheads – powerful 'rubble bouncers' in the stark and ruthless language of nuclear conflict.

Their crews have shown in trials that they can fire their missiles while the boats are alongside the piers, within nine to 15 minutes after receiving the launch authorisation codes from the General Staff. But, of course, by being in port, these boats and weapon systems have lost the submarine's great strategic advantage: no longer can they avoid detection by hiding in the depths of the sea. US reconnaissance satellites, which can identify objects on the Earth's surface of less than three feet in size, can readily spot their location. Inevitably, attacking missiles could target and destroy them.

In 1995, Russia had a total of 754 ICBMs, armed with 3,708 warheads, declared operational under the 1991 Strategic Arms Reduction Treaty (START 1) Of these, 366 (or 49%) were located in the silo fields in the remote birch forests of the Russian Federation. The remainder were less vulnerable to sneak pinpoint attack, being launched from railway trucks or mobile all-terrain vehicles. Most were ageing, with some verging on obsolescence, with designs dating back to the end of the 1960s, in the case of the SS-18 'Satan' and SS-19 'Stiletto' missiles, 97% of the silo-based force. With declines in funding for maintenance, how many would have worked on the day?

Of course false alarms are not the sole prerogative of Russia's nuclear forces: the USA has been afflicted by this problem too.

There was the well-documented event at 08.50 on the morning of November 9, 1979, when US Air Force Minuteman missile crews were warned that a massive Soviet ICBM attack was en route to destroy US nuclear forces and the command infrastructure. They prepared to launch their missiles, unaware that a training tape had mistakenly been loaded onto the USA's early warning system computers that had generated the false alarm.

The attack showed up on displays at Strategic Air Command's bunker beneath Cheyenne Mountain in Colorado, at the Pentagon's National Military Command Center and at the Alternate National Military Command Center at Fort Ritchie, Maryland. The National Emergency Airborne Command Post took off, (bizarrely, without the President on board), and a very senior officers' threat assessment conference was hastily convened.

Within six minutes, the American network of early warning satellites and early warning radars had confirmed no Soviet launches had occurred and the alert was stood down. No doubt, whoever inadvertently fed the training tape into the system saw their career prospects suddenly and dramatically limited. After an independent investigation of the incident by the US General Accounting Office, a special off-site facility was created to run training or test tapes, outside the loop of the military command structure.

Seven months later, at 2.25 a.m. on June 3, 1980, another false alarm triggered a second preliminary warning to Minuteman crews to get ready to launch. Displays at the command bunkers showed attacking missiles but in an odd sequence; indicating the launch of 200 Soviet ICBMs, then zero missiles, then just two. Moreover, the numbers across the various command post tote boards did not tally. Again, data from watching US satellites was consulted – but again, no threat was present. The alert was exactly replicated three days later and the cause was found to be a rogue computer chip that was failing randomly, generating the figure 2 instead of the correct zeros.

With the possible survival of humanity at stake, it was natural for both superpowers to examine ways of minimising the risk of accidental missile launches, later perhaps impelled by publicly unannounced fears on all sides over the decay of the Russian early warning system.

In 1987, Nuclear Risk Reduction Centres (NRRCs) in Moscow and Washington were set up, linked by secure Group III fax link via satellite communications, so that if accidental or unauthorised missile launches occurred, both the US and Russian Presidents could exchange information and prevent rapid escalation into full-scale nuclear war, rather than rely on the slow telex of the old 'hot line'. (Concerns over the Millennium Bug (Y2K) and its potential impact on the creaking Russian command structure, prompted the creation of a temporary joint US-Russian Y2K centre in Colorado Springs over the New Year 2000 period to negate any computer-generated false alarms. None occurred.) These NRRCs may have been superseded by the agreement to set up a Joint Ballistic Missile Early Warning Centre outside Moscow by June 2002, with separate US and Russian data monitoring ballistic missile and space vehicle launches. Any discrepancies between the information would be able to be resolved by the American and Russian monitoring teams. Eventually, the centre will handle information on launches by other countries such as North Korea and Iran, and will be accessible to up to 200 users.

On December 16, 2000, the USA and Russia signed a Memorandum of Understanding extending the process governing the notification of missile launches between both sides and to other states. An earlier agreement, signed in 1988, bound Washington and Moscow to provide at least 24 hours warning of all ICBM and submarine-launched ballistic missiles   (SLBM), with details of the launch and impact areas.

Do these measures provide any comfort to those quite properly worried about the deterioration of the Russian early warning system and the likelihood of accidental nuclear war? On paper, they look good. In practice, they may be less than adequate. Take the jointly manned centre in Moscow. In reality, it is based in a renovated former school, outside the city centre. It is clear the Russians place little reliance on its usefulness because in their heart of hearts, they cannot bring themselves to believe that the US side would confirm that an American missile launch showing up on the computer screens was the real thing. It takes more than a piece of paper with high-flown diplomatic phrases to erase the suspicions of two generations of Cold War thinking.

Such treaties are more presentation than substance – like the 1994 deal removing targeting information from US and Russian missiles. The default targets now held by US missiles are located harmlessly in the ocean wastes. Russian missiles, launched without targeting data, reportedly revert to the previously programmed targets. In addition, everyone knows that new target data can anyway be fed into both nations' missile systems within seconds.

And the Russians? The temporary Y2K centre in Colorado Springs indicates perhaps their true level of nervousness over the robustness of their nuclear command and control, for all the reassuring words put out to the international community by the Foreign Ministry and General Staff in Moscow.

It may take two or three years for the Russian network of early-warning satellites to be brought back to full operational capability at a cost of perhaps $1 billion, even though this is the preferred route to remedy the shortcomings in the Kremlin's system. The US has offered to fund the construction of new early warning radars but their location would not close the blind corridors currently leaving the Russian Federation open to sneak Trident SLBM attack. The Defence Ministry in Moscow has talked of plans for new radar technologies and mobile missile attack warning radars, but as ever, funding remains a problem.

Meanwhile, some crumb of comfort may be gleaned from signs that the Russian early warning system has now deteriorated to the point where its data may not be relied upon for a LOW decision to launch a retaliatory strike. Perhaps such a doctrine is now problematic for the Russian leadership, given the poor readiness status of the missile forces. Certainly, Moscow insists that the chances of an accidental launch remain very low.

After Putin ordered a switch in funding to conventional forces, Russia's strategic assets are now rapidly decaying. There is no need for any international treaty to reduce its number of warheads; it's happening anyway through shortage of cash. Moscow's missile forces are now being reorganised to be able to launch 'up to 1,000 warheads' via what the Russians call a 'flexible response', enabling the General Staff, via Perimetr or direct links with the missile silos, to transmit the authorisation and unlock codes in a very short timespan.

On what quality of information that decision is based, remains conjectural.

CHAPTER 2

THUNDER FROM THE SKY

THE SECOND WORLD WAR saw sophisticated technology employed for the first time to deliberately and calculatingly inflict mass destruction on both sides' civilian populations. The concept was not new to the 1940s: just the sheer scale of the onslaught and the massive tonnage of explosives used. More than two decades before, during the last stages of the First World War, German 'Gotha' and Riesen-type 'Giant' heavy bombers mounted 27 raids on targets in mainland Britain, killing 836 people (353 of them civilians), and injuring a further 1,994. Bombing missions by the ungainly, hydrogen-filled Zeppelin airships, beginning in January 1915, together with a few sneak attacks by single-engined aircraft, killed a further 577. Britain's Royal Air Force's (RAF) own bombing offensive against Germany in 1918 killed more than 700 civilians and wounded 1,800 more during 242 raids in six months.

Compared with the overall slaughter of the First World War, particularly on the blood-soaked battlefields of the Western Front in France and Flanders, these figures, by themselves, are statistically insignificant, dwarfed by the daily butcher's bill of casualties caused by trench fighting and artillery bombardment. But a clear lesson of the perceived value of bombing civilian targets had been learnt and, with the benefit of emerging technology, would be ruthlessly and relentlessly applied, day after day, over the cities of Britain and Germany during the Second World War.

In the run-up period to these hostilities, there were dour forecasts of violent death, from high explosive and chemical agent bombs raining from the skies, triggering futile international attempts to outlaw bombing of civilian targets.* The British Prime Minister, Stanley Baldwin, warned in 1932: 'I think it is well for the man in the street to realise that there is no power on earth that can protect him from being bombed. Whatever people may tell him, the bomber will always get through.' He stressed: 'The only defence is in offence, which means that you have to kill more women and children more quickly than the enemy if you want to save yourselves.' Ironically, even as the World Disarmament Conference was convening in Geneva in February of that year, Japanese naval aircraft bombed the Chinese residential Chapei district of Shanghai, (attacks they repeated on the city in August, 1937). The bombing of towns in the Spanish Civil War heightened European populations' fears of this weapon of mass destruction.

Aerial bombing had become a *strategic weapon*, designed to terrorise your adversary's population, diminish war production and disrupt his communications, and stretch the enemy nation's ability to care, feed and shelter its people beyond breaking point. Later, the British Prime Minister Winston Churchill, no doubt recalling the notorious German night raid on Coventry on November 13, 1940, in which 554 civilians died and 865 were seriously wounded, wrote the following year: 'We need to make the enemy burn and bleed in every way.' In the face of such determined onslaughts, their will to fight would therefore seep away – or that was the theory enthusiastically propounded by strategists. The aim was simply to bomb them into submission.

In military terms, it was very much a blunt instrument. Academics and strategists argue to this day whether such *conventional* bombing campaigns could ever be effective war winners. Certainly, an official British report after the cessation of hostilities in 1945 admitted that bombing had a "remarkably small" impact on German war production output. Although prolonged carpet bombing and the subsequent horrific firestorms of the Second World War caused misery, fear, panic and unimaginable suffering amongst non-combatants, civilian morale both in Britain and Germany did not suffer the total collapse confidently predicted by the war planners in London and Berlin. But mass destruction there certainly was. Much of urban Britain and Germany was just one huge heap of pulverised rubble and dust by 1945.

* A British Chief of Staffs' secret report on the effects of an aerial gas attack on Britain's population, written in 1933, has still not yet been released to public view in the Public Record Office, London.

Despite all the arguments over morality and military value, terror as a high-technology weapon of war had been delivered into the arsenals of the powerful. Everyone was aware of the overwhelming explosive power of bigger and better bombs. But what the air forces sought was the means to safely and surely *deliver* destruction to the target, preferably and literally, out of the blue, to maximise the efficiency of the strike.

Delivery is everything. No matter how powerful or awesome is a weapon of mass destruction; it is totally worthless in deterrent value, or in strategic war-winning terms, unless it can be accurately brought to its target to fulfil its grim role of dealing out death and obliteration.   German ingenuity came up with the answer in the Second World War – the development of *Vergeltungswaffe* weapons, unmanned terror missiles heaping 'vengeance' or 'reprisals' on the hapless heads of enemy populations in England and Belgium. After the horrors of the earlier German aerial 'Blitz' against Britain there was something somehow more terrible in the realisation, in those drab days of 1944–5, that a human being would not physically release the instrument of destruction in the skies above the target. An unthinking metal machine would mercilessly cause all those deaths, all that massive damage to homes, hospitals and schools, safely launched from far away by merely pressing a button. Those responsible could not see the blast, smoke and rubble of the explosion, or the consequent suffering. There was not even the remote chance of last-minute pity or remorse above the target.

In the creation of these missiles, Germany planted the seeds from which germinated the Cold War's weapons of mass destruction, the same weapons that continue to overshadow our lives today, still designed to blast, obliterate and cow into submission.

Between September 1940 and May 1941, the German Luftwaffe's 'Blitz' offensive against Britain, with high explosive bombs and incendiaries, had killed 43,000 civilians as well as seriously injuring another 87,000. More than 1,400,000 were rendered homeless by bomb damage, with around 60% of total homes destroyed in some areas of the main target: London. More women and children were killed in these mainly night-bombing raids than British soldiers dying in battle until midway through the Second World War. But the cost to the Luftwaffe was unacceptably high: 1,449 pilots were killed between July and September 1940 with a further 1,914 missing in action and

530 wounded. A total of 1,882 aircraft were destroyed in that brief campaign. Many of the elitist Luftwaffe's highly trained and motivated aircrew had disappeared in the smoke of combat in the blue skies above Britain and the English Channel.

By June 1942, Britain's RAF Bomber Command, in turn, was mounting night 'saturation' or area bombing raids on German cities, with the main objective of attacking the 'morale of the enemy's civilian population and in particular, of the industrial workers.' After an incendiary bomb raid on Lübeck, north Germany, on March 28, 1942, in which all the buildings in a 200-acre area were totally destroyed, the furious German dictator Adolf Hitler ordered retaliatory terror attacks and a month later authorised development of new weapons of reprisal. The Luftwaffe, bloodied by air combat with British Spitfire and Hurricane fighters over Britain and preoccupied by the heavy demands of the campaigns in Russia and the Mediterranean, looked to safer, less costly methods of bringing destruction to British mainland targets without the haemorrhaging loss of skilled aircrew or expensive aircraft.

A small and cheap expendable robot bomb looked likely to provide the answer and eventually was to become the first cruise missile, the direct ancestor of today's long-range, precision-targeted munitions, used in the Gulf War and against Yugoslavia and Afghanistan, launched from surface ships, submarines and bombers. As a parsimonious Hitler later pointed out, with this weapon, the Luftwaffe didn't even need fuel for a return flight.

In 1942, much of the technology required was already developed. The German engineer Paul Schmidt had invented an air-breathing 'pulse jet' engine in the early 1930s. The AS 014 version chosen to power the flying bomb had the advantage of providing 600 lbs thrust, but using ordinary petrol rather than scarce, strategically vital, high-octane aviation spirit utilised to fuel the Luftwaffe's fighters and bombers. The weapon project, designated the Fi-103, quickly got under way at the Wehrmacht experimental station at Peenemünde, on Wolgast island, on Germany's Baltic coast, disguised by the cover name *Flakzielgerat 76,* or 'anti-aircraft target, number 76'.

A number of prototypes were quickly built, including one, marked V83, fitted with a dummy warhead of concrete that crashed in a turnip field on the Danish island of Bornholm, in the Baltic Sea, between Germany and Sweden, on August 22, 1942. It was photographed and sketched by the local Danish naval officer in charge who secretly sent the documents to London. There, the initial belief among experts was that the 14ft long fuselage was a new variant of the German HS 293 glide bombs then being deployed successfully against Allied shipping in the Mediterranean. But later that year, reports from agents within the Polish resistance, prosaically codenamed PING-PONG, confirmed that development was underway of a terror weapon to be used against London. The British had been tipped off about the new German secret missile.

The Fieseler Werke company designed the flying bomb with its engine developed by Argus-Schmidt and the guidance system by Siemens, fitted with an Askania gyroscope. It was quick to build, needing just 500 man-hours for each missile, used only sheet steel for the fuselage and plywood for the stubby wings, and cost only around £350 each to manufacture. Mass destruction can come cheaply. More than 30,000 flying bombs were to be manufactured in the Volkswagen, Mittelwerke and Henschel plants in Germany (although a 60,000 production run was planned), and at peak output, around 6,000 a month rolled off the assembly lines.

The first glide test of the new weapon came in early December 1942, when a Fi-103 was dropped from a Focke-Wulf FW-200 Kondor aircraft flying over the Baltic. A powered flight followed on December 24 but, disappointingly, it only flew just over half a mile. Subsequent flights indicated recurrent stability problems and several development prototypes plunged into the ground or sea immediately after launch. The cause of these crashes was only discovered after a tiny cockpit fitted with rudimentary flying controls was inserted into the Fi-103's fuselage in place of the warhead and the redoubtable and dashing 30-year-old Luftwaffe test pilot *Flugkapitan* Hanna Reitsch bravely volunteered to fly this manned version. During several highly dangerous test flights she discovered that the missile's guidance system responded badly to a combination of cross winds and the airframe vibration caused by the pulse jet. Modifications were made to the design and further test flights of production prototypes, codenamed *Kirshkern,* or 'Cherrystone', proved more successful, though the weapon still remained frustratingly liable to occasional instability and, more seriously, eccentric flight paths.

On May 23, 1943, full production of the Fi-103 was authorised by Berlin. Reichsmarschall Hermann Goering, the corpulent and boastful head of the Luftwaffe, ordered construction to begin on 96 launching sites in the Pas de Calais area of north-west France, facing the Dover Straits and 143 miles from the planned symbolic aiming point: Tower Bridge in the heart of London. Each site had two 157ft long concrete ski-jump launching ramps. A special air force unit to transport and fire the missiles, Flakregiment 155W, was formed the following August, under the command of Colonel Max Wachtel, the formation's title maintaining the Luftwaffe's attempts to deceive British intelligence into believing the weapon had an anti-aircraft training role. The German High Command believed the unit could fire salvoes of 1,000 flying bombs *per day* at London, each one armed with a 1,870lb Trialen high explosive (HE) warhead.

Hitler, enchanted with Wagnerian fantasies of Valkyrian retribution from the skies, was delighted with the opportunity of paying back the British, with additional interest, for the destruction so relentlessly meted out over Germany by RAF Bomber Command. His Information Ministry, quickly sensing the propaganda power of the flying bomb, triumphantly coined the name *Vergeltungswaffe Eins*, or V-1, for the weapon.

Swift and ruthless vengeance against the British for their incessant and punishing air raids had to wait, however. Flakregiment 155W's training immediately began in earnest on the western edge of the Peenemünde site and continued throughout the winter and into 1944. Test firings aimed at establishing range and accuracy were staged over the Baltic, but these were not always successful: six V-1s accidentally crashed in neutral southern Sweden, near Karlskrona, Ystad and Brösarp, between November 1943 and November 1944. All were subsequently recovered by the Swedish army and examined by experts from Stockholm's defence aeronautical institute, the FFA or *Flygtekniska Försöksanstalken*. Technical details of the V-1 had leaked out.

And because of further reliability problems with the flying bomb, full production was not achieved until April 1944, with 1,000 V-1s completed that month on the Volkswagen production line at Fallersleben. The first 2,000 missiles produced were found to be faulty and were scrapped.

British intelligence meanwhile had been assembling a dossier on the V-1 and the concurrent development, the A4 ballistic missile, later named the V-2, also under development at Peenemünde. On June 29, the British War Cabinet, concerned at the contents of the growing pile of reports on work on secret weapons there, ordered an all-out attack on the site.

In Operation HYDRA, RAF Bomber Command despatched a force of 596 heavy Lancaster four-engined bombers from 5 Group on the moonlit night of August 17–18, 1943, using, for the first time, marker bombs – called 'red spot fire' – to pinpoint three widely separated targets: the experimental station itself, the scientists' accommodation and the co-located V-2 production factory. It was a carefully thought-out tactical plan. German night-fighter patrols were deliberately distracted and diverted by a feint attack on Berlin itself by Mosquito light bombers in Operation WHITEBAIT, to allow the Lancasters to mount the raid. The Peenemünde attack, despite dropping more than 2,000 tons of high explosive, failed to disrupt either the V-1 or V-2 programmes, the latter resuming production after a two months' delay. But among the 700 casualties on the ground (sadly, mainly from the accidental bombing of a slave labour camp at Trassenheide, two miles away), was Dr Walter Thiel, director of V-2 propulsion development at the research centre. The RAF force lost 40 aircraft to enemy action, a further 32 were damaged, and 290 aircrew killed.

Following the raid, the Luftwaffe dispersed some of the V-1 development work into Poland, out of the reach of the Lancasters.

RAF photo-reconnaissance of the Peenemünde site continued and in November, analysis of images taken at high altitude clearly showed a short aircraft with stubby wings on a concrete launching ramp built there. In a draft press statement on the vengeance weapons produced by the British Chiefs of Staffs after the war, they described the images showing 'inclined ramps, apparently fitted with rails. Around some of these the ground was darkened by long dark streaks such as might have been caused by hot blast.' The last piece in an intelligence jigsaw that began with the photograph and sketches from Bornholm had been put into place. This secret weapon was secret no more.

The V-1 and V-2 posed a conundrum for the Allied war leaders. Were they designed as true weapons of vengeance? Were they armed with chemical or biological agents instead of high explosive? Or were they intended to achieve much more telling strategic objectives such as the interruption and delay of the invasion of Europe, now imminent, or to attack the Allied air force bases, to blunt or stifle the continuing bombing campaign against Germany? Could their deployment halt the accelerating Allied momentum towards victory –

and plunge the conflict into a frustrating stalemate? Could the V weapons become Hitler's ticket to the international negotiating table and an eventual permanent cessation of hostilities?

Little did those know within those worrying secret discussions in London that Germany had been motivated solely by naked revenge in developing these weapons – although V-1 launch ramps had begun to be constructed on the Cherbourg peninsula to target the invasion ports of Plymouth and Southampton. (These sites were quickly captured after the D-Day landings in Normandy.) Hitler, like a reeling, punch-drunk prize-fighter, was merely set on standing toe-to-toe to the Allies, exchanging blows, looking for ways to hurt them, to wreak massive destruction and casualties on the prime target, London. In German thinking, it was truly a case of 'an eye for an eye'. Armed with the V-weapons, 'We will', Hitler ranted, 'force England to her knees.' History would show that he had missed a great strategic opportunity. It was only later that the V-weapons target was switched to the Belgian port of Antwerp in a bid to interdict Allied lines of supply to its ground forces, an action motivated much more by the need to achieve a purely military objective.

In Whitehall, it was decided that there was too great a risk in not taking at face value the repeated, thinly veiled German hints that the British capital was *the* target and the creation of terror was Berlin's goal. Plans were hurriedly laid to protect the population of London from this new, but still unquantified menace. The city's civil defence planners were warned in December 1943 of imminent attacks by the V-1 (and later, the V-2), and told to expect the horrifying effects of massive 10-ton warheads said to be fitted to each weapon. The Home Security Ministry ordered a further 100,000 pre-fabricated steel indoor family shelters – named 'Morrison' after the Home Secretary – in October and others stored throughout England were moved nearer the capital, ready for immediate issue. Around 9,000 were distributed to London residents in January and February 1944. Eight new deep concrete public shelters were hurriedly completed at Underground (tube) stations 100ft beneath the London streets: each one was fitted with enough multiple tier sleeping bunks for 8,000 people and was equipped with canteens and medical facilities. These were located below stations at Belsize Park, Camden Town, Clapham North and South, Chancery Lane, Goodge Street, Stockwell and Clapham Common. The last four were retained for government use: Chancery

Lane and Clapham Common were to be used as citadels during the V-1 and V-2 attacks, to allow the machinery of government to continue throughout the attacks. Stockwell was earmarked to protect US troops based in London. The National Fire Service hastily built a network of observation posts perched on tall buildings to quickly locate the V-weapons' impact points. Existing evacuation plans for women and children were dusted off and revised to enable them to escape London, out into the safety of the countryside. In the event, 1,500,000 fled the capital.

For their part, the Germans knew the Allied invasion of Europe (the so-called 'second front') was looming, but because of an Anglo-American campaign of military deception, mainly based on misleading signals traffic, they were convinced, wrongly, that the landings would come on the flat, sandy beaches of the Pas de Calais – the area where the V-1 launching sites were under construction. It was in this area that most of the Wehrmacht armoured forces in France were positioned.

The German High Command wanted to initiate the attack on London late in 1943 but work on the sites had been proceeding at a slower pace than planned, hindered by continual bombing raids. A total of 55 were due to be completed by this time, but only 10 were ready operationally. There was also a shortage of equipment and spare parts at most locations, again caused by disruptive bombing.

Allied photo-reconnaissance had picked up the construction work on four large concrete 'ready-use' weapon storage bunkers in the Calais and Contentin areas as soon as it began in May 1943 and these had been speedily bombed. Six months later, the first of the 96 V-1 launching ramps had been identified and were attacked both by the RAF and the US Army Air Force's (USAAF) Eighth Air Force's B-17 bombers in the long-running Operation CROSSBOW. In addition, effective low-altitude sorties were flown by Republic P-47 Thunderbolt fighter-bombers of the US Ninth Air Force, dropping 1,000 and 2,000lb bombs, a methodology developed and practised at the proving ground at Eglin Air Force base in north-west Florida. Carpet or area bombing of these small, dispersed targets had been ruled out because of the fear of accidentally killing French civilians: thus, these were dangerous, precision attacks. Seventy-three sites were destroyed in 25,100 CROSSBOW sorties, the missions expending almost 8% of the total tonnage of bombs dropped altogether by the RAF and USAAF during the period December 1943–June 1944. The Anglo-American air forces lost 154 aircraft and 771 aircrew in this frenetic and desperate phase of the CROSSBOW campaign.

Unsurprisingly, the Germans abandoned the prominent concrete ramps by the spring of 1944 as too vulnerable to air attack and instead created camouflaged, lightweight launching ramps that were more difficult to spot and destroy. But British and American bomber raids on French railways continued to disrupt transportation of the missiles to their launching areas.

After much delay, Flakregiment 155W had been moved to the Pas de Calais and was ordered to begin the V-1 attacks in June 1944. The flying bombs and the equipment needed to launch them did not arrive until June 12. The Germans, bent on revenge, had missed the unique chance to attack the massive Allied invasion fleets off Normandy, further down the French coast, on D-Day, June 6, at the moment of their greatest vulnerability. But despite the shortages, at long last, Wachtel and his men were now ready to launch.

The V-1 was a simple, robust weapon, but suffered from a number of design and operational defects. It was 25.4ft long, with a wingspan of 17.7ft and weighed 4,760lbs. Within the nose was the warhead with its 1,870lbs of HE, fired by an electrical fuze. Mounted on the tail was the long cylindrical pod containing the pulse jet engine.

The flying bomb was launched by Walter steam catapult, after the engine had been fired up, at a speed of 235 mph. It was designed to fly at an altitude of around 2,000 to 3,000ft, guided by a set of gyroscopes and a pre-set magnetic compass to control direction. By completing a number of pre-set revolutions, a spinner or propeller in the nose armed the weapon after flying about 60 miles and this timer mechanism also determined when it would nosedive to its target, after locking the tailplane elevators and raising airflow spoilers. This action normally stalled the engine. Maximum speed was about 390mph and the flying bomb took around 22 minutes to reach its target, although there was enough petrol to take it more than 160 miles. Later, increased fuel capacity extended the potential range to 250 miles.

The engine worked by sucking in air through movable flaps in the front of the housing to mix with the fuel before ignition. These flaps closed during combustion and reopened again for the next cycle, a process repeated up to 500 times per minute. This created the characteristic loud drone of the V-1 engine; a rapid and repetitive throbbing that was like no other aircraft sound and spawned the Londoners' contemptuous nickname of 'buzz bomb' or the more profane 'farting fury'. The popular sobriquet 'doodlebug' apparently comes from Royal New Zealand Air Force personnel, who coined the name after a noisy insect they knew back at home. The sudden silence as the engine cut out indicated an imminent and nearby explosion around 10 seconds later. It brought terror to many of those crouched, holding their breath, beneath whatever protective shelter they could find. Not for nothing was the V-1 codenamed DIVER by the British authorities.

Wachtel and his team launched the first V-1 around 03.00 on the morning of June 13, followed by nine more flying bombs in rapid succession as Operation RUMPELKAMMER began. Of those catapulted into the sky, just four reached England. Four exploded soon after take-off; two more plunged uselessly into the English Channel. Of the four successful flights, only one hit London, destroying a railway bridge at Bethnal Green, three miles east of the Tower Bridge aiming point, and killing six people. Three fell short of the capital, the second exploding at 04.20 at a farm at Cuckfield, West Sussex, the blast blowing off the door of a pigsty and releasing a number of terrified animals. The remaining two landed in Kent and Surrey without inflicting casualties.

For the Germans, it was an inauspicious start to their much-vaunted campaign of vengeance. The Allies reacted surprisingly mildly with just one sortie by 36 USAAF B-17 aircraft dropping 101 tons of bombs on a V-1 supply site. After a brief pause, no doubt because of shortage of hardware, Wachtel resumed his launches on the night of June 15–16, but this time from 55 sites, catapulting 244 flying bombs into the sky, of which 73 impacted on London and another 71 exploded between the capital and the south coast of England, around 60 miles away. One hundred V-1s failed to cross the Channel and of these, 45 crashed in the seconds immediately following launch, one in a nearby French village where ten civilians were killed in the blast. Premature explosions, on take-off, seriously damaged nine sites.

Despite this poor strike rate, Hitler was jubilant. He flew to France on June 17 specifically to shower congratulations on Wachtel and his men of Flakregiment 155W. During the visit, the Führer insisted that London should remain the sole target. The production rate of his new wonder weapons would be stepped up. Amid all the celebrations and unknown to Hitler, his audience were only too aware that one rogue V-1 had made an unplanned U-turn in its flight and had crashed in a huge explosion near the command post he was scheduled to visit later that day.

The campaign, however, continued relentlessly. That same day, Wachtel launched his 500th V-1 and by June 29, the number despatched had climbed to 2,000. At last for Berlin, the long-awaited massive bombardment of London was underway.

RAF Bomber Command quickly mounted a raid by 740 Lancaster, Halifax and Mosquito aircraft on the night of June 24, hitting identified V-1 launch sites at Prouville, Rimeux, Pommereval, Le Grande Rossignol, Bamieres and Flers in the Pas de Calais, losing 87 bombers in ferocious anti-aircraft fire and night-fighter attacks.

The British Government's Regional Commissioner for London, Sir Ernest Gowers, told the Home Office in early August that the V-1 offensive had gone on 'for day and night with intervals which sometimes lasted several hours. As many as 15 have been known to land in the London region almost simultaneously. The largest number to fall in any 24 hours was 98. Not one of the 95 local authority areas in the Region has escaped. As all the orthodox form of shelters afford excellent protection, we have been lucky in having fewer casualties than might have been expected. The worst disasters were at the Guards Chapel during morning service (119 killed) and a block of US Army flats in Chelsea (74 killed).'

By the end of August, a total of 5,126 civilians had been killed and 14,712 wounded in V-1 attacks. Although one flying bomb hit the headquarters of Gen. Dwight D. Eisenhower, the Supreme Allied Commander, many fell short of their target, because the Germans failed to receive accurate information on the impact points and so could not adjust their aim. One of the worst-hit areas in the entire V-1 offensive was the Borough of Croydon, 12 miles south of London, which received 141 direct hits, killing 211, seriously injuring 697 and destroying 1,400 homes. A further 54,000 dwellings were damaged. A workforce of 5,000 labourers was recruited to clear the rubble in the London streets and keep road communications open. One and a half million residents left the city to escape the attacks.

Churchill was enraged by the attacks. He wrote: 'One landed near my home in Westerham, killing by cruel mischance, 22 homeless children and five grown-ups collected in a refuge made for them in the woods.' He urged his War Cabinet colleagues to allow him to order the RAF to drop Britain's considerable stockpile of chemical weapons on German cities in retaliation for the V-1 attacks. With his experience of the bitter fighting on the Western Front nearly 30 years before, he was less squeamish than many others in his readiness to deploy poison gas. The British Prime Minister was dissuaded by two more realistic arguments. Firstly, this would almost certainly dramatically escalate the conflict, with the Germans also resorting to chemical warfare against civilians in a tit for tat reprisal. Secondly, the RAF still believed that conventional high explosive and incendiary bombs were far more effective in achieving Britain's war aims. (Ironically, the Germans considered fitting a chemical warhead on the V-1, but believing the British possessed the new nerve gases they themselves had developed and fearing reprisal in kind, they scrapped the plan.)

The Allied response took two forms. At home, the defences for London and the South-East were considerably beefed up after initial largely ineffective attempts to shoot down the intruders. The defences eventually formed three lines of interception: what was to become a total of 2,015 huge gas-filled barrage balloons, tethered up to 5,000ft above the ground, positioned in a line along the southern perimeter of greater London, protecting the capital's south-east flank; a gun line of anti-aircraft ordnance and finally, a number of fighter squadrons specifically tasked to shoot down the flying bombs.

There were operational problems. At first, the ground gun crews could not fire freely at low-altitude targets for fear of hitting their own intercepting fighters. The very visible barrage balloons amounted to little more than a psychological prop for Londoners rather than an effective countermeasure: their cables brought down 232 V-1s, but some later-model flying bombs were reportedly fitted with cable cutters. The fighters also had problems keeping up with the high speed of the flying bombs.

Fighters capable of greater speed —Vickers Supermarine Spitfire F-XIV, Hawker Tempest Vs, the Rolls-Royce Merlin-engined North American Mustang III and the De Havilland Mosquito, all with speeds in excess of 350mph – were then brought into play. Fifteen day-light and nine night-fighter squadrons were assigned to the defence of London. The revolutionary Gloster Meteor jet, capable of 485mph and armed with four 20mm cannon, which made its first flight on March 5, 1943, was rushed into service and made its operational debut countering the V-1 threat, seven joining 616 Squadron in July.

For the pilots, shooting down the flying bomb presented great hazards because of the danger of the warhead exploding when their cannon fire ripped into the V-1. Tactics were refined into making a dive attack from above and astern of the target and opening fire from about 1,000ft. A safer technique was to fly alongside, slide the tip of the fighter's wing under the missile's stubby plywood wings and flip it up, throwing out the guidance gyroscope. The flying bomb would then nosedive and crash to earth. Fighters accounted for 1,847 V-1s, in the two phases of the flying bomb offensive, with Squadron Leader Joseph Berry, a Tempest V pilot, accounting for 59. The Meteors' tally was 13.

The British military leaders' 'official' description of the battle against the vengeance weapons after the war, commented:

> Some time ago, a special trial was arranged for him [Hitler] in the Baltic. A German fighter ace flying a captured Spitfire demonstrated to the Führer that British fighters did not possess the necessary speed to intercept the flying bomb. They reckoned without the increased efficiency of our latest types and without the superior skill and resource of our pilots.

The remaining defence was the gun line, close to London. Because of the problems of 'friendly fire' against defending British aircraft and the danger of both crashing V-1s and falling shrapnel to civilians on the ground, the gun positions had clearly to be moved forward. In July, it was decided to establish a new defensive line along the south-east coast where the incoming V-1s could be shot down over the sea without fear of them causing damage to life or property as they crashed. 'No go' flying zones for the British fighters could also be established, to avert the risk of shooting down their own pilots. If any V-1 escaped the barrage of shells thrown up by the gun line, there were still six to seven minutes in which the fighters could neutralise the threat before the flying bomb reached London.

In just four days and by July 19, nearly 600 heavy anti-aircraft guns, 200 rocket batteries and 500 Bofors 40 mm cannon and other light calibre weapons of Anti-Aircraft Command were transported and placed in new positions, from Newhaven in East Sussex, to St Margaret's Bay, in Kent. It was a massive logistical operation, involving 23,000 personnel and the laying of 3,000 miles of new telephone cable. As there was no time to build concrete emplacements, the guns were placed on hastily built platforms made of wooden railway sleepers and rail lines. Deployment of mobile 3.7in AA guns was abandoned, as the manually operated ordnance just could not move quickly enough to track the fast-flying V-1s. Instead the British relied on static guns, remotely controlled and automatically laid on their targets. American-manned batteries were added, fitted with the new SCR-548 gun-laying radar to automatically track and predict the V-1 flight paths. Their 90mm guns fired shells armed with new proximity fuzes, to explode near the missile rather than relying on a direct hit. In all, the gun line accounted for 1,878 V-1s.

By August, an average of 81 V-1s were being launched each day – including a peak of 316 on August 2. By the end of the month the defences were becoming more than a match for the intruders. On August 28, 90 of 94 flying bombs crossing the English Channel coast were destroyed, 65 of them shot down by the re-sited gun line, and by the month end, an average of only one in seven V-1s were penetrating the defences and hitting its target in London.

The second Allied response was another phase of CROSSBOW, launched six days after the V-1 attacks began. Eisenhower, the Allied supremo, was concerned that his invasion supply lines would be destroyed and he ordered that bombing raids on V-1 targets should receive 'first priority over all targets, either in France or Germany'. Within 14 days, 8,310 missions, dropping 23,341 tons of bombs were diverted from other targets and during July and August, 250 V-1 associated targets were attacked.

But some eventual relief for the hard-pressed Londoners and those in peril beneath the flight path over south-east England came from another direction – the invasion forces breaking out north-eastwards in France from the Normandy bridgehead. V-1 operations were halted on September 3 when 155 Flakregiment W was forced to evacuate across the river Somme because of advancing Allied ground forces. By mid-September, all the launching sites in the Pas de Calais had been captured. A total of around 9,400 V-1s had been launched against London, of which around 2,000 had hit the British capital.

The V-1 offensive was not over, however. In early July, a number of V-1s had hit targets some way from London, in Manchester and Gloucester and the extra range of the attacks initially puzzled British intelligence. These had been launched from modified Heinkel He-111 bombers, flying from Dutch airfields About 30 bombers could carry the flying bomb under the port wing, inboard of the engine, of which 20 were operational at any one time. The aircraft approached England at low altitude to evade radar detection, climbed to an altitude of about 20,000ft, set the V-1's gyroscope and then fired the engine. The weapon was released, dropped for a few hundred feet, and then headed off on its lethal mission. It was a dangerous business for the German bomber crews. The V-1s had a distressing habit of exploding prematurely. The Luftwaffe launched 1,200 V-1s on these sorties but lost 77 aircraft through accidents, 12 in just two missions when the warheads blew up as the aircraft took off from the runway. Faced with these losses, the air-launched V-1 campaign was halted in mid-January 1945.

The British Chiefs of Staff, trying to predict future attacks, reported to the War Cabinet on September 25:

> There is evidence of experiments with other types of aircraft for launching the flying bomb. If the [Dornier] 217, [Focke-Wulf] 200 or the [Heinkel] He-177 were to be used for this purpose, suitable bases could be found in Norway, Denmark and the greater part of Germany, the likely scale of attack by flying bombs would be proportionately increased.

If this occurred, they forecast new V-1 attacks down England's east coast, particularly around Tyneside and Hull. But the experiments with new aircraft came to nothing.

Simultaneously with the Heinkel launches, the Germans had developed an extended range version of the flying bomb and constructed new sites in the occupied Netherlands to continue the campaign against England, still focusing on London. By increasing the fuel capacity and reducing the size (and thus weight) of the warhead, this later model V-1 could fly 250 miles. These attacks commenced in March 1945, but ended on March 29 after about 275 had been launched.

In all, the V-1 attacks against Britain killed 6,781 civilians and injured 17,981, together with a further 1,200 service casualties, both killed and wounded. It destroyed 130,000 homes in England and damaged a further 750,000 dwellings.

As we have seen, the Germans turned their attentions to other targets as the advancing Allied ground forces pushed them back. The important Belgian re-supply port of Antwerp was liberated by the British 11th. Armoured Division on September 1944, its extensive docks capable of handling 100,000 tons of freight per day, still miraculously intact. On October 13 1944, the V-1 assault against the city

began. During 154 consecutive days, it received 2,448 V-1 hits, most in
or near its centre, killing 3,470 civilians, 682 Allied servicemen and
injuring 10,606 people. Only 211 hit the harbour area. A total of 5,600
were targeted on Antwerp but largescale deployment of American,
British and Polish anti-aircraft batteries to the north west of Antwerp
were major contributors to the 2,100 V-1s destroyed before they could
hit their targets. The port remained open throughout the attacks. A
further 3,141 hit the Belgian city of Liège. The attacks finally ended on
March 26 as German forces began pulling out of the Netherlands.

German development of the V-1 had not finished with the
extended-range version. Bizarrely, a plan emerged in May 1944, to
build a manned version, used in what amounted to suicide missions
against high-value naval targets like aircraft carriers, battleships and
heavy cruisers, and to destroy important heavily defended targets on
land. The idea is a measure perhaps, of the scale of German desperation
at this stage in the conflict, to find and deploy a war-winner. It may
also indicate German mounting frustration at the flying bomb's inherent inaccuracy. After Hanna Reitsch's earlier perilous V-1
development flights at Peenemünde, not much new work needed to
be done; mere adaptation of the airframe. Within a fortnight, four prototypes had been built, with a cramped cockpit inserted just forward
of the propulsion pod. Flight tests began almost immediately.

The project was codenamed REICHENBERG. The plan was for the
manned version of the V-1, designated Fi-103R, to be carried towards
its target, slung under the wing of a Heinkel He-111 bomber from the
Luftwaffe's special operations wing, in the manner of the less-than-
successful air-launched flying bomb. After release, the manned missile
would be flown to its target and during its final dive, at speeds
approaching 500mph, the pilot would release the cockpit canopy and
scramble out, parachuting to safety. That was the theory, anyway. In
practice, of course, the pilot stood precious little chance of survival;
the AS 014 pulse jet's air duct was immediately behind and above
the canopy and opening it and escaping would have been almost
impossible.

The Fi-103R was 27ft long, almost 18 inches longer than the parent
design, and carried a 1,874lb explosive warhead in the nose. Range,
from a launch height of just over 8,000ft, was estimated at 200 miles.
Flying instruments were very basic – an altimeter, airspeed indicator,
attitude indicator, a clock and the all-important warhead arming

switch. Three training versions were produced, one with two seats including one in the nose for the student, and all fitted with flaps and primitive landing gear, such as a skid. About 175 flying bombs were converted to the piloted model.

Proving the concept, in September 1944 and subsequent training flights, was problematical. The first two crashed. Manoeuvrability was poor and landing, at high speeds, hazardous. There were a number of further crashes, before test flights were handed over to Hanna Reitsch, who herself suffered some narrow escapes. Meanwhile, volunteers were sought to fly the missions: called, ominously, *Selbstopfermänner,* or 'self-sacrifice men'. Amazingly, 70 applied for training.

But the Luftwaffe, distracted by the rapid onslaught of the Allied forces into the Fatherland, cancelled the project in October 1944. No Reichenberg flying bombs were ever used operationally.

Berlin's plans to deal out vengeance were not fully played out, however. Germany had been secretly developing and producing other *Vergeltungswaffe* weapons, one of which we have briefly met before – the V-2. If the noisy and inaccurate V-1 is the forerunner of today's cruise missiles, the liquid-propelled and guided V-2 is the father of the Cold War intercontinental ballistic missile.

The weapon was born out of the innocent hobbyist rocket clubs that flourished in Germany in the 1920s and early 1930s, all intrigued by the possibilities of travel in space, free of the Earth's gravity. One of these young enthusiasts, Werner von Braun, began research into using rockets as long-range artillery for the German army in 1932, before graduating from Friedrich-Wilhelm-Universität with a Ph.D in physics. The Wehrmacht's interest in rockets was sparked by its desire to circumvent the restrictions placed on the range and calibre of its guns by the 1919 Treaty of Versailles and still retain some vestiges of legality. Because no one, after the First World War, saw rocketry as a serious military weapon – in modern parlance, 'no real threat' - they were not included in the clauses covering artillery. That viewpoint was to change as a result of the experiments at Peenemünde.

Encouraged by early tests of small rockets at the Kummersdorf range, near Berlin, in 1936 the German army began building a huge research and development facility at Peenemünde for continuing work on rockets; the following April, the vanguard of nearly 2,000 scientists and 4,000 other personnel moved there, led by von Braun, as technical director, and a German army officer, Walter Dornberger, who was in charge of the overall rocket projects. The site was code-named *Heimat Artillerie Park II*, or home artillery park.

The immediate priority for von Braun's team was to develop the A3 rocket, a 21ft long ballistic missile, powered by a mixture of liquid oxygen and ethyl alcohol. After a number of tests on this prototype, the Wehrmacht ordnance department in 1938 ordered the development of a rocket with a range of between 150 to 200 miles, capable of carrying one ton of explosives as a warhead. A further development version, designated A5, was built and flight-tested at the end of 1938 and into the following two years. One vertical launch achieved an altitude of 7.5 miles.

Test data from these launches was used in the design of a powerful new rocket, designated A4 (later to become the V-2), with the aerodynamics confirmed using models in a small wind tunnel at Peenemünde. However, von Braun's test programme of prototypes of this new ballistic missile began badly. Before firings began, one was damaged during fuelling when it slipped out of its holding device on the launch pad and crashed to the ground. The first launch came on June 13 1942, but the rocket spiralled out of control because of a failure in the internal fuel to the rocket motor. The next launch, on August 16, also failed in its objective, but success finally came on October 3, when the A4 reached a height of 55.9 miles and achieved a range of 170 miles, splashing down into the Baltic. This was the greatest altitude achieved by any projectile at that time. The flight confirmed the efficacy of the liquid fuel propulsion and met the Army's operational requirement.

Further launches proved similarly successful, although at least one A4 exploded over Sweden, near Bäckebo, where a crater remains to this day. Another, taking part in experiments with the prototype radio guidance system for the planned *Wasserfall* ('Waterfall') surface-to-air missile, crashed on Swedish territory in June 1944 and the debris was sent to England for examination, despite Berlin's desperate attempts to recover it, in return for new British radar technology. It was painstakingly reconstructed at the Royal Aircraft Establishment at Farnborough, Hampshire and the potential performance of what came to be called 'the Swedish model' by the British analysed by technical experts. Further information became available via interrogations of German prisoners, formerly based at Peenemünde, who surrendered in the fighting after D-Day. Some mysterious documents on the

V-2 were also captured in Normandy, which provided help in the Farnborough reconstruction.

Back in Germany, production of the missile was soon authorised by Berlin and the A4 assembly lines at Peenemünde began work. But, as we have seen, the RAF HYDRA raid on the site on the night of August 17–18, 1943 damaged the rocket assembly facilities, delaying production by two months, as well as killing a vital team member, Dr Walter Thiel, head of the V-2 propulsion project.

Probably, as a result, the feared *Schutzstaffel* or SS, under Reichsführer Heinrich Himmler, seized control of the project from the Army within 24 hours of the raid and with it, the resources and organisation of components manufacture and weapon assembly. A bomb-proof underground factory, codenamed MITTELWERKE, was quickly created in former mine-workings beneath Kohnstein mountain, in the Harz Mountains, a few miles north-west of the city of Nordhausen in Thüringia, central Germany, specifically to assemble both the V-2 and the V-1.

The complex had begun in the mid-1930s as a gypsum mine and the workings were later used to store strategic materials such as petrol and rubber, as well as stockpiles of chemical munitions. Work on extending the storage space had continued there from 1940 and two large curved tunnels had been excavated with a number of communicating lateral galleries. Now it was to be transformed into what was, at that time, the world's largest underground munitions factory.

The SS, quick off the mark, transported the first consignments of slave labour from the Buchenwald forced labour concentration camp, near Weimar, more than 50 miles away, to the Mittelwerke site on August 28, 1943 to begin work to extend the tunnel system. Later, slave labour installed the equipment for the V-2 assembly lines. After completion, the gigantic concrete-lined complex consisted of the two main tunnels, named A and B, each 6,200ft long, 23ft in height and 36ft in width and with its own small-gauge railway track. These tunnels were connected along their course by 48 lateral galleries, or halls, 600ft in length, also used for production work. Tunnel B contained two adjacent assembly lines for the V-2. Production of the V-1 was sited at one end of Tunnel A and other sections of the complex housed the separate manufacture of aircraft engines.

Prisoners from adjacent concentration camps provided most of the labour force: the new 'Dora' camp, with 58 barrack blocks, eventually housing 20,000 inmates, was located just 500 yards outside the factory's south entrance. A network of other camps was sited around Nordhausen. Altogether, some 60,000 camp inmates were forced to work in the barbarous, inhumane conditions of the subterranean assembly lines in 12-hour shifts, around the clock. Of these, about 25,000 ultimately perished from malnourishment, disease, frequent beatings and in mass punishment executions by SS guards. Some were strung up by the neck from wires in the tunnels as a gruesome example to fellow workers. About 100 bodies of those who had died, too weak to continue working, were disposed of daily, like so much worthless detritus, in a specially built crematorium nearby.

Aside from those manufactured for developmental tests, total Mittelwerke output of operational V-2s between August 1944 and March 1945 was 4,575 rockets. Work there halted on April 10 because of advancing American troops.

Despite the use of slave labour, the V-2 was far more expensive to fabricate than its sister weapon of vengeance, the V-1, mainly because of its more complex design, necessarily higher engineering standards and the thousands of components required for each rocket. Unit cost of the ballistic missile was estimated at more than £12,000. Total German expenditure on the V-2 project is believed to have been more than £500,000 in 1940s' prices. But the human cost of production was far higher: nearly six slave labourers died for each V-2 assembled at Mittelwerke – piquantly, a higher rate than enemy civilians killed by its operational use.

The V-2 infrastructure contained a host of supporting industrial facilities throughout Germany and Austria, manufacturing components or engaged in quality assurance and calibration of instruments. At Lehesten, 80 miles south-east of Mittelwerke, a quarry site was utilised to build a hardened complex to test-fire V-2 engines, the labour provided by its own concentration camp at Schmiedebach.

The project was gathering momentum. In late December 1942, only two months after the first successful flight-test of the rocket, Hitler ordered the speedy construction of three special concrete-protected sites in northern France for launching the V-2. These would include accommodation barracks, dedicated anti-aircraft defences, and storage and assembly buildings, as well as the associated concrete launch pads. New manufacturing plant for the liquid oxygen (LOX) used for the rocket propulsion system was also desperately needed: the

Third Reich just did not possess the industrial capacity to produce enough LOX to support Hitler's hoped-for but totally unrealistic tally of 144 V-2 launches every day against England.

After a quick search for suitable sites, a team of experts visited the St-Omer area in the Pas-de-Calais at the end of December and selected a site within the Forêt d'Eperlecques, eight miles from Watten, on the road to Calais, well beyond the range of British heavy naval guns, but still close to good rail, road and canal communications links.

Within two months, the German forced labour administration, the *Organisation Todt*, completed plans for the complex and construction began in late March. The work on the two-storey structure, 92ft tall, was to end just six months later, 30 days ahead of schedule and would involve 30,000 mainly French and Russian slave labourers and huge numbers of earth-moving machines, together with an estimated 120,000 cubic yards of reinforced concrete. The main blast-proof door, made of steel, weighed 216 tons. A dedicated railway spur line was also constructed, as was a special bunker containing electricity generators. In timing and construction, it was a marvel of civil engineering.

The Germans codenamed the huge bunker, or blockhouse, KRAFTWERKE NORDWEST, or 'power station north-west' as a cover for its true role.

The complex contained a factory to produce LOX and halls where the V-2s were assembled after their rail journey from the Mittelwerke plant. Finally, the warheads were fitted before the completed missile was moved out to launch pads 100ft away. The plan was for 36 V-2s to be launched each day from the Eperlecques complex.

RAF photo-reconnaissance picked up the construction work on the site on May 16, 1943, but the British were mystified as to the role of the gigantic concrete structure. The first raid on the site came on August 27, when 185 USAAF B-17 Flying Fortresses attacked, dropping 366 2,000lb bombs. The northern sector of the bunker, where the concrete had not yet dried, was devastated.

It was the first of 21 raids launched up to August 25, 1944, two of which involved the dropping, by 5 Group's Lancasters, of more than 15 of the RAF's new 'Tallboy' 14,000lb deep-penetration bombs, specially developed by the inventor Barnes Wallis (of Dambuster fame) to destroy hardened bunkers. Most of these fearsome weapons unfortunately missed but the explosions shook the massive bunker.

Work resumed on the site in November 1943, with the Organisation Todt deciding to complete the liquid oxygen plant in the
southern portion of the complex, beneath a 15ft-thick concrete roof,
the output to support V-2 operations elsewhere. This was completed
in January the following year but the 'Tallboy' raids convinced the
Germans that the site was unusable and it was abandoned. Eperlecques
was finally overrun by Canadian troops on September 6, 1944.

Two more V-2 sites were under construction. Work on a second
assembly and launching site began in November 1943 at an old chalk
quarry at Wizernes, near St-Omer, codenamed SCHOTTERWERKE
NORDWEST, or 'rubbleworks north-west', as a back-up for the bombed
Eperlecques facility. To avoid the unwelcome attention of Bomber
Command and the USAAF, here the complex was hidden within 11
miles of tunnels, protected by a huge 15ft-thick dome, formed from
55,000 tons of reinforced concrete – hence the name *La Coupole*, for
the present-day museum on the site. It included another LOX plant
and an underground hospital was constructed near by in the quarry.
Completed V-2s would be moved down two tunnels, nicknamed
'Gretchen' and 'Gustav' by German engineers with a touch of homely
humour, through the protective 5ft-thick blast doors, to launching
pads outside.

Again the Allies were slow to recognise the true purpose of the
Wizernes complex and the first bombing raid was not made until
March 11, 1944 when 34 American B-24 aircraft dropped 248 1,000lb
bombs on the site. In the five months following, however, a further 15
raids were mounted, totalling more than 2,900 tons of bombs, including two which dropped the Tallboy 'earthquake' weapons. The last of
these blew the hillside apart, threatening the stability of the concrete
dome, though not seriously damaging it. Hitler ordered the site to be
evacuated soon after the attacks, in July 1944.

(As an aside, German capabilities in concrete construction in the
Second World War became legendary. At an airfield at Karup, in then
occupied Denmark, the Luftwaffe built a huge command bunker
which after the war ended, was of little use to the Danish air force.
Various expert allied demolition teams tried unsuccessfully to destroy
it, including, perhaps anecdotally, a Royal Navy team which confidently filled it with water and exploded a powerful depth charge
inside, believing the mighty shock waves would shatter the concrete

casement. All was to no avail. After every explosion, there was no sign of damage, not even a crack. Eventually, NATO took it over as a regional headquarters, called, in the Alliance's curious language of acronyms, BALTAP, covering the Baltic approaches.)

Thirteen miles from Wizernes, a V-2 guidance site was constructed at Roquetoire, codenamed UMSPANNWERKE C, or transformer station C. To achieve greater accuracy, the Peenemünde team had developed a system in November 1940 where the V-2 would 'ride' radio beams projected towards its target – the first appearance of a guidance technology used by many tactical missiles in the 1960s and early 1970s. The Roquetoire site, located within a 12ft-thick concrete bunker, 22ft tall, contained a 500-watt, 45 MHz transmitter to generate the *Leitstrahl* radio beam for missiles launched from the Wizernes site. It never became operational because of the scrapping of the Wizernes project.

The third and final permanent V-2 site was at Sottevast, about eight miles south of Cherbourg, begun in October 1943. This was, however, overrun by Allied forces whilst still under construction soon after D-Day. Another at Brécourt, also on the Cherbourg peninsula, was begun, codenamed WASSERWERKE 2 ('waterworks 2') but plans for V-2s to be deployed there were subsequently dropped and its role was changed to launch V-1s instead. After all the frenetic construction work, not one of the permanent sites had fired, or even come close to firing, a V-2 in anger. Another method of launching had to be found.

General Walter Dornberger, who had led the research and development at Peenemünde, always favoured firing the V-2 from pre-surveyed sites, with the missiles being moved around on mobile launchers that were difficult to detect and interdict from the air. This became the solution, although it involved the development of a large logistical operation, involving 30 vehicles, to transport, fuel, arm and fire each missile. In France, the Germans laid a number of concrete launching pads, hidden away in forests and woods in Normandy, called *regenwürmstellungen*, literally 'earthworm position' – a telling reference to their low profile, almost impossible to spot by photo-reconnaissance. In the event, once operational, the Germans fired V-2s from unprepared sites or on roads or any flat surface, moving them around on 16-wheeled *meillerwagens*, designed by the Peenemünde engineers – what today would be called a 'transporter/erector/launcher' or TEL vehicle.

This tactic in the deployment of ballistic missiles, developed by the

Germans in the Second World War, is all too familiar to us in the 21st century. During the 1991 Gulf War in Iraq, substantial coalition forces, both in the air and, covertly on the ground, were assigned to destroy mobile launchers before their missiles could be fired at Israel and Saudi Arabia. A number evaded the pre-emptive strikes and were launched.

It is time to examine the nature of the beast.

The V-2 was the first large guided ballistic missile used in war. Resembling a stubby, fat metal cigar, it measured 46ft 1in in length and had a diameter, at its widest part, of 5ft 6in, with fins, at the base, extending the overall width to 12ft. The outer skin was made of thin steel sheet. The 6ft-long nose of the rocket held the warhead, amounting to 2,204lbs of amatol HE – just under a ton. Immediately below, was the section containing the automatic gyroscopes electrically controlling four movable vanes or rudders fitted to the base of the fins to maintain stability (or pitch, roll and yaw) in flight. Also in this 5ft section was other instrumentation and the radio guidance system, receiving the 'Leitstrahl' guidance beam that shut down the fuel supply, via another gyroscope, when the missile was approaching the target. This system was only suitable for short-range operations and only around 25% of V-2 attacks used this guidance method. Radio antennae were attached to the lower outer edges of the fins.

Below the guidance compartment was a 20ft section carrying the fuel tank, containing 8,180lbs of a mixture of 75% ethyl alcohol and 25% water, above another tank holding 10,805lbs of liquid oxygen at a temperature of -183° C. The fuel and oxygenant were pumped into the engines by 3,800 revolutions-per-minute steam turbines, powered by secondary fuel consisting of volatile hydrogen peroxide and the catalyst, sodium permanganate. Below the rocket motor, or combustion chamber, operating at around 2,700°C, in the 15ft-long base section, were four movable jet vanes that also steered the missile. Overall weight of the fully fuelled rocket was 12.5 tons.

The motor generated 69,000lbs of thrust at ignition, lifting the missile vertically off its launch pad relatively slowly, but quickly developing its designed maximum of 160,000 lbs and accelerating to speeds of around 5,000ft per second. After about four seconds, the V-2 settled into its short flight at its programmed angle – around 45° – to achieve the maximum range. The rocket motor burnt for about 65 seconds, pushing it to a height of 55 miles above the Earth's surface. Range was between 150 and 220 miles. The missile impacted its target at around 2,000mph, three times the speed of sound, between five and seven minutes after launch. Often the kinetic energy would drive the weapon 30ft into the earth before the warhead exploded.

The V-2 missiles were placed under the command of SS General Hans Kammler on August 31, 1944 with Dornberger relegated to organising the field training of the launch and support crews. Within two months, he had eight V-2 'artillery' batteries ready for operations within LXV Corps assigned for 'special employment', headquartered at Haaksbergen in the Twente region of the Netherlands, just west of the German frontier.

Launching the V-2 was a complex operation. The missiles were transported to storage zones by flatbed rail car from the Mittelwerke factory and lifted off the wagons by mobile 16-ton cranes and laid onto horizontal cradles fitted to the *meillerwagens*. Each V-2 battery had five platoons of 39 troops each, handling launch, fuelling, logistics and testing, communications (including operating the radio guidance) and surveying and finally, command duties, with a fire-control vehicle, called the *feuerleitpanzer*.

There were three launch units, with three *meillerwagens* per group. The fuelling group had special vehicles to tank the liquid oxygen, alcohol and hydrogen peroxide. Once a launch site was selected, the missile was erected onto its 10ft welded iron rotatable ring launch platform, fuelled from the support vehicles, its flight path programmed in, and final checks completed – a process that took, on average, around 90 minutes. Three V-2s were normally fired in one salvo. The firing battery then hastily moved to another camouflaged launch site, in a manoeuvre now known as 'shoot and scoot'.

Hitler ordered Operation PENGUIN, the V-2 attack on the English mainland, to begin by September 15, 1944. Because of the Allied advance, only Dutch and German territory remained as launch sites for his potential targets for vengeance – France had been liberated.

And France, so recently wrested from German occupation, marked the V-2's debut as a weapon of terror. Like the V-1, the beginning was unfortunate from the Germans' point of view. On September 6, at just after 09.00, two missiles were launched at Paris, 180 miles away, by a battery of 444 (Motorised) Artillery Battalion at a site 11 miles south-east of Malmédy, Belgium, near the German border. Both failed, falling back on their firing platforms. The following day, in London, Churchill's son-in-law, Duncan Sandys, Parliamentary Secretary to the Ministry of Supply, told a press conference that as far as the V-1 offensive was concerned, 'except possibly for a few last parting shots, what has come to be known as the Battle of London is over'. Londoners, battered and terrified by the 'doodlebug' onslaught, were delighted to read his confident statement when they opened their newspapers the next morning, September 8. The sigh of relief throughout the capital was almost audible. They had suffered death and destruction at the hands of Hitler's hated buzz bomb. It was good to know the end was in sight.

That evening, at precisely 6.43 p.m., the first V-2 impacted on London, in Staveley Road, Chiswick, in the western suburbs, and killed three civilians, and seriously wounding another 10. It left a crater 18ft deep and 25ft wide. Another demolished some wooden sheds in Parndon Woods, 3.5 miles north of Epping, to the north-east of London, 16 seconds later. Both were launched from road junctions in Wassenaar, a district of The Hague, the Dutch capital, 200 miles away, by the second battery of 485 (Motorised) Artillery Battalion, who had soon departed the scene.

Death, unannounced, had reached down from the skies.

This time there was no throbbing engine note to warn of the attack. No air-raid sirens were sounded. Just a distinctive double-crack explosion caused by the rocket's blast wave hitting the ground, then the explosion of the huge warhead itself. The V-2 flew so fast that the roaring, rushing noise of its rocket motor was heard *after impact*, as the slower sound waves caught up, amid the immediate noise of rubble falling. There was no time to take cover. And there was absolutely no protection, nor could there be: no fighters yet dreamt of, no gun-line, no barrage balloon could counter the speed and the threat of this new weapon of vengeance.

The British government sought to massage the morale of the 6,800,000 Londoners. The explosions, the public were initially told, were merely caused by leaks of town gas from the mains. Nothing to worry about: just an unfortunate series of accidents. The War Cabinet repeatedly considered whether to disclose the nature of the attacks. On September 26, it decided that 'it would be best to leave well alone and say nothing – at any rate until we could definitely say that no further threat existed.' They asked the British Chiefs of Staff to ask their American counterparts to 'take steps to restrain publication [of news of the V-2 attacks] in America' as 'any reference to the attack would be seized upon by the Germans, and so magnified so as to provide sorely needed encouragement for their people.'

On October 7, the British chiefs sent a top secret telegram in cipher to their liaison team in Washington, repeating the request to the US combined chiefs, following the publication of an article in the *New York Times* about the V-2 attacks on London.

It was not until November 10 that Churchill told the British Parliament that the Germans had launched long-range rockets against England but his words, stating what was painfully obvious, were merely confirming a statement from Berlin of two days before.

The British became increasingly worried by the power of the V-2. On September 14, a junior War Transport Minister, Philip Noel-Baker, told the War Cabinet, in an admirable example of British under-statement, that the missile was:

> more capable of piercing the under-river Tube than the flying bomb. The consequences of such an occurrence would be exceedingly serious. In the absence of an effective warning system,★ however, there appeared to be no alternative to either closing the Tube more or less permanently, or taking no action. The former would create a serious traffic problem and in view of the [then] lightness of the scale of the attacks, the Ministry [of War Transport] was for the present taking no action.

The Vice Chief of the Imperial General Staff sent this 'Most Secret' telegram in cipher to the irascible Field Marshal Bernard Montgomery, British commander of Allied forces advancing through Belgium:

> Two rockets, so-called V-2 landed in England yesterday. Believed to have been fired from areas near Rotterdam and Amsterdam. Will you please report urgently by what approximate date you consider you can rope off the coastal area contained by Antwerp, Utrecht, Rotterdam. When this area is in our hands, the threat from this weapon will probably have disappeared.

Although conventional defences against the missile attacks, code-named BIG BEN, by the British Chiefs of Staff, were denied them, radar plots and a series of swift reports by a very efficient and certainly

★ The section of the Tube or metro which ran under the River Thames between stations at Waterloo and Leicester Square was always closed during an air raid alert because of fears of damage that would flood the entire London system.

gallant Dutch resistance sometimes enabled the launch sites to be pin-
pointed. The RAF were tasked to attack these sites but never
succeeded in interdicting a V-2 launch, although one fighter, by
chance, unsuccessfully opened fire on a missile as it was launched from
some trees. To try to provide faster information, the Chiefs of Staff
recalled No 10. Survey Regiment, Royal Artillery, from 21 Army
Group, fighting in Europe, to provide a sound ranging and spotting
capability in south-east England. They also searched for effective
countermeasures, requesting the loan of 16 B-24 Liberator aircraft
from the USAAF, fitted with radio jamming equipment to disrupt the
V-2 guidance system. In addition they positioned 36 ground radio
jammers and two 50 kW 'cigar' sets along the known flight path over
England and sent another 2 kW set across the English Channel from
Southampton to use in Belgium.

    (Meanwhile, the ill-fated 444 Artillery Battalion suffered another
failure in its launches. On the same day of the first successful V-2
attacks on London, the unit launched another missile at Paris, but it
exploded harmlessly at high altitude. The second, launched on September 8, hit south-east Paris, killing six and injuring 36.)

    A total of 517 V-2s were to hit London in the seven months before
the Allied advance into Germany would push the weapon out of
range. Altogether, 2,724 Londoners were killed and 6,500 injured in
the attacks. Most of the impact points were in the east and south of the
city: the poorer area of Hackney received 10 V-2 hits; the borough of
West Ham, 27. By November, the capital was suffering four V-2
impacts per day. The explosive power was awesome.

    Among a number of terrible incidents, 160 civilians were killed and
108 injured when a V-2 demolished a Woolworth's department store in
New Cross, south east London, on November 25. No trace of 11
people known to be in the store at the time was ever found. A total of
129 died when a missile hit the Smithfield meat market on the outskirts of the city's financial district on March 8, 1945 and on March 27,
on what was to be the last morning of the V-2 attacks, Hughes Man-
sions, a block of flats in Stepney was pulverised and 134 killed and 49
injured.

    A further 44 V-2 attacks were made on Norwich and near the east
coast port of Ipswich. Destruction was also the order of the day: the
London Repair Executive was set up within 48 hours of the first V-2
salvoes to co-ordinate the renovation and rebuilding of London's bat-

tered housing stock and road and rail communications.

The Germans, firing from a multitude of sites in the Netherlands, and later from western Germany – 80% from The Hague and its environs – failed to mount the expected scale of offensive against England. Only around 40% of those targeted on London actually reached the British capital. A further 598 V-2s impacted in eastern and southern England. Shortage of parts or LOX hampered the operation, together with repeated and fierce Allied air attacks on rail supply networks and The Hague, identified by the Dutch resistance.

There was an estimated 8% firing failures, due to corroded components or some other form of mechanical malfunction. On October 26, a V-2 fired in The Hague immediately spiralled out of control, just 350ft above the ground, fell back onto the launch site and exploded, killing 12 German soldiers. Others lost stability and crashed near their launch sites, killing Dutch civilians and destroying buildings, one of the worst incidents occurring on January 1, when a V-2 landed just over half a mile away from launching, killing 38 residents of The Hague.

If London and England were bruised by the V-2 campaign, the Belgian port of Antwerp was again to suffer a far heavier bombardment. Here, 1,134 civilians and Allied soldiers were killed and more than 1,300 wounded in the attacks. The worst incident in Antwerp, and indeed throughout all the V-2 campaign, occurred on December 16, 1944, when a missile, fired from Germany, hit the Rex cinema in the city. It was a full house that afternoon with many US, British and Canadian soldiers enjoying rest and recuperation away from the fighting. A total of 567 military and civilians died and 291 were injured in the blast that destroyed 11 nearby houses.

A further 2,579 V-2s were fired at European targets, 2,419 of them at Antwerp in an attempt to slow up the Allied advance. In October 1944, Paris was reselected as a target with 22 missiles hitting the outskirts fired from Merzig in southern Germany. Belgian targets also included Luttich (27), Hasselt (13), Mons (three), Tournai (nine) and Diest (two). In France, (in addition to Paris), Lille was hit by 25 V-2s, Tourcoing by 19, Arras by six and Cambrai, four. On March 17, 11 V-2s were fired from Hellendoorn, targeted at the Remagen bridge, crossing the Rhine, which had been captured in a lightning attack by US troops. One impacted just 1,000 yards from the bridge, killing three American soldiers.

But the V-2's thunder from the skies was to be short-lived. The last rocket to be fired against England was launched at 16.48 on March 27 from The Hague and impacted five minutes later in Orpington, Kent, killing one and injuring 23. The last V-2 to be launched against Antwerp came six hours later, killing 23, injuring 62 and destroying 29 homes. On March 29, with the V-2 battalions in full retreat, 485 Artillery Battalion, which had opened the campaign against London, fired its last two missiles in anger near Fallingbostal, near Hanover, in Germany. Their impacts are unknown.

Viewed coldly and clinically, in purely strategic terms as a weapon of mass destruction, the V-2, with its warhead of nearly one ton of explosive was no match for the RAF's Lancaster bomber, which could carry a load of explosives seven times that weight in repeated missions, night after night. With the V-2, there was also no horrific firestorm, caused by the oxygen in the atmosphere over a city target being sucked up by the intensity of an incendiary attack, and fuelling the holocaust. But its psychological power to terrorise a civilian population was perhaps many times greater because of the uncertainty of when an attack would come and the suddenness of its arrival. There was something rather terrible about the fact that the first you knew of a V-2 attack was when the explosion sent rubble, dust and debris high into the air, and the ground shuddered and shook under the reverberations of the blast.

The weapon's strategic power to influence the war turned out to be very limited. If it had been deployed earlier, against the Allied armies massing for the invasion of Europe in southern England, it might have become a war-winner. Its guidance system was being improved all the time, and recent German reports suggest that this could eventually have provided a capability for the High Command to be very selective and more precise in their targeting. It was the first guided ballistic missile used in conflict, the direct ancestor of those military weapons used in the 'war of the cities' in the first Gulf War, between Iran and Iraq in the 1980s, but also of the civilian Saturn rockets that took the first men to the Moon in 1969. Indeed, the Saturn was engineered by Werner von Braun himself and some of the team from Peenemünde.

In the Second World War, they also took a step nearer a fully fledged ICBM with the abortive development of a longer-range version of the V-2, the A9, or A4b, beginning in 1940. Work on this was suspended between October 1942 and June 1944 while attention focused on ensuring the V-2's operational effectiveness, but as the fortunes of war inexorably turned against Berlin, efforts were renewed.

The A9 was a V-2 with wings attached to enable it to glide to its target in the last stages of its flight at subsonic speeds. This glide sequence would extend its range to 400 miles to include targets in northern England from launch sites in France. The first test launch at Peenemünde, on December 27, 1944, was unsuccessful because of a guidance system failure.   The third launch, on January 24, 1945 achieved a height of 48 miles and a speed of 2,700mph. The glide failed, however, because one of the wings broke off during this section of the flight. Time was running out at Peenemünde, with the advance of Russian forces, and no further tests were staged.

Simultaneously, the ambitious German rocket engineers were working on a two-stage variant, called the A9/10, with a 3,000-mile range, far enough to strike the cities of the USA's eastern seaboard. With the entry of America into the war, the idea was rejuvenated in December 1941, by the V-2 propulsion expert, Dr Walter Thiel and design work began.

It was an audacious plan. New York and Washington DC were among the intended targets. The first stage would consist of an A10 rocket, with several motors fuelled by a benzol mixture and nitric acid, developing a massive thrust of 375,000 lbs. These would lift the 84ft-high missile off the ground and burn for 50 seconds, before the second stage, a winged A9, separated in the upper atmosphere and its rocket motor ignited, pushing the weapon to a height of more than 200 miles and to the breathtaking maximum speed of 6,600mph. The two-stage missile would have weighed about 55 tons and was planned to be armed with a one-ton HE warhead. But it was only a paper missile – fortunately for the USA, the design never left the Peenemünde drawing boards.

The Germans, ever concerned about increasing accuracy, also worked on a manned version of the A9/10, fitted with a pressurised cockpit in place of the warhead in the nose and a ramjet engine for cruise flight. The brave (or perhaps foolhardy) pilot would be guided by radio transmissions from U-boats specially positioned in the North Atlantic and would depart the 46ft-long missile immediately after crossing the USA coastline, via a primitive ejection seat. Planned range was 2,699 miles. Design speeds compared well with the future experimental American X-15 rocket-powered plane of the 1950s. Again, probably to the benefit of Luftwaffe volunteer pilots, the war ended too soon for developmental work to be undertaken.

Germany had one last vengeance weapon in its arsenal – the V-3, or *Hochdruckpumpe* ('high pressure pump') codenamed WIESE, or 'meadow'. This was a super gun capable of delivering a 310lb shell more than 100 miles and was a direct descendant of 'Big Bertha', the First World War 8.27in rail-mounted gun used by the German army to shell Paris in 1918. This could hurl a 264lb shell up to an altitude of 25 miles and to a range of around 80 miles. It was fired 351 times, killing 256 civilians and wounding a further 620. In 1937–41, the German armaments company Krupp developed 'Dora', a massive 32.5in railway cannon, originally designed to travel through Spain to attack the vital British naval base and fortress at Gibraltar at the gateway to the Mediterranean. It was deployed in more temperate climes, however, at the German siege of Sebastopol in June 1942, when one of its 48 shells blew up a heavily protected magazine. One of the major drawbacks of the 1,350-ton giant, was the 4,500 personnel needed to crew and defend it.

The V-3 was no mere piece of steel ordnance. Attached to its 460ft-long smooth-bore barrel were a number of side chambers with electrically-fired extra propellant charges to accelerate each fin-stabilised shell's velocity as it moved towards the muzzle – resulting in a speed of 4,920ft per second as it left the gun muzzle. A 60ft-long prototype with a calibre of less than an inch was built at a test site at Miedzyzdroje in Poland and was demonstrated in April and May 1943. Despite grave misgivings among the German general staff, Hitler was impressed and immediately ordered 50 of the super guns to be based in special bunkers near the French coast. The target was once again London, 103 miles away.

Work by slave labour began on a facility in a hillside at Mimoyecques, between Calais and Boulogne in September 1943, to house a battery of 25 5.9in V-3s, each angled at 34° and mounted five to a shaft. The SS planned that these super guns would fire 200 shells per hour at the British capital. A number of munitions companies began production of the special finned shells: 20,000 were manufactured by mid-1944. But just before the first bombardment was to commence, RAF Bomber Command stepped into the ring. British intelligence was unaware of the true purpose of the concrete construction at Mimoyecques but firmly believed that the site was another V-1, or possibly V-2 launch location. Lancaster bombers, in one raid on July 6 1944, managed to drop three 'Tallboy' earth penetrators straight down one gun shaft and these exploded 100ft below the surface, wrecking the site and flooding the lower levels. The Germans were forced to scrap any idea of using the site to house this latest vengeance weapon on London.

A version of the V-3 *was* used in combat against Luxembourg city (which had been liberated by American forces in September 1944), in support of the German offensive in the Ardennes, the so-called 'Battle of the Bulge'. Under orders from SS General Hans Kammler, operational commander of the V-2 and V-3 vengeance weapons, two shortened, 164ft-long gun tubes were positioned, angled at 36°, facing west, at Lampaden, eight miles south-east of the city of Trier in southern Germany. The first gun opened fire on December 30, firing 215lb shells, five of which hit the centre of Luxembourg, 28 miles away. Between those opening shots and February 22, a total of 183 projectiles were fired by both guns, with Luxembourg the only target, killing 10 civilians and wounding 35. Shortly afterwards the guns were captured by American ground forces. Both were shipped to the USA, together with any remaining ammunition, and were evaluated in test firings at the US Army's Aberdeen Proving Ground in Maryland before being scrapped in 1948.

So the V-3 went the way of the V-1 and V-2. All were stunning military ideas, certainly innovative designs, but perhaps too far ahead of their times. The technology available in the 1940s just could not provide the operational reliability necessary for any effective weapon of war. If the missiles were the ancestors of today's powerful weapons of destruction, the V-3 laid down the principles later adopted by Iraq's Saddam Hussein with his own super gun, dismantled under the supervision of the UN weapons inspectors following the 1991 Gulf War.

Aside from the terrible human cost, in stark terms, compared with the strategic conventional bombing of Germany by RAF Bomber Command and the USAAF Eighth Air Force, the death toll inflicted by Hitler's vengeance weapons pales into statistical insignificance. When the bombing campaign was at its peak, both Allied air forces deployed 28,000 aircraft and a total of 1,335,000 men to fly and maintain them. About 593,000 Germans died in air attacks on 61 cities with about 1.5 million tons of bombs dropped on the Third Reich between 1939 and 1945, half a million tons in 1945 alone. More than 3.6 million homes were destroyed – 20% of the total housing stock – and 7.5 million Germans made homeless. Despite this horrific toll of death and destruction, the campaign failed to reduce overall German war production, or significantly damage civilian morale, although it had some impact on oil production. The cost to the RAF and USAAF was also high: Bomber Command lost 55,573 aircrew dead or missing, a further 8,403 wounded and 9,838 captured. The American Eighth Air Force suffered 43,742 dead. Together, the Allies lost 40,000 aircraft in the campaign.

The bomber *had* got through, night after night, but at a terrible cost to both sides.

CHAPTER 3
DAWN OF DETERRENCE

A T THE END OF THE SECOND World War, there was an unseemly scramble by the USA, Britain and the Soviet Union to get their hands on the secrets of German missile technology. To the victors, the spoils. With an eye to the future, all three nations also wanted to deny that valuable knowledge to their former Allies. In the chaos and confusion of now-occupied Germany, there was an indecorous and sometimes embittered race by the former comrades-in-arms to scoop up any half-built missiles and their components before another ally could sequester them. The tensions and anxieties of the imminent Cold War were immediately becoming all too apparent.

There was a frenetic quest for human expertise too. Werner von Braun, whom we met earlier as the father of the V-2 project, had earlier fled Peenemünde with a number of his team as the victorious Russian forces advanced westwards into Germany. On May 2, 1945, they, together with General Walter Dornberger, who had been in charge of the research site, surrendered to a surprised anti-tank unit of the American 44th Infantry Division, on patrol at Reutte, near the present-day border with Austria. They underwent preliminary interrogation and their future worth to Uncle Sam was quickly appreciated by the US War Department back in Washington.

The allocation of captured V-2 weapons and parts became a major source of friction. On May 1, 1945, the Supreme Allied Commander, General Dwight Eisenhower, sent a coded signal to the US Combined Chiefs of Staff, copied to their British counterparts:

French pressing request of samples of captured V-2s. Present state of allocation:

Required by British: 4. Allocated: 2.

Required by US: 100. Allocated: 7.

Required by French: 3. Allocated: 0.

British request likely to be considerably increased. Capture of additional V-2s anticipated − though not in sufficient numbers to fill all requests.

As supply of V-1s have exceeded demand, samples have been furnished to the French. Other secret weapons such as rockets, rocket-assisted shells, controlled Glider bombs − HS 293 and successive types − likely to be in short supply, will probably be requested by French when information leaks out. Request general allocation policy on secret weapons.

The British subsequently increased their requirement to 100 V-2s. In the confusion, the Americans decided on direct action. At the V-2/V-1 underground factory at Mittelwerke in the Harz mountains, American troops from a unit called 'Special Mission V-2', frantically searched the 23-mile maze of tunnels for partially completed V-2 missiles and spare parts to ship back to the USA. The complex was, according to one US technical expert, 'like a magician's cave'. The first of several shipments of booty was despatched to the Belgian port of Antwerp, via a guarded 40-wagon railway train on May 22. Eventually, 16 'Liberty' freighter ships ferried the components back to New Orleans. There were sufficient to assemble more than 50 V-2s for test-firings at the White Sands site in New Mexico. Meanwhile, 1,000 German V-2 technicians and their families were evacuated from around Nordhausen to the American occupation zone, just 24 hours before Russian troops arrived in the area.

Washington badly wanted the V-2 as their own potential weapon and didn't care whom they offended in their attempts to capture the secrets of ballistic missile technology. The British, originally promised half of all captured V-2s in a deal with the Americans, were eventually allowed into the Mittelwerke to scavenge for what was left, before Russian forces took over the site. There was probably enough material remaining to build eight V-2s, but the British found they were still missing some key components to enable the missiles to be fired. Frustration and anger began to taint senior Anglo-American military relations at the very moment of victory. .

During his flight from the Russians, Von Braun had hidden 14 tons of V-2 plans and documents in wooden crates in an abandoned salt mine outside the village of Dornten and, as a precaution against prying eyes, had blown in the entrance to the tunnel with explosives. American interrogation of some of the Peenemünde team revealed the existence of this hidden cache of blueprints and after locating the site, US troops desperately excavated the blast debris. After breaking into the mine, they managed to recover all the plans by May 27, only a few days before the British army was due to assume administrative responsibility for the area.

The British, like both the Americans and Russians, were keen to evaluate the V-2 for their post-war arsenals. With memories still fresh of the horrors of the rocket's campaign against London and Antwerp, they were only too aware of its destructive power. A unit was set up, euphemistically called the Special Projectile Operations Group, supported by 307 Infantry Brigade, to utilise captured German scientists and missile troops to test-fire V-2s at the former Kriegsmarine artillery range at Altenwalde, near Cuxhaven in northern Germany, in an operation codenamed BACKFIRE. However, the British were still short of vital parts for their V-2 war booty and a huge search by British soldiers, chosen for their fluency in German, was mounted to hunt down the missing components throughout all the former occupied European countries. Eventually, 250,000 separate parts and a number of the 16-wheeled *meillerwagen* transporter/launcher vehicles were painfully retrieved and transported to Cuxhaven where a concrete launch site had been hastily constructed. Around 79 Peenemünde scientists and 400 soldiers from former V-2 batteries were mustered at the firing range by the British to assist in the complicated assembly and firing of the rockets.

On October 1, 1945 the first launch took place – but failed because of a faulty ignition system. A second was staged the next day and this was successful, the rocket spectacularly splashing down in the Baltic a few minutes later. A final test, on October 15, was watched by American and Soviet officials, invited in a magnanimous gesture by the British military. The V-2 happily hit its target zone in the North Sea.

London was initially unwilling to have any Allied observers at Cuxhaven. The War Office, responsible for BACKFIRE, told the British Chiefs of Staff in a memorandum:

> There is no viewpoint near the firing point, which is concealed in a wood. Spectators would have to watch from the nearest hill, some 2,000 yards away. From this hill, the rocket would not be visible until it was launched and then it would only be visible for a few seconds.

Hardly welcoming. The Chiefs of Staffs in London rather half-heartedly signalled their American counterparts on September 27:

> We would of course welcome the presence of experts who the Combined Chiefs of Staff wish to send. Accommodation is, however, very limited and it is feared that visitors will inevitably be faced with some discomfort and may not see very much.

There was now increasingly heated wrangling between the military authorities in London and Washington over the eventual fate of the Peenemünde scientists and engineers. The British at one stage, apparently wanted to try Dornberger for war crimes. The US Army, rather more pragmatic and with their eyes more on the future than on retribution for the past, offered generous contracts to von Braun and 120 of his colleagues to work for the ordnance department in the USA; they were sent to Washington in Operation PAPERCLIP, arriving on November 17, to be followed by 350 more specialists a few months later.

There was a furious exchange of signals over the fate of 12 Peenemünde scientists borrowed from American custody for the BACKFIRE launches. Under OVERCAST signed on June 14, one of the many covert deals between the USA and Britain, all German munitions scientists were to be handed over to the War Department in Washington, 'for exploitation in the development of weapons to. be used against the Japanese'. During the BACKFIRE operation, the Americans suddenly wanted them back, but the British huffily declined to accede to repeated requests for their return, signalling on September 3:

> We cannot believe a delay of less than two months would seriously inconvenience the US Chiefs of Staff, since the end of the Japanese war means that they can only be required for work on long-term research projects and BACKFIRE research will be made available to the USA.

Ultimately, the British had to agree. The once-friendly US armed forces had become suspicious and were now unwilling to share missile development information with their erstwhile allies. The end of hostilities meant suddenly, all bets were off. On February 3, 1946 British officials in Washington reported to their masters sitting on the newly-formed Co-ordinating Committee on Guided and Propellant Missiles in London:

It must be realised that all liaison results are achieved almost entirely by the personal contacts made by our representatives. We are not, with two exceptions, on the official distribution lists for American reports on these matters ... All air force branches and laboratories have been instructed not to disclose information on any development started since 2nd September 1945, the closing date of Lend Lease.*

The British were on their own.

Across the Atlantic, the US Army had become interested in ballistic missiles in the early 1940s, developing their own very crude prototypes. In December 1944, 24 ugly and ungainly winged 'Private A' rockets, fitted with boosters, were fired down the range at Camp Irvin, California, performing only 'satisfactorily' in the terse, clipped words of the subsequent Army report. A later version, the 'Private F' was tested at Hueco range at Fort Bliss, Texas, in April 1945, to overcome recurrent stability problems and high-speed drag in flight. In the V-2, the US Army had an operational weapon and the tried, tested and expensively won German technology allowed them to leapfrog many developmental hazards. If they saw the ballistic missile as a future long-range weapon, they must build on the V-2's pioneering technology.

At the newly constructed White Sands range, the V-2 material was finally arriving from Europe. Some idea of the scale of the American recovery operation can be gauged by the fact that every railway siding in the 210 miles separating El Paso, Texas and Belen, New Mexico, was sometimes fully occupied by freight trucks, brimming with salvaged V-2 missile sections and parts. Around 300 rail wagons eventually arrived, bearing a cargo of 215 combustion chambers, 180 sets of propellant tanks, 100 sets of graphite jet vanes and 200 turbopumps. No rockets arrived in flyable condition – all had to be reconstructed, with defence company General Electric providing reverse-engineered parts later in the flight-test programme. A total of 67 V-2s were ultimately assembled.

A new concrete control blockhouse was specially built at White Sands for the V-2 tests (now designated a National Historical Landmark by the US National Park Service), together with a special launch gantry.

* The Anglo-American agreement on the exchange of information, defence equipment and munitions.

The initial firing was a static test of the motors on March 15, 1946. The first launch came on April 16, when a rocket reached an altitude of 18,000ft.

It was the dawn of many heady days in the new, exciting science of rocketry in the USA.

The American V-2 test programme, which totalled 64 launches (the last in September 1952), created a number of milestones, not all of them concerned with purely military research. The first motion pictures showing the curvature of the Earth's surface came on October 24, 1946 – heralding the advent of space travel in the 1960s. The first separation in space, of a missile nose cone, had occurred just over three months earlier, a harbinger of the technology required for the delivery of ICBM nuclear warheads in the future. As a forerunner of today's remotely guided rockets, a V-2 fitted with a true automatic pilot was successfully tested on January 23, 1947. The programme included the first attempts at biological experiments in the then brief periods of weightlessness in space. There were also some embarrassments: on May 29, 1947, a rogue V-2 crashed just outside the town of Juarez, across the border in Mexico. Fortunately, no one was killed or injured.

American missile development went into top gear. Other associated programmes included Operation BUMPER, an army ordnance project to develop a two-stage rocket (with a V-2 as the launch vehicle), first tested on May 13, 1948 with five further launches following. This was the first rocket to leave the tenuous upper atmosphere of the earth and enter true outer space. Operation SANDY was an astonishing plan to launch a V-2 from the flight deck of the brand-new US aircraft carrier *Midway*, whilst underway in the Atlantic, almost miraculously achieved on September 6, 1947 without the loss of the ship. (To be fair, the earlier Operation PUSHOVER evaluated the effects of a potential launch accident, by deliberately exploding a fuelled V-2 on a White Sands mock-up of a ship deck.)

Out of all this research and other American development work came the USA's first guided ballistic missile, the 45ft-long Corporal, first fired on May 22, 1947, using aniline as a fuel and a particularly unpleasant chemical, red fuming nitric acid as the oxidiser. This army weapon, after a rather tortured career path flawed by continual unreliability, was deployed to Germany and Italy in February 1955, armed either with a conventional HE or nuclear warhead. It had a range of 25 to 75 miles and a circular error probability (CEP, the measurement of

accuracy used for missiles), of less than 984ft around the target. Around
900 Corporals were manufactured, 113 of them produced for the
British Army as a tactical nuclear weapon delivery system from 1955.

A direct derivative of the V-2 was the US Army's SSM-A-14 Redstone, designed and developed by von Braun and his 100-strong team
at Redstone Arsenal, Alabama, in the early 1950s. Its test programme
was stunningly successful: only one missile failed during the first 15
launches in 1953–6. The 69ft-long missile was capable of carrying a
HE or 1–2 megaton (MT, or a million tons of TNT equivalent)
nuclear warhead more than 200 miles. A force of 60 Redstone missiles
entered service with US forces in Germany in 1959 and was withdrawn in 1965. The weapon enabled the creation of the Jupiter rocket,
also designed by von Braun beginning in 1954, the first American
intermediate range ballistic missile, with a range of 1,500 miles. It was
based in Europe in 1959–65, with 45 operated by the Italian and
Turkish air forces from surface launch pads, but with the W-49 1.44
MT nuclear warheads firmly under American control. The Jupiter
went on, with modifications, to become the first-stage launch vehicle
for the American Juno satellites.

The USA's interest in the V-1 and cruise missile technology had not
disappeared. They had suffered a number of setbacks in the development of their own radio-controlled flying bombs and before the end
of the Second World War, in July 1944, after a number of French
launching sites had been overrun, captured V-1 components were
shipped to Wright-Patterson air base in Ohio for reassembly and eval-
uation. Within 21 days, the weapon had been re-created, and then
reverse-engineered, with the Republic Aviation Corporation building the airframe and the Ford Motor Company the pulse jet engine.
The USAAF, perhaps incautiously, ordered 1,000 of the weapons, now
designated JB-2 ('jet bomb') but given the rather uncomplimentary
title of 'Loon', named after a sea bird. First test flight was in October
1944, from Eglin air base in Florida. Although launching off a rail,
using a rocket booster, was normal practice, the USAAF also evaluated
air-launches, dropping the missile from B-17 and B-29 bombers.

The US Navy also procured the JB-2 and some were reportedly
embarked on an aircraft carrier for possible deployment during the
planned invasion of Japan. The Navy saw the missile as a potent
weapon with which to bombard distant shore targets. Its own version,
the KUW-1, went to sea in two modified submarines, *Cusk* (SS-348)

and *Carbonero* (SS-337) in 1948–9. In February 1948, *Cusk* became the first submarine to launch a guided missile from her deck.* The Loons were stored in a bulbous metal watertight hanger on the boats' forward casing, and launched, while the submarine was surfaced, off a clumsy fixed raised ramp, using solid rocket boosters. The Navy also modified the seaplane tender *Norton Sound*, 9,090 tons, as a flying bomb launch platform.

The USAAF had begun development of the Atlas ICBM in 1945 but cancelled the programme two years later because of concerns about the ability of ballistic missiles to accurately deliver nuclear warheads onto a target. Their decision was made despite technical studies that suggested that cruise missiles, given the technology of the day, would be not only more expensive but hardly a precision weapon in practice. So, before 1954, when its viewpoint dramatically changed, the Air Force enthusiastically forged ahead with cruise missiles.

The next-generation weapon of this type was the USAAF's 'Matador', tested from 1949. It resembled the streamlined designs of early jet fighters, with swept-back wings and a wingspan of 28.5ft, yet looked far less graceful. It was more a pilotless aircraft than a cruise missile. This ground-launched weapon, armed with the massive punch of a W-28 1 MT nuclear warhead, had a range of just over 600 miles, but suffered from inherent guidance problems. More than 1,200 were produced and the Matador entered service in what was now the US Air Force (USAF) in 1954 and became operational in Germany the next year. A follow-up missile, the MGM-13B 'Mace', had a range extended to 1,380 miles, and early versions were guided by a primitive terrain-matching system which compared radar images of the weapon's ground track with a map held within the missile's system. Later marks of the Mace were retired in 1971.

The Air Force also sought a long-range cruise missile that could hit targets 5,000 miles away. With the icy tentacles of the Cold War grasping international relations in the late 1940s, Russia was already firmly in the American military's weapon sights. The result was the SM-62 Snark, later to become the Super Snark, a huge airframe with two jettisonable solid fuel boosters slung under the wings. It looked more like an infant bomber than a missile, with a huge wingspan of 42-feet, a

---

* The US submarine *Halibut* was the first *designed and built* to launch guided missiles. It launched a Regulus 2 missile whilst *en route* to Australia on March 25 1960.

length of 67ft, and a launch weight of 4.5 tons. The weapon was ground-launched and would ramp up its speed into supersonic flight for the last phase of attack. Its nose cone, with a W-39 1 MT warhead, was designed to separate just before reaching the target and continue on a ballistic trajectory. But the Snark was an operational disaster. Testing began in 1952 and soon proved the missile unreliable. Only one of the last ten launches achieved the planned range, but an optimistic USAF still authorised production.

The Snark was embarrassingly inaccurate; test flights demonstrated a CEP of 20 miles at shorter range, instead of the designed 500 yards, and it was said there was only a one-in-three chance of the missile getting off the ground. Wags in the USAF said the waters around the weapon's Florida test site were 'Snark-infested' because of the missiles that had splashed into the sea in failed launches. One flight disappeared completely from the radar screens after launch and this may have been the errant Snark reportedly discovered in the Brazilian rainforests in 1982.

The missile entered service in 1960 but was deactivated in June 1961 after newly elected President John F. Kennedy decided it was already obsolete and of marginal military value, compared with the new USAF and Navy ballistic missiles then entering service. The ill-fated Snark probably had the shortest service life of any American weapon system.

The Navy had better luck with the Regulus sea-launched cruise missile, developed from 1947 onwards by Chance Vought. Again the appearance was like a small aircraft with delta wings and a swept-back tail fin, but the launch was assisted by a solid propellant booster mounted beneath the airframe, before the J79 turbojet motor took over. Guidance was by radio command but the system had a weakness in that the flight path had to be determined and corrected by a chase aircraft. Shoot that aircraft down and the missile's track became confused and erratic. Regulus, with a range of 459 miles in its early version and armed with a 45 kT nuclear warhead, entered service in 1955, with launchers fitted to five submarines, four cruisers and 10 aircraft carriers. It formed the USA's first sea-borne nuclear deterrent from 1959 in the Pacific, completing 40 patrols.

Undaunted, the USAF pressed on with cruise missiles, producing the elegant GAM-77 'Hound Dog' in the late 1950s. This too had wings and was powered by a Pratt & Whitney J52-P-3 turbojet engine, developing a maximum speed of twice the speed of sound. The 43ft-long 'Hound Dog' was designed as a defence suppression weapon, with more than 500 miles range. Two were carried on pylons beneath the wings of Strategic Air Command's giant B-52 Strato-fortress bombers and would have knocked out Soviet air defences with its massive 4 MT nuclear warhead, to create a safe passage for the parent bomber wing to press home their attacks with freefall atomic bombs. The weapon entered service in February 1960 and was only phased out in 1976.

Regulus meanwhile continued faithful service until 1964, two years after the first Minuteman I ICBMs became operational at Malmstrom air force base, Montana, five years after the Atlas 'D' ICBM entered service and four years after the Polaris A1 submarine-launched missile first went to sea in *George Washington*. Ballistic missiles had taken over as America's main strike weapon in the Cold War.

Badly burned by their experiences with cruise missiles, the USAF switched to developing ballistic missiles and reawakened the Atlas ICBM programme in the belief that with this, they could have a true strategic weapon up and running by 1960. At the same time, they embarked on the silo-based Thor intermediate range and the Minute-man and Titan ICBM projects. Both the Atlas and Titan had nuclear warheads with massive yields – later versions with 3.75 MT and 9 MTs respectively – for use against 'undefended soft targets', a polite strategic euphemism for Russian cities. Mass destruction on a punishing scale was the objective. The age of deterrence had dawned and with it, the dreadful jargon of all-out global nuclear war.

On the other side of what had become the Iron Curtain, Russian forces had captured the Peenemünde research station on May 4, 1945 and later rounded up a number of the scientists and engineers who had worked there. By June 1947, the first group of 234 specialists were settled on Gordomlya Island on Lake Seliga, between Novgorod and Rzhev, in the western USSR, on a site previously used for research into animal diseases. A German V-2 was test-fired from the giant new range at Kapustin Yar, near Stalingrad (now Volgograd) on October 18 1947, no doubt after the usual nightmare re-assembly process, but it immediately veered off course. Undeterred, the Russians pressed on and within a month, all 10 V-2s they had captured in parts had been rebuilt and launched.

The race with the West to develop new ballistic missile technology and deploy ever more powerful weapons had begun. The government decree founding Russia's embryo rocket industry was signed in 1946. That autumn, Marshal Pavel Zhigarev, commander-in-chief of *Voyenno-Vozdushnyye Sily* (VVS), the Soviet air forces, acknowledged:

> We must admit that our V-2 type rockets do not satisfy our long-term needs: they were good to frighten England, but should there be an Ameri-can-Soviet war, they would be useless. What we really need are long-range, reliable rockets – capable of hitting target areas on the Ameri-can continent.

So, in a development programme which mirrored that going on in the USA, the Soviet Union produced its first ballistic missile, again very much a V-2 derivative, in 1950, designated the SS-1A 'Scunner' by NATO intelligence, although the Russians rather prosaically called it the 'R-1' for *raketa* or rocket. (In passing, it should be noted that NATO codenames are normally chosen from a list of randomly selected words, but one wonders how 'Scunner' arrived on that list in the first place. Dictionaries tell us it is an obscure Scottish dialect word meaning 'object of loathing', or 'to feel sick or nauseated'. NATO's selection of codewords is not normally so emotive.)

What we would know now as ICBM technology was out of the Russians' immediate reach. As a first step, they needed to be able to demonstrably strike at a foe nearer home. By April 1947, the Kremlin was seeking a missile with a 1,860-mile range that could hit targets in Britain, with authorisation to develop various candidate missile designs signed by the Soviet Council of Ministers on December 4 1950. Cruise missiles were tried and initially abandoned, but later used for tactical purposes.

Two separate design teams, one purely Soviet under the leadership of Sergei P. Korolev, and the other comprising the émigré German sci-entists, led by Helmut Gröttrup, had produced two separate competing designs for a short-range liquid-propelled ballistic missile, both based on the V-2. The Soviet Council of Ministers' approval for the project was signed on April 14 1948. Both versions were flight-tested that year in two series of launches at Kapustin Yar, beginning on September 17, unfortunately with a failure caused by a control system failure. In the end, the Russian team's design, which had scored 17 suc-cessful launches out of 20, was chosen for further development. The

German scientists were disappointed, suspecting the Soviet leadership was suffering from an early manifestation of the 'not invented here' syndrome.

The 48ft-long Scunner, armed with a 2,200lb HE warhead, had a range of 185 miles, and was guided by radio command. It entered service with the Soviet Army in 1950 and was succeeded in 1953 by the SS-2 'Sibling' and SS-3 'Shyster' missiles. The Soviet Navy developed its own version of the Scunner, called 'Golem', but this missile was never deployed operationally.

Korolev then proposed the 'R-2' with larger propellant tanks and a more powerful motor, the RD-101, and incorporating up to 100 design improvements suggested by the German team, based on their experience at Peenemünde. This was to become the SS-2 'Sibling,' 58ft long, again with a HE warhead, this time weighing 3,300lbs. Range was still only 375 miles. The missile entered service in 1952 but was not deployed widely.

With the next missile in this early surface-to-surface series, the Russians moved on from the German designs captured in 1945 in an attempt to develop their own technology. In appearance, the weapon was a complete transformation from its stubby V-2 ancestor into an elegant single-stage pencil-thin rocket, more than 60ft tall. The 'R-5', (NATO's SS-3 'Shyster'), pushed the striking range of Soviet ballistic missiles out to 750 miles. The R-5M version, which entered service in late 1956, became the first Soviet nuclear delivery vehicle, with an 80 kT warhead, although it could also carry a chemical weapon. A total of 48 were initially deployed, mainly in the western USSR, close to the border. Large warheads, up to 1 MT yield, were also later fitted, according to recent Russian reports. The V-2 mixture of liquid oxygen and alcohol powered early versions but the propellant was later changed to kerosene, increasing the missile's range. R-5M designs were passed to China in 1958 – an early example of missile proliferation. It remained in Soviet service until 1967.

The single-stage R-12 (SS-4 'Sandel') evolved from the 'Shyster' with testing beginning in 1955 and operational deployment in 1959 in the western USSR. One version was fired from a fixed ground launcher, supported by 12 vehicles; the other from four silos at the Dvina launch complex from January 1, 1963. Range was 1,250 miles. The missile had a re-entry vehicle that separated in space from the nose casing after motor burnout by a pneumatic device. The single warhead had a yield of between 2 and 2.3 MT. Sandel had a long and reliable operational life with a maximum of 608 deployed: it was replaced by the SS-20 'Saber', beginning in 1977, but at the time of the Intermediate Nuclear Force reduction treaty in December 1987, the Soviet Union declared it still had 65 SS-4s deployed with 105 more in storage. These were all destroyed by May 22, 1990 at the Lesnaya missile elimination facility under the terms of the agreement.

The follow-on missile, the SS-5 'Skean', or R-14, was another development of the 'Shyster', fitted with a single 2 MT warhead, but later versions were armed with two re-entry vehicles, each with a 300 kT warhead. Range was 2,800 miles, a quantum jump in Soviet strike capability. Skean entered service in 1961 and during peak deployment around 1965, nearly 100 were aimed at Western European targets.

The medium-range SS-4 was the missile covertly deployed by Moscow at two sites in Cuba in 1962 – the immediate cause of the Cuban missile crisis.

The first Soviet attempt at an ICBM was the towering and ungainly two-stage R-7 (SS-6 or 'Sapwood'), fondly known to rocket force personnel as *Semyorka*, the 'Old Seven'. Informal approval to proceed with the design was given in April 1953, with full-scale development authorised on May 20, 1954 by Soviet ministers. The first successful test flight came on August 21, 1957 from Baikonur, but a material failure in the missile nose cone caused the dummy warhead to disintegrate over the Kamchatka peninsula in the far east of Russia. None the less, the Kremlin triumphantly announced five days later, through the then state news agency TASS, the successful test flight of a 'super long distance intercontinental multi-stage ballistic rocket … a few days ago'.

Clustered from its tail up to two-thirds its 100ft length were four angled, strap-on liquid propellant boosters which, with its sharply pointed nose cone, made the missile look more like a stately Victorian Gothic church tower than a weapon of war. Range of later models was 6,000 miles – capable of reaching the eastern seaboard of the USA if fired from the western Soviet Union, and capable of delivering a massive single 3–5 MT warhead in airburst detonations over American cities. 'Sapwood' entered service at five sites on a specially constructed base at Angara, later known as Plesetsk, near Archangelsk, on October 31, 1959. Its warhead was tested at a yield of 2.9 MT in an airburst at the Novaya Zemlya range on October 6, 1957, the most powerful Soviet test up to that time. But 'Sapwood' never proved reliable because the cryogenic liquid fuel was unstable and it took more than 24 hours to fuel the missile up. Hardly a quick reaction force. Moreover, it could not be fired from protective silos. Only ten ever became operational and these were stood down in 1964–8.

Although, at long last, Moscow had a long-range nuclear strike weapon able to heap considerable devastation on the heads of the hated Yankee capitalists, the 'Sapwood' missile was less than a surefire success, although a modified version was used to launch the first two Russian 'Sputnik' artificial satellites into orbit in October and November 1957... Luckily, the Kremlin had another shot in its locker in the shape of the R-16 (SS-7 or 'Saddler'), the first Soviet ICBM to be widely deployed.

This is one of the few Soviet missiles *not* to have been proudly rolled through Red Square during the interminable and almost inevitably freezing May Day parades. Little is known of its development, save for reports that one R-16 exploded on its launch pad at Baikonur just before the first test flight on October 24, 1960, the resultant fire killing between 74 and 100 people, including, embarrassingly, Marshal of Strategic Rocket Forces Mitrofan Nedelin. The accident was apparently due to premature ignition of the second-stage motor while the fuelled missile was being prepared for a delayed firing.

Tests restarted on February 2, 1961 with the first successful flight following on April 2. 'Saddler' had a design range of between 7,000 and 8,100 miles, depending on variant, and provided Soviet nuclear war planners with a lengthy list of potential US targets. The missile, armed with a 5–6 MT warhead, was clearly conceived as a city killer. It entered service on surface launch pads on November 1, 1961 at the Desna-V complex, but the later model was held in long, low hardened concrete shelters resembling, perhaps appropriately, fat coffins, or, from February 1963, in three specially designed silos, with steel and concrete hatches, underground command centres and fuel storage facilities. Maximum deployment totalled 186 missiles in 1965 but the missile was retired by 1976 in line with the requirements of the Strategic Arms Limitation Treaty (START) of 1972.

The appearance of the Soviet 'Sapwood' ICBM in 1957 caused a reaction approaching panic within the 70 miles of dingy corridors within the Pentagon. The initial USAF disenchantment with ballistic missiles had delayed development of the Atlas and belatedly, work began in earnest on this weapon and concurrently on the Titan 1 in 1955, but the USA was still some way off operational deployment. A yawning 'missile gap' had appeared between the capabilities of the Soviet and American strategic arsenals and this gave the Pentagon generals many an uneasy night.

The USAF's first operational ICBM, the two-stage 'D' version of the Atlas, began deployment in 1959, stored horizontally on an above-ground 'soft' launcher, unprotected from the effects of nuclear blast or radiation. It had a range of 8,700 miles and was armed with a single W-49 1.44 MT nuclear warhead. The Atlas 'E/F' versions had similar ranges, but were armed with the more powerful W-38 3.75 MT warhead. They were launched either from semi-hardened coffin-type launchers, or in the case of the 'F' model, stored in protective under-ground silos and lifted to the surface for firing. A total of 125 missiles of all types were eventually deployed with 13 USAF Strategic Air Command squadrons at 11 air bases in the mid-West of the USA, before their retirement, brought forward from the planned FY 1968 to FY 1965.

The liquid-fuelled Titan 1 entered operational service in 1961. It was the largest USAF ICBM yet developed, more than 100ft tall and 10ft in diameter, and armed with the W-38 3.75 MT warhead, like the later model Atlas. Titan 1 was retired in 1965, being replaced by Titan 2, with 3,100 miles added range (to total 9,321) and the huge W-53 9 MT warhead, similar to the obscenely fat 8,848lb B53 freefall hydro-gen bomb carried on B-52 bombers from 1962. The first operational Titan 2 unit was the 570th Strategic Missile Squadron, at Davis-Monthan air base in Arizona, which went on alert on June 8, 1963. A total of 49 were deployed; 15 at Davis-Monthan, 17 at Little Rock, Arkansas, and 17 at McConnell, Kansas.

The missile suffered three disastrous accidents that destroyed two sites and killed four airmen, casting nagging and embarrassing doubts over its safety and reliability. The USAF has confirmed there were 125 accidents involving Titan 2 sites in 1975–9, but potentially the most dangerous was on September 18, 1980 at Damascus, within the Little Rock base. A maintenance crewman at work in a silo reportedly dropped a heavy socket wrench that bounced and holed the fuselage of a missile, creating a leak in the pressurised fuel tank. Eight and a half hours later, the fuel vapour ignited, blew off the 740-ton protective steel and concrete silo door and hurled the missile's W-53 warhead

600ft into the air. It landed about 300 yards away, with only slight impact damage. There was no nuclear explosion (warheads are not armed within silos) and no radiation contamination, but one airman was killed and 21 other USAF personnel were injured in the explosion. (The accident prompted the USAF to set up a small team of communications experts, called Hammer ACE, to provide secure voice communications between response teams and command posts during nuclear weapons accidents. There were clearly serious shortcomings in response procedures.) Earlier, on August 24, 1978 two airmen were killed by an accidental release of oxidiser gas inside a silo, also at Little Rock.

These accidents led to some hard thinking in Washington about the viability of the Titan 2. By 1981, it had been in service for eight years longer than its predicted life and the Pentagon decided to retire it under operation RIVET CAP. The last Titan 2 was lifted from its silo at Little Rock on June 27, 1987, finally ending the USAF's use of liquid-propelled ICBMs.

During this period, the British were scrambling to keep up with both friendly and potential enemy weapon developments, eventually producing thermonuclear free-fall bombs like the 750 kT-1 MT YELLOW SUN and the 1–3 MT GREEN GRANITE in the late 1950s. They had to rely on RAF or Royal Navy bombers to deliver these weapons in the teeth of increasingly sophisticated Soviet air defences. What the air marshals required was a 'stand-off weapon' – a missile launched some distance from the target, enabling its parent aircraft to survive the worst of the expected hostile SAM barrage. The answer came with the liquid propellant BLUE STEEL guided missile, virtually a powered bomb, fitted with the OR141 RED SNOW 1 MT warhead. Development began in 1954 for deployment on the RAF's giant Mk2 Vulcan and Victor 'V' bombers.

To fill the temporary capability gap in Britain's nuclear strike power, in 1958–9 the USA lent 60 Thor 1,700-mile range missiles, armed with American W-49 1.44 MT warheads. These became available for unprotected surface launches from clusters of RAF stations between 1958 and 1962 at Feltwell and North Pickenham, Norfolk; Bardney, Caistor, Coleby Grange and Ludford Magna, Lincolnshire, Shepherd's Grove and Tuddenham, Suffolk, Mepal, Cambridgeshire; Driffield, Folkingham, Carnaby, Full Sutton, Catfoss, Breighton and Hemswell, Yorkshire; Harrington and

Polebrook, Northamptonshire, North Luffenham, Rutland and Melton Mowbray, Leicestershire.

The blunt-nosed missiles were fired by two separate keys, one operated by an American Authentification Officer, normally a captain, under orders from his American superiors at the headquarters of the USAF's 7th Air Division (co-located at RAF Bomber Command at High Wycombe), the other by an RAF squadron leader.

The Thor missile needed a lengthy countdown and plenty of warning of an impending launch. The warheads were stored some distance away from the 20 RAF missile squadrons, at a former Second World War bomber base at Faldingworth, Lincolnshire and these had to be transported, under tight security, to the Thor bases during any period of tension. Once fitted and the missile taken out of its hangar and fuelled up, at least 15 minutes would elapse between receipt of the positive launch order from High Wycombe and both keys turned simultaneously to arm and fire the weapon.

In 1962, Washington decided to focus on ICBM developments. US Defense Secretary Robert McNamara told his British counterpart on May 1 that American logistic support would not be available for the British Thor squadrons after October 31, 1964. By this time, the threat posed by increasing numbers of Soviet intermediate range missiles such as the 'Skean' in 1961, with improved terminal accuracy, also reduced the credibility of the unprotected Thor surface launch pads as a survivable deterrent. The missiles were returned to the USA by December 1963 and later some became anti-satellite weapons, based at Johnson Island in the Pacific in 1964–75.

The British meantime had brought BLUE STEEL to operational capability. Unfortunately, the range was limited to 100–186 miles but the missile had the ability to take evasive action through changes in course and altitude. Its guidance system could not be jammed, as it did not depend on navigation data transmitted from its parent aircraft.

It was a sophisticated weapon, in advance of its time. Early trials at the Woomera range in Australia were disappointing, but despite these results, 57 missiles eventually entered service in 1963, fitted to 24 Vulcan and 12 Victor bombers. In the event of an alert, these aircraft would be dispersed to a number of airfields throughout Britain, with no more than four bombers per site, to avoid pre-emptive strikes knocking out the RAF nuclear retaliatory force. Aircrews could remain at 15 minutes readiness for 30 days at these dispersal airfields.

Fastest time into the air was about two minutes, 30 seconds after the order to scramble.

Improvements to Soviet defences then forced the RAF into adopting very demanding low-level tactics, their ponderous aircraft flying in beneath radar detection at speed to avoid high-altitude SAMs. BLUE STEEL had to be adapted and an improved version entered service in 1964.

In war, the V-bombers would accelerate to maximum speed at low level before pulling up into a programmed climb, releasing both weapons at around 300 knots equivalent air speed, the so-called 'pop-up manoeuvre'. The aircraft had special protection against the thermal effects of the nuclear explosion they had released, with anti-flash screens fitted to the cockpit windows. Their crews were issued with strict instructions as to the minimum altitudes, depending on cloud cover ('slightly less than 10,000-feet'), to drop both BLUE STEEL and the YELLOW SUN freefall bombs with ground-burst yields of 750 kT - 1 MT.

BLUE STEEL had some unsatisfactory operational problems. It took up to an hour to fuel with its kerosene fuel and the high-test peroxide oxidiser that required service crews to wear bulky protective clothing. Its short range implied a high attrition rate amongst V-bomber crews during attacks. A longer-range version, with BRJ.800 ramjets fitted to boost its reach out to 300 miles, began development but the project was cancelled in 1960.

BLUE STEEL Mk 1 was phased out between 1968 and 1970s, with the British looking to the USA for its successor.

Britain had meanwhile been working on its own medium-range, silo-launched ballistic missile to overcome the growing vulnerabilities of the manned bomber. In April 1954, Washington suggested the USA and Britain should explore joint ballistic missile programmes, with the USAF concentrating on ICBMs and the UK on medium-range weapons. The Royal Navy had suggested development of a submarine-launched missile in March 1954 but the British government turned down this innovative idea on both technical and cost grounds. The American idea of co-operation was formally accepted in London in August 1954, and Britain began working on a missile, BLUE STREAK, with a design range of 2,500 miles and armed with the 750 kT ORANGE HERALD nuclear warhead, with what seems a wildly optimistic project costing of £50 million.

The first engine tests were conducted at the RAF range at Spadeadam in Cumbria in August 1959. The missile used kerosene as a fuel and cryogenic oxygen as the oxidiser, like the American Atlas and Titan ICBMs, and the limitations this placed on storage and transportation dictated that BLUE STREAK had to be launched from a static position. With deployment of new Soviet medium-range missiles and the shorter warning times involved, unprotected surface launch sites like those used by the Thor would be too vulnerable to attack. So the British decided on hardened silo-launches in a project codenamed K-11, with a planned reaction time of less than ten minutes from the order to launch. Design work on a below-ground six-storey concrete and steel silo, with the launch control room located three floors down, fitted with a blast-proof 750-ton movable concrete door on rails, was completed. But the Treasury refused to fund any further work, because by 1959, estimated total project costs had soared to between £278 million and £320 million. The budget vultures had begun to gather around the project.

When doubts about the survivability of a British silo-based nuclear deterrent finally surfaced, the Chiefs of Staff recommended the immediate cancellation of BLUE STREAK in a secret memorandum to the Defence Minister Harold Watkinson on February 5, 1960. The project was now dead in the water and was finally cancelled on April 13, with the UK government picking up the bill of £60 million spent in research and development.

As a footnote, the missile was seen as the first stage rocket in the civilian satellite programme being organised by the European Launcher Development Organisation (ELDO). The French were very interested in the British project but there were grave suspicions in Whitehall that this stemmed from their requirements for missile technology. London was hamstrung by its agreement with the USA on the exchange of this type of information. For example, the BLUE STREAK's re-entry vehicle was said to be invulnerable to countermeasures of the day ('it is so advanced that neither the US nor ourselves can conceive a counter to it', according to one British document of the period). Information about its radar signature was classified top secret and 'would be of great value to the French', the government's chief scientist Sir Solly Zuckerman told ministers on January 20, 1961:

The most advanced work in this field is British and is acknowledged by the US to be ahead of their work. It is thought that future US warheads may be based on this British work.

Release of this information would be contrary to I and II of para. 3 [of the Anglo-American agreement] in that it could provide an enemy with a ballistic weapon against which we could see no defence and it would prejudice American weapons. ...It is recommended that this information should not be released.

Information on ... [decoys] would [also] contravene [the agreement]. This is a sensitive Top Secret field in which we are well ahead of the USA who accordingly would be apprehensive if we released information to the French.

The British were forced to politely avoid discussion of any details about the re-entry vehicle with the French.

So the UK pulled out of the strategic systems business – a decision they were to regret a few years later when trying to develop a new system to upgrade their American Polaris A3 missiles to counter the growing threat posed by Moscow's anti-ballistic missile defences.

In the meantime Britain was faced with the desperate need for a new independent deterrent if it was to remain a member of the exclusive nuclear weapons club. Ownership of such an arsenal was regarded in London, and later in Paris, as a prerequisite for international diplomatic clout in the United Nations security council and elsewhere, as well as being a source of great national pride.

The Americans obligingly offered the Douglas AGM-87A Skybolt, an air-launched two-stage, solid propellant ballistic missile they were developing for air-launch by their B-52 bombers as a defence suppression weapon. Deployment of Skybolt would overcome the British bombers' vulnerabilities to Soviet air defences, as it had a range of 1,100 miles and they could safely launch without coming into reach of Soviet missile batteries. The USAF planned to buy 1,000 missiles, enough to equip 22 of its squadrons, in a programme costing $15.3 billion in 1960 prices. The British chipped in with their order for 144 Skybolts in March 1960, to arm Vulcan Mk.2 bombers, one under each giant delta wing. London was given firm assurances that the project would go ahead.

In a secret addendum to the Anglo-American Skybolt agreement, signed on June 6, 1960 the British Prime Minister, Harold Macmillan offered President Eisenhower the use of Holy Loch in Scotland as a US Navy submarine facility for use by Polaris missile-firing boats, whose limited range dictated they needed a forward operating base nearer their Soviet targets than their bases in the USA.

But the Skybolt project was beset with technical problems and costs were inevitably rising. The flight tests, using both US aircraft and a single RAF Vulcan, failed to achieve much quantifiable progress; the first five being partial failures.

This was, no doubt, the reason why the prudent British set up an inter-departmental study group to examine various weapon options 'as we could not be certain that Skybolt would be available'. The group reported that:

> Only a long endurance ballistic missile system could give a reasonable assurance of being effective in all circumstances. For the period 1965-70, the only weapons likely to be available were the American missiles, Skybolt and Polaris. When Blue Streak was cancelled it had been accepted that if an American weapon could not be obtained there would be a gap before a British weapon became available. A new British weapon to replace Skybolt would be a major development project and would take at least eight years to complete.

Despite this uncompromising verdict, pressures were growing within Whitehall, particularly from the aviation lobby, for a new British-designed weapon that could be carried by the V-bombers and the advanced low-level strike aircraft, the TSR-2, then under development,* for squadron deployment in 1966.

The RAF created a set of operational requirements that laid down that such a weapon should be launched outside 'concentrated enemy defences' with a range of at least 1,150 miles, and with a low-level terminal flight phase of at least 150 miles. The missile should be guided by terrain-matching technology, fly at no more than 300ft above the ground, with speeds of three to four times the speed of sound at its initial high-level phase of flight. Overall accuracy should be no worse than a diameter of 2.88 miles around the target.

Two designs were submitted: the Avro W130 and the British Aircraft Corporation's X-12, a long-range ramjet. Costs of the project were

* And subsequently brutally cancelled: even the manufacturing machine tool jigs were broken up.

estimated at around £100 million, but the cynical Treasury had seen those kinds of estimates before. Their implacable opposition, the fact that these were still 'paper missiles', and that any weapon could not conceivably be in service before 1968–9, leaving a capability gap in the deterrent, killed off the final British attempt to create a brand-new strategic system from scratch.

London was right to be suspicious about Skybolt. US Defense Secretary Robert McNamara recommended to President Kennedy, on November 21, 1962, that the project should be scrapped. Less than a month later, Skybolt was gone.

The programme had cost the Pentagon $2.6 billion and President Kennedy offered the British all the information and materials from the project in return for a token one-off payment of $100 million and their promise to continue it. A generous offer made by an embarrassed ally. But Britain was by now very wary of any indigenous ballistic missile development and graciously declined. Instead, Prime Minister Macmillan had his sights set on buying into the US Navy's more ambitious Polaris programme, already operational at sea. After some persuasion, Kennedy eventually agreed, despite strong opposition from his State Department, concerned at the precedent such a deal would set amongst other allies.

Another area of nuclear weaponry where the British were again less than successful was in the design of atomic demolition munitions (ADMs), a little-known facet of the Cold War. In the years following the Second World War, intelligence reports continually highlighted the overwhelming strength of Soviet ground forces in Europe and their supposed ability to roll over NATO's opposition and drive on to the English Channel ports in France and Belgium within a matter of weeks, if not days. Once the Russian forces had crossed the River Elbe, time would be very limited to rush in reinforcements from across the Atlantic and from elsewhere in Europe. World War Three could be over in a matter of hours – with the Western democracies the losers.

A delaying tactic was necessary: something that would destroy large areas of buildings or strategically vital transport hubs and thus hinder, slow up, the speed of the Soviet advance on the ground. Both the UK and US worked on ADMs – called 'defensive nuclear weapons' – that would be buried under their wartime targets in advance of hostilities and only detonated if the pressing tactical need arose.

Few details about these controversial weapons have entered the public domain. In 1953, the British began work on the charmingly codeworded BROWN BUNNY (later BLUE BUNNY* and eventually BLUE PEACOCK), a 20 kT weapon weighing more than 7.5 tons, carried around on the back of a flatbed lorry. Two prototypes were built under plans to deploy 10 such ADMs to the British Rhine Army's area of Germany in 1958–9, but the weight of the weapon ironically meant the truck could not be driven off the roads. The project was abandoned.

The British Army then produced new plans for a smaller, lighter atomic weapon for this role, codenamed VIOLET MIST, using a modified RED BEARD nuclear bomb with a yield of 15 kT. But this was scrapped in 1961 because of budget considerations.

Around 600 American ADMs were manufactured and put in place in the 1960s, 30 of them reportedly along the Yugoslav border and others positioned to block Alpine passes on the road and rail approaches to Italy. There was a public outcry in Germany in 1964 when it emerged that the then German Defence Minister was considering an American plan for 200 such weapons to be sited in a 'nuclear mine belt' along the Inner German border with East Germany. Other nuclear munitions of this type were to be laid behind enemy lines by American special forces to destroy tunnels or bridges to interdict his reinforcements or re-supply lines.

The American ADMs were of two main types: the Medium Atomic Demolition Munition, or MADM, which weighed less than 400 lbs and deployed in 1965, armed with a variable 1–15 kT yield W-45 warhead. The smaller version was the Special Atomic Demolition Munition, weighing just 163 lbs, with a yield of 0.01 kTs and carried in a metal suitcase. The American weapons were only decommissioned after the collapse of the Soviet Union in the early 1990s and have now been destroyed. Other US ADMs were positioned in South Korea and also stored on Guam.

The Soviet Union developed similar weapons for use by their Spetsnatz special forces against targets well inside Western Europe after the outbreak of war. There were reportedly about 115 ADMs in the Soviet arsenal, each one with a yield of 1 kT. A number are said to have gone missing during the Soviet Army's withdrawal from what was East

* The codename was changed because the name BLUE BUNNY was compromised. The Russians knew what it signified.

Germany after the collapse of communism. According to some Western intelligence sources, China retains ADMs for possible use in conflict.

One of the more bizarre nuclear weapons developed by the USA in the 1950s was the 'Davy Crockett', the infantry's own atomic weapon with ranges of between 1,000 and 13,000ft. This was a recoilless rifle, or bazooka, that fired a spin-stabilised, unguided nuclear projectile, to destroy large enemy tank concentrations short distances away. The bulbous warhead, weighing only 51lbs, contained the W-54 warhead with a variable yield of 0.01 to 1 kT, fitted with a time fuze. Around 2,100 of these astonishing weapons were deployed with the US Army from 1956, each one served by a three-man crew. Two were tested on July 7 and 17, 1962 at the Nevada test site in the LITTLE FELLAH series of nuclear trials. In the second test, a Davy Crockett 0.02 kT warhead was fired from its stationary 155mm launcher and detonated 40ft above the ground over its target 1.7 miles away. The system was withdrawn from service in 1971.

Both sides in the Cold War also deployed nuclear artillery shells as short-range tactical weapons – the so-called atomic cannon. While not strictly weapons of mass destruction, the opposing forces would have seen their use as another step in the escalatory ladder to full-scale nuclear conflict. Largest of these was the US Army's M65 280mm gun, 42ft long and weighing 42,500lbs, which could hurl a nuclear-armed artillery shell 20 miles. A total of 20 of these clumsy leviathans were manufactured at Watervliet Arsenal, New York, entering service in 1952 and being decommissioned 11 years later. On May 25, 1953 one cannon fired a 15 kT shell at Frenchman Flat at the Nevada Test Site in the GRABLE nuclear shot. It exploded in an air burst seven miles from the gun, 528ft above an area littered with bridges, vehicles and railway carriages to test the destructive effects. Seven atomic cannon remain on public display in the USA.*

What of the French? We saw how the Anglo-American allies sought to deny France the secrets of German missile technology in 1945 and the concern in the 1960s about revealing details of the Blue Streak re-entry vehicle to the European Launcher Development

* The surviving atomic cannon are at Yuma Proving Ground, Yuma, Arizona; Junction City, Kansas; Atomic Museum, Albuquerque, New Mexico; Fort Sill Museum, Oklahoma; US Army Ordnance Museum, Aberdeen, Maryland; Virginia War Memorial Museum,. Newport News, Virginia and Watervliet Arsenal, Watervliet, New York.

Organisation because of fears the technology might be used by the French military.

Political instability in France delayed nuclear weapons research in the 1940–50s and it was not until December 5 1956 that a Committee for Military Applications of Atomic Energy was secretly set up in Paris, with approval for a nuclear freefall bomb given two weeks later. When de Gaulle assumed power in May 1958, he accelerated the programme. The first French test, GERBOISE BLEUE, on February 13, 1960, was a 65 kT bomb detonated atop a 300ft tower at Reggane, in the Algerian Sahara, 200 miles south of Colomb Bechar. This was a development version of the AN-11 gravity bomb, 40 of which armed Mirage IVA bombers in 1964–8. A live drop followed on July 19, 1966.

France had become the world's fourth nuclear power.

The last of three further atmospheric tests in Algeria, on April 25, 1961 was a detonation of just 0.5 kT, reportedly exploded to remove any chance of it falling into the hands of the disaffected French Army which had mutinied in the French colony.

Development work on the S-2, an intermediate-range missile with a 120 kT MR-31 warhead, was also underway, with the first test-firing on December 1, 1968. Nine *Sol-Sol-Balistique-Stratégique* missiles, based in hardened silos in the Plateau d'Albion, between Marseille and Lyon, became operational on August 1, 1971 with a further nine the following April, all able to reach targets in the western USSR. The missiles formed the major portion of the French *force de frappe* – the nuclear strike force – later renamed with elegant Gallic subtlety, the *force de dissuasion*. They were replaced from 1980 by 18 S-3 silo-based missiles with a 2,200-mile range and armed with a single hardened TN-61 1.2 MT warhead and a range of penetration aids.

Up to the late 1950s, any nuclear-armed missiles carried by submarines were launched while the boat was on the surface. The US Navy mounted regular deterrent patrols with its Regulus cruise missile system and the Soviet Navy introduced ballistic missiles to the oceans with the less-than-effective R-11FM naval version of the short-range land missile 'Scud', first tested in 1955 and becoming operational four years later.

After being beaten to the punch with ICBMs, the USA stole a vital but temporary march on their Russian counterparts with the Navy's two-stage solid-propelled UGM-27 Polaris missile – the first to be capable of being launched while submerged. Now strategic nuclear weapons lurked silently in the depths of the sea.

The war-fighting advantages of submarines as missile-firing platforms, or SSBNs, are enormous. Not only are the weapons platforms mobile, but also they are also extremely difficult to detect within the vastness of the ocean deeps. Just where do you start searching for them? Draw a circle on the map from their likely targets, based on a diameter provided by their missiles' known range, and any part of the sea contained within that circle may be a hiding place for your enemy SSBN. Trying to track them down and destroy them before they can fire their missiles ties up considerable naval and aviation resources, together with substantial investments in technology – nuclear 'hunter-killer' submarines, underwater sensors, torpedo or missile developments. The task seems hopeless.

Both sides in the Cold War routinely tried to track the opposing SSBNs. They still do. It is proudly claimed that the Russians have never detected Royal Navy missile boats on patrol. Stealth, silence and, if necessary, speed, are the watchwords of any missile-firing submarine. The old submariners' phrase 'run silent, run deep' encapsulates this little-known battlefield between the nuclear powers.

Much of the deadly cat and mouse game between the SSBN and its hunters was and still is fought in the unfriendly alien environment of the icy waters north of the Arctic Circle – indeed beneath the Polar Ice Cap. One later class of Soviet submarine, the huge, mighty 'Typhoon' class, was designed in the 1970s solely with the aim of safely sitting out, beneath the pack-ice, the early nuclear exchanges in any East–West conflict, only breaking through to the surface to launch Moscow's retaliatory strikes.

Development of Polaris, the first true submarine-launched ballistic missile, began in 1956 with the first test flight coming in 1959, the same year as the first US SSBN submarine, *George Washington*, was commissioned. A new version of the missile, the A2 entered service in 1961 with the *Ethan Allen* test-firing a round carrying a W-47 warhead in 1962. A third version, almost wholly a new missile, the A3, was deployed from 1964 in US Navy boats, as well as four Royal Navy 'Resolution' class submarines, following the cancellation of Skybolt. The 1,370-mile range of the A1 version was extended to 2,900 miles for the A3. Warhead accuracy improved too, with the CEP being halved from 5,940ft to 2,970ft.

The USA was now armed with its much-vaunted 'triad' of nuclear deterrence, comprising air, land and sea weapons. There were the silo- and submarine-launched missiles in addition to the Short-Range Attack Missiles (SRAM) and the B53 nuclear bombs carried by the lumbering B-52 bombers, some of which were always airborne, constantly on alert, awaiting the order to attack from the US President.

With the advent of Polaris, now Moscow was suffering its own gap in missile capability with no sea-based deterrent capable of effectively striking the USA. The Russians accelerated their research and development programmes. The first true Soviet naval missile was the R-13 (SS-N-4) deployed from 1963 to 1965 in 23 diesel-electric powered 'Golf' submarines and the first Russian nuclear-powered boats, the eight-strong 'Hotel' class. The system lost much of the submarine's great advantage, because the boat had to be surfaced for firing and so was vulnerable to aircraft attack.

The first Russian missile to be launched from a submerged submarine was the 882-mile-range single-stage R-21 (SS-N-5 'Sark'), armed with either an 800 kT or 1 MT warhead, which began development in 1959 and entered service in 1963 – the short timespan an indicator of the high priority Moscow was placing on its sea-based deterrent. The R-21 was fitted in existing 'Golf' and 'Hotel' class submarines, three missiles to a boat contained in vertical tubes within the fin, and was launched from depths of 150ft by the ejection of cold gases from nozzles at the base of the missile before the main motors fired. The 'Sark' provided a short-range rudimentary capability for the Soviet Navy, but was less than satisfactory.

More effective was the two-stage R-27 (SS-N-6 'Serb') that equipped 34 'Yankee' class, the first true Soviet ballistic missile-firing submarine design. The weapon entered service in 1968, carried in 16 tubes in each boat's hull behind the fin or conning tower. Earlier models had ranges of more than 1,500 miles, later extended to 1,900 miles. The Northern Fleet submarines were positioned in the western North Atlantic off the east coast of the USA and their mission was to attack cities and other targets on the USA's eastern seaboard with the 1 MT (later three 200 kT weapons), fired at intervals of eight seconds from beneath the waves.

The French also took their strategic nuclear weapons to sea, with the COELACANTHE project to develop a ballistic missile submarine squadron, called the *Force Océanique Stratégique,* or FOST. The

'Redoubtable' boats, their first class of *Sous-Marines Nucléaire Lanceur d'engines balistique,* (SNLE) were deployed from 1972 and are still operational (until 2004) in *L'Indomptable.* Initially, they were armed with the M-1 missile carrying the TN-60/61 family of warheads, France's first thermonuclear weapons, developed from 1968. Successive missile developments culminated in the squat, round-nosed M-45, carrying six 100 kT TN-75 warheads with a range of 3,730 miles, now at sea in the successor *Le Triomphant* class with 16 launch tubes apiece.

China was also anxious to develop SSBNs but was to suffer continual frustrating setbacks to her ability to deploy a credible SSBN deterrent. In the early 1960s, there were experiments with two Soviet-design 'Golf' diesel-electric submarines and seven 'Scud' R-11F missiles, originally built for short-range attacks for the Soviet Army, generously supplied by Moscow.

These proved less than successful and Beijing began painful and problematic development of its own submarine-launched ballistic missile in 1967, the two-stage, solid-fuel Ju-Lang (JL) 1 ('Giant Wave') or CCS-N-3. First test-firing came on April 30, 1982 from a submerged pontoon barge near Huludao, followed by further launches from a converted 'Golf' class trials boat. The missile has a range of 1,340 miles and is armed with a single 250 kT warhead. It became operational on the People's Liberation Army (Navy) SSBN, the single 6,500-ton 'Xia' class in 1987, four years after the boat, *Changzheng 6,* was available for service. There are persistent but unconfirmed reports that a second boat was built, but was lost in an accident in 1985. The 'Xia' boat underwent an extensive refit in 1995–2000, probably to improve its nuclear propulsion and to fit an improved missile, the JL-1A, armed with a variable yield warhead in the 20–150 kT range. It is deployed in China's Northern Fleet, based at Qingdao, and never operates in the waters outside Chinese territorial limits – perhaps a sign of official unease over her operational reliability, or known lack of capability to defend against Western (or indeed Russian) anti-submarine warfare weapons and techniques.

China is now building a second class of SSBN at Luhudao shipyard, called the Type 094, with a planned operational date of around 2005–6, although problems with the nuclear reactor may delay entry into service of the first boat. Four to six submarines are planned to be built, armed with 12 or 16 of Beijing's new JL-2 missile. This has the greater range of 2,700 miles, enabling targets in most of the USA to be reachable from a boat submerged off the Chinese coast.

Up to the 1990s, therefore, the 'official' nuclear weapons 'club' consisted of the USA, Britain, France, the Soviet Union and China. The three Western nations became increasingly reliant on their submarine-launched weapons for strategic nuclear capability; the US Trident D-5 missiles carried in its giant 'Ohio' class submarines, and Britain's Royal Navy with their own Tridents, arming its 'Vanguard' boats (but with British warheads) and the French with their two classes of SSBN, armed with the M45 and M4 missiles.

The USA upgraded its silo-based force of ICBMs from 1962 with various marks of the Minuteman missile, with a maximum of 1,000 operational in the early 1980s.

The technology of MIRVing warheads means that a missile's weapons can be programmed to hit multiple and widely dispersed targets at the same time.

From 1986, it also deployed the more advanced three-stage Peacekeeper, once planned as a mobile weapon on railway cars to avoid pre-emptive strikes but now silo-based, with a new post boost vehicle carrying 10 W-87 warheads with yields of 300–475 kT. They are "sown" from the vehicle by attachments being unlatched by gas pressure from an explosive cartridge broken by small, exploding bolts. Range is greater than 6,000 miles and the missile's CEP is just 270ft – a level of accuracy enabling it to be used to destroy enemy missile silos with a high level of confidence. Fifty Peacekeepers remain in service at Francis E. Warren air base, Wyoming, but after ratification of the START 2 treaty, all will be withdrawn after 2007. As well as the Peacekeepers, 500 of the latest three-stage Minuteman version, Mk III, are deployed at Malmstom, Montana; Warren and Minot, North Dakota (the latter base covering almost 8,500 square miles) armed with up to three W-62 170 kT or W-78 350 kT warheads. Minuteman has a range of more than 8,000 miles and a CEP of 396ft and its service life will be extended until 2020. Both missiles can provide immediate reaction and drop a multitude of warheads on their planned targets within 30 minutes of the order to launch. Overwhelming nuclear retribution can come swiftly.

The airborne element of the American nuclear triad is represented by the AGM-86B/C air-launched cruise missile, carried by the now venerable B-52G/H bombers, the last upgraded version carrying eight missiles in a rotary launcher in its bomb bay. The aircraft has an unrefuelled combat range in excess of 8,800 miles. The weapon will also be cleared for deployment on the B-2A 'Spirit' bat-winged stealth bomber with up to five missiles carried internally. The cruise missile, guided by terrain-matching radar, has a range of 1,550 miles, a CEP of 100ft, and is armed with a 200 kT single warhead – an incredibly accurate weapon, designed for precision strikes on enemy high-value targets.

Both bombers can also carry the B83 nuclear bomb, with an explosive power equivalent to 1-2 MT, for use against hardened targets such as missile silos, or concrete command post bunkers, in low-level drops, either by 'laying down' precisely on the target (with detonation delayed by two minutes to enable the delivery aircraft to escape the blast) or by a retarded drop, using three small parachutes to slow descent. The USAF has 500 of these weapons in store for operational use, out of 1,400 originally manufactured in 1983–7.

The B61 bomb can be delivered at high speeds from as low as 350ft, with airburst, ground burst or time delay explosions of its variable 10–500 kT device. One variant, the 100 to 500 kT yield B61-11, was developed in 1996 to penetrate the ground's surface by between seven and 50ft before detonation, in order to create a powerful shockwave to destroy underground fortifications.

Both the B61 and B83 bombs are fitted with a range of safety and anti-tamper devices, called Permissive Action Links (PALs), which enable the weapons to be made live or safe, as well as preventing disassembly or unauthorised detonation, by punching in various numerical codes. The final arrow in the airborne nuclear quiver is the B57 depth charge, of which 150 were retained in 1994 for delivery by a range of other US ground and maritime attack aircraft against submarines. It has variable yields ranging from five to 10 kTs.

Eighteen US Navy 'Ohio' class SSBNs, each one armed with 24 Trident missiles, are available for patrol in the North Atlantic and Barents Sea and the Pacific. Each patrol area totals more than one million square miles of ocean – a graphic indication of the problem the adversary has in tracking them down. Most of the missiles are the D5 version, with a range of 7,500 miles, a CEP of 300ft, and eight W-76 or W-88 warheads with yields of 100–475 kTs.

Today, the USA's nuclear forces are controlled by a unified command formed from the merger of the Space and Strategic Commands, headquartered at Offutt air base in Nebraska and responsible for early warning and military space operations as well as the triad of nuclear weapons. The size of the force has seen substantial reduction, both by treaty and by a re-assessment of the threat facing the USA following the end of the Cold War. Take the example of nuclear depth charges: around 1,000 were deployed in 1983 for use by American ships and naval aviation in all potential theatres of war. By 1993 that number had dropped to 425 and today only 150 are in store in the USA, the remainder destroyed.

Britain retains the Trident D-5, operational on four 'Vanguard' class SSBNs, with 16 launch tubes each. The missiles use the American Mk 4 re-entry vehicles, but with up to eight UK designed and built warheads, similar to the 100 kT W-76. Each boat carries a maximum of 48 warheads, suggesting that the 16 missiles either have three each, or there is a mix of single and multiple warheads. Following the withdrawal from service of the RAF's W-177 tactical nuclear freefall bomb, the British government decided in 1996 to use some D5s in what was called a 'sub-strategic role' with some fitted with a single warhead of less than 10 kTs. The kind of scenarios that would trigger use of these lower yield weapons probably involve, for example, retaliation in response to a massive chemical or biological attack on mainland Britain by a clearly defined culprit state who owns a target of value or national prestige.

France renounced development of new nuclear systems at the end of the Cold War, withdrawing the Pluton battlefield nuclear-armed missile, cancelling its Hades successor in 1996, dismantling its S-3 missiles on the Plateau d'Albion and also retiring the AN-52 freefall bomb and the Mirage IVP bombers. It has dismantled all its nuclear test facilities in the Pacific and since mid-1996 has ended production of fissile material for nuclear weapon production. No doubt France can recycle old warheads to make new versions if it needs to. It still retains a strategic nuclear capability in its four SSBNs and tactically, with its three squadrons of Mirage 2000N bombers and naval Super Etendard aircraft, equipped with 80–90 *Air-Sol Moyenne Portée* (ASMP) air-launched missiles, capable of 155-mile range and each fitted with a 300 kT warhead. A new version, the ASMP-A will enter service in 2007, arming the Mirage 2000N and the new Rafale fighter.

Russia's missile forces are in decline, driven down in numbers by arms reduction treaty obligations, a shortage of cash and a switch of resources to Moscow's hard-pressed conventional forces. At peak levels, in 1990, there were 1,064 ICBMs based in silos, armed with 4,278 warheads. The land-based ICBM force is now based on five fourth- and fifth-generation missile types, the RS-20 (SS-18 'Satan'), RS-18 (SS-19 'Sickle'), RS-22 (SS-24 'Scalpel'), RS-12M (SS-25 'Sickle') and the RS-12M1 (SS-27 Topol-M).

The RS-20 SS-18 Satan (another graphic NATO codeword!) was deployed in 1975 with later versions entering service up to 1988, with the highest operational number totalling 308 in silos in 1991 in Russia and what is now Kazakhstan. The collapse of the Soviet Union meant that all 104 Kazakhstan missiles, at Derzhavinsk and Zhangiz-Tobe, were withdrawn and destroyed, as were their launch silos by September 1996. The START-2 Treaty, ratified by the Russian *Duma* or parliament in May 2000, lays down that the remaining Satans must be removed from their silos and destroyed by 2007. This now began at a special destruction plant at Surovatikha, near Nizhny Novgorod, with up to 30 missiles a year being cut up. The first six of the 30 SS-18 silos were destroyed at Aleysk in 2000. As at January 2001, 180 missiles were still operational in Russia with ranges of more than 9,000 miles, each armed with 10 550 kT MIRVed warheads.

The last of the Soviet fourth-generation ICBMs, the RS-18 SS-18 Stiletto, with six 500 kT MIRVed warheads and a range of more than 6,000 miles, became operational in 1975, with peak deployment of 360 seven years ago in four silo fields in Russia and Ukraine. The 130 Ukrainian-based missiles were deactivated and destroyed at a special plant at Dnepropetrovsk by January 1999. The Russian force level dropped to 150 missiles by June 2001 and of these, almost a third will be withdrawn from service by 2007 and the remainder, totalling 105, will be converted to carry a single warhead, probably with a yield of 550 kTs.

Moscow, like the USA, became concerned about the survivability of its silo-based ICBM force in the early 1970s, and developed the RS-22 SS-24 Scalpel as a mobile-launched missile, carried on specially designed railway trucks, drawn by three diesel locomotives, complete with a command post. The objective is to constantly move each train to prevent accurate targeting by attacking enemy missiles. The trains has three launchers with hinged roofs that swing out sideways to allow the missile, within its canister, to be erected for firing. The trains can travel at 75mph and were based at Bershet, Kostromo and Krasnoyarsk from 1987, although the force is now substantially reduced and probably totals less than 25 launchers. Because of problems affecting the accuracy of the missile guidance system when fired from the rail launchers, the Soviets also deployed the Scalpel in silos from 1989 at Tatischevo in Russia and Pervomaysk in the Ukraine. The latter were all destroyed by December 2001. By June that year, only six of the 6,000-mile-range missiles, each armed with ten 550 kT warheads, remained operational in their silos and these are due to be phased out and cut up by 2007.

The Russian designers then moved on to much more accurate, single warhead ICBMs, with the development of the three-stage RS-12M SS-25 Sickle or Topol ('poplar tree') in the 1980s. They sought rationalisation of the land-based missile force by reducing the number of weapon types in service, so simplifying maintenance, training and storage issues. With better guidance technology now available, improving accuracy, the new missiles could be armed with single warheads. Two were envisaged under a project codenamed UNIVERSAL. The first was again designed for mobile launchers, being carried in huge, clumsy 14-wheeled transporter-erector-launchers (TELs) to pre-surveyed launch sites in protective, thickly wooded areas, hidden from the prying eyes of spy satellites. This entered service in 1988 at nine sites in the Soviet Union, two in what was to become the independent republic of Belarus. Around 450 missiles were built before production ended in 1994. They have a range of more than 6,500 miles, a CEP of less than 600ft, and a single warhead with a yield of 550 kt. START 2 restricted the missiles to their garrison areas but allowed some to be based in converted and upgraded SS-18 silos. The Belarus missiles were reclaimed by Russia with the last despatched in November 1996.

About 350 Sickles remained operational in January 2000. The last in a series of proving flights to test reliability was in February 2001 when a Sickle was launched from Plesetsk and successfully hit its target on the Kura proving ground in the Kamchatka peninsula. A few months later, in July 2001, a Sickle launch occurred with the missile apparently fitted with an experimental scramjet to power the last stage, capable of speeds well in excess of five times the speed of sound. Whilst Moscow denied the report, it seems likely that this is part of a plan to develop brand-new countermeasures to foil attempts to destroy a warhead – such as the USA's new national missile defence shield.

The second UNIVERSAL missile was the RS-12M1 Topol-M, designed in the late 1980s to be both silo-based and road-mobile. But development was stopped dead by the collapse of the Soviet Union and was only restarted in February 1993. The new missile has a heavier but more powerful first stage and a brand-new re-entry vehicle and single warhead, rated at 550 kTs. This may well include new counter-measures, as Russian reports have emphasised the Topol-M's ability to defeat known or projected anti-ballistic missile defences, including the USA's new system. It is known that the re-entry vehicle is agile, able to manoeuvre in space to evade attacking missiles, and the warhead has been hardened to withstand explosions closer than 1,500ft away. Guidance is via the Russian Glonass satellite system, providing warhead accuracy of less than 1,000ft around its target.

The silo-based version became operational in December 1998 at the refurbished launch complex at Tatischevo, with two missile regiments. A third unit was declared operational in December 2001 but is armed with only four missiles, instead of the normal ten – a symptom of budget constraints. The mobile version entered service 12 months later. Although production has been cut back, it is expected that the Topol-M will become the mainstay of the Russian ICBM force in the foreseeable future with around 90 missiles located in converted SS-18 silos at Uzhur, Aleysk and Kartaly and the mobile launchers based at Altaif and Valdaif.

The Russian submarine-launched missile force is in a state approaching disarray. With the withdrawal of all but two of the monster Typhoon class submarines – they proved too expensive to operate – and their Sturgeon missiles, the core of the modern sea-based deterrent remains in the hands of the SS-N-23 'Skiff' missiles that arm seven Delta IV submarines. These boats can launch the missiles from depths of up to 180ft whilst on the move underwater at speeds of around five knots. Skiff, which entered service in 1986, is carried in 16 vertical launch tubes in a massive box-like structure behind the boat's fin. It has a range of more than 5,000 miles and is fitted with four MIRVed 100 kT warheads.

The other main Russian naval strategic weapon is the now ageing SS-N-18 'Stingray' carried by the six venerable 'Delta III' submarines remaining in service, also with 16 launch tubes apiece. The latest version of this missile has seven MIRVed warheads of 100 kT apiece.

Finally, two 'Delta I' submarines, conceived in the 1960s and built between 1971 and 1979, deploy the SS-N-8 'Sawfly' SLBM, which began development in 1961 and is now armed with a single 800 kT warhead. These submarines and their missiles are likely to be withdrawn from service shortly.

Most of the Russian SSBNs in the Northern and Pacific Fleet now spend little time at sea because of lack of funding and poor training levels. Although they can fire their missiles whilst tied up alongside the jetty, the clear strategic advantage of the submarine is lost in these circumstances. If you know where they are, a surprise pre-emptive attack can neutralise them.

Lastly, China. We have already looked at the single less-than-effective Chinese ballistic missile submarine, but Beijing also has an increasingly effective land-based deterrent.

In the late 1950s, the Soviet Union supplied a small number of 'Shyster' missiles to China that were rapidly reverse-engineered and produced domestically. These were the parents of a range of Chinese short- and intermediate-range missiles that culminated in the Dong Feng 5 (DF-5) ('East Wind') ICBM, that entered service in 1971 in hardened silos in central China, with a range of 7,500 miles and a single warhead with yields varying between 1 and 3 MTs. These were modernised in the mid-1980s, fitted with four to six MIRVed warheads of 350 kT each. Between 20 and 30 are now based in the Tai-hai mountains, some stored in protective horizontal tunnels. The missiles are likely to be withdrawn from service in 2005, to be replaced by up to 20 of the new ICBM, the DF-41, developed, reportedly with the aid of stolen American technology, from 1986.

This 7,500-mile-range missile, armed with a single 1 MT or 3 MIRVed warheads of up to 120 kTs each, is solid-propelled, providing faster reaction times. It is likely to be based in silos or in mobile launchers, either rail carriages or seven-wheeled trucks, and stored in mountain caves.

The DF-31, which entered service in 1999, is a close relation of the JL-2 submarine-launched missile, planned to enter service, as we have seen, with the new Chinese SSBN. This 6,000-mile-range ICBM is again stored in caves and deployed either by rail or road to pre-surveyed launch sites, to prevent detection. Test flights included three MIRVed warheads, believed to be up to 150 kT yield, and a range of penetration aids. Between 10 and 20 missiles were reported in the first production batch.

So the four members of the old nuclear club have lined up their weapons of terrifying might and increasing accuracy, providing them with the ability to strike against an adversary's military installations and cities with devastating and crushing power. The Cold War has ended, but the weapons remain as potent and as dangerous as ever with the ability to kill the world's population many times over. Deterrence remains in place – hopefully.

But no longer are these countries the only ones to possess ballistic missiles. Others have emerged from development in a wide range of countries fitted with nuclear, chemical and perhaps biological weapon warheads. These weapons have become the new symbols of prestige in nationhood – the ultimate phallic symbol. Everyone wants them. And some now deploy them as means to control events regionally – and perhaps further afield – to their advantage.

CHAPTER 4
A TERRIBLE MUSHROOM CLOUD

THE OFFICIAL ORDER FOR THE FIRST RELEASE of a nuclear weapon in anger was signed on July 25, 1945 by General Thomas Handy, acting Chief of Staff of the US Army, after its approval by President Truman and Secretary of War Henry Stimson who were attending the Potsdam conference of the Second World War allied leaders. Directed to General Carl Spaatz, commander of the USAAF Strategic Air Force, it ordered the 509 Composite Group, 20th Air Force to deliver its first 'special' bomb

as soon as weather will permit visual bombing after about August 3 1945 on one of the targets: Hiroshima, Kokura, Niigata and Nagasaki. To carry military and civilian scientific personnel from the War Department to observe and record the effects of the explosion of the bomb, additional aircraft will accompany the airplane carrying the bomb. The observing planes will stay several miles distant from the point of impact of the bomb. Additional bombs will be delivered on the above targets as soon as made ready by the project staff. Further instructions will be issued concerning targets other than those listed above.

The targeting committee, meeting on May 10 and 11, had reviewed Kyoto, Hiroshima, Yokohama, Kokura arsenal, and Niigata as potential objectives. Hiroshima was said to be

an important army depot and port of embarkation in the middle of an urban industrial area. It is a good radar target and it is such a size that a large part of the city could be extensively damaged. There are adjacent hills, which are likely to produce a focusing effect which would considerably increase the blast damage. Due to rivers, it is not a good incendiary target.

It was rated as an 'AA target' and the second choice behind Kyoto. The advisers also considered bombing the Japanese Emperor's palace. They agreed that

we should not recommend it, but that any action for this bombing should come from authorities on military policy. It was agreed we should obtain information from which we could determine the effectiveness of our weapon against this target.

But later it was decided that the palace would have least strategic value. Kyoto was also dropped from the target list. The planners were looking for the best effects from what was to be called 'a demonstration shot' in modern nuclear parlance. The psychological factors in target selection 'were of the greatest value' within Japan and 'making the initial use sufficiently spectacular for the importance of the weapon to be internationally recognised.' The USAAF was ordered not to firebomb the potential targets to maximise the impact of the atomic weapon attacks.

Looking back, more than five decades later, this all sounds coldly calculating. Today, after surviving the Cold War, our viewpoint is more humane. Then, it *was* full-scale war against the Imperial Japanese empire, and the Allies were looking to a quick end to the bloody conflict and to avoid a costly invasion of the Japanese homeland islands. It's important to remember that in the Second World War, death rained from the skies night after night. On March 9, 1945 the USAAF dropped around 2,000 tons of incendiary bombs over Tokyo, creating a horrendous firestorm, whipped up by 25mph winds, which totally destroyed 16 square miles of offices, factories and homes and caused 185,000 civilian casualties, 80,000 of them deaths. Or expressed in the grim statistics of strategic aerial bombing, 37.2 deaths per ton of ordnance dropped. That was just one raid on one target. There were many, many others. In purely military terms, aside from the terrible human suffering, conventional bombing by the RAF on Hamburg and the USAAF on Tokyo alone produced more immediate deaths than the nuclear weapon dropped on Hiroshima.

The political requirement for the power of the atomic bomb to be 'internationally recognised' had strong undertones of the need to establish military power and diplomatic clout in the years following the end of hostilities.

There was, of course, a moral debate before the atomic bombs were dropped. The Committee on Political and Social Problems attached to the MANHATTAN project – the American codename for the development of these weapons – had grave misgivings about the awesome power that had come into the hands of the Western allies. Their secret report, dated June 11, 1945, stated:

> Scientists have often before been accused of providing new weapons for the mutual destruction of nations, instead of improving their well-being. It is undoubtedly true that the discovery of flying ... has so far brought much more misery than enjoyment or profit to humanity. In the past, scientists could disclaim direct responsibility for the use to which mankind had put in their disinterested discoveries. We cannot take the same attitude now because the success we have achieved in the development of nuclear power is fraught with infinitely greater dangers than were all the developments of the past.
>
> All of us, familiar with the present state of nucleonics, live with the vision before our eyes of sudden destruction visited on our own country, of a Pearl Harbor disaster, repeated in thousand-fold magnification, in every one of our major cities.

They urged that the new weapon should be demonstrated to United Nations representatives 'on the desert or a barren island' rather than against Japan – as a method of achieving an international agreement on the prevention of nuclear warfare. They also prophetically talked of a nuclear armaments race.

But their plan for a peaceful detonation was not to be.

On July 16, 1945 at 12.29 GMT, the first detonation of an atomic weapon, a plutonium implosion device, was staged in the Jornada del Muerto ('Journey of Death') valley near Alamogordo, New Mexico, codenamed TRINITY. The 19.3 kT weapon, nicknamed 'Gadget' for security reasons, was exploded on a 100ft steel tower above the desert, producing a huge red fireball. Observers 20 miles away felt the heat of the blast on their exposed skin. Brigadier General Thomas F. Farrell, found the affects 'beautiful, stupendous and terrifying':

The whole country was lighted by a searing light with the intensity many times that of the midday sun. It was golden, purple, violet, grey and blue. It lighted every peak, crevasse and ridge of the nearby mountain range with a clarity and beauty that cannot be described but must be seen to be imagined.

General Leslie Groves, in charge of MANHATTAN, in his official report, talked of the massive cloud that 'surged and billowed upward with tremendous power' reaching a height of 41,000ft in about five minutes. The explosion created

a crater from which all vegetation had vanished with a diameter of 1,200-feet ... the center was a shallow bowl 130-feet in diameter and six feet in depth. The steel from the tower was evaporated. Fifteen hundred feet away there was a four-inch iron pipe 16-feet high set in concrete and strongly guyed. It disappeared completely.

Other steel and concrete structures, simulating buildings, were set up half a mile from the detonation point.

The blast tore the tower from its foundation, twisted it, ripped it apart and left it flat on the ground. The effects on the tower indicate, at that distance, unshielded permanent steel and masonry buildings would have been destroyed. I no longer consider the Pentagon a safe shelter from such a bomb.

Julius Robert Oppenheimer, (1904–67) technical director of the MANHATTAN project, was less lyrical, more soberly realistic, in his assessment. Afterwards, he commented: 'We knew the world would not be the same.' At the time, as the ground shook and the blast wave raced across the early morning desert, into his mind came the words of a Hindu text, the *Bhagavad-Gita*: 'I am become death: the destroyer of worlds.' That destruction was shortly to be heaped upon Hiroshima, built on flat ground on six islands in the Ota River, surrounded by hills climbing to heights of 700ft. The 26-square-mile city, after an evacuation ordered by the Japanese government in the face of conventional bombing attacks, housed about 255,000 people at the time of the attack. Three-quarters lived in a densely built-up area in the city centre. Hiroshima contained the headquarters of the 2nd Army, in command of the defences of southern Japan. It also served as a major assembly point for troops and equipment.

On August 6, 1945 at 2 a.m., the four-engined B-29 bomber 'Enola Gay' took off from the USAAF airfield on Tinian Island in the Mariana group in the North Pacific, an ungainly, 10ft long, 9,000lb uranium weapon nicknamed 'Little Boy'* carried in its forward bomb bay. Two chase aircraft carrying observers and scientific measuring equipment followed immediately afterwards on the 1,500-mile flight north to Japan.

A hour or so later, the bomb was armed by Capt. William Parsons, chief of ordnance for the MANHATTAN project and the aircraft commander, Col. Paul Tibbetts, told the 11-man crew for the first time that 'Enola Gay' was carrying an atomic weapon. Around 7.15, Japanese radar detected the approaching B-29s at very high altitude and air-raid sirens alerted the population of Hiroshima. At 8.00 a.m. local radar determined that only three aircraft were involved in the raid and radio broadcasts warned civilians that no raid was expected as these were probably reconnaissance planes.

At 8.09, 'Enola Gay' was at 25,000ft above the city and received confirmation that the weather was suitable for dropping the weapon. At 8.16, 'Little Boy' was released from the bomb bay.

At that moment, the Hiroshima radio station went off the air. The Japanese Broadcasting Corporation in Tokyo tried to contact the station by telephone but the lines were dead.

'Little Boy' had exploded with the explosive force equivalent to 15,000 tons of TNT – or 15 kilotons (kTs) – in an airburst, 1,900ft above the city.

Sixty-six thousand people were killed instantly in the fireball, their bodies vaporised in temperatures hotter than the sun. Roof tiles were melted up to 4,000ft from the explosion. The blast wave destroyed or severely damaged more than 60,000 of the city's 90,000 buildings, although some reinforced concrete buildings, built to withstand earthquake shocks, remained standing but were burnt out in a firestorm that raged in a 6,000ft radius from the aiming point.

The total death toll was 118,661. A further 79,130 people were

---

* The US government failed to block the sale of two green circuitry plugs, part of the safety devices used in 'Little Boy' at an auction in San Francisco in 2002.

injured. Tibbetts' view of the explosion was related later in the magazine *Newsweek:*

> A bright light filled the plane. We turned back to look at Hiroshima. The city was hidden by that awful cloud … boiling up, mushrooming.

The survivors suffered appalling injuries, burns from the bomb's thermal radiation peeling the skin in scorched and charred tatters from their bodies. There was no treatment available. Fire-fighting and rescue units were stripped of men and equipment. More than 70,000 water pipes were fractured by the blast and heat effects. Ninety per cent of all doctors and nurses in Hiroshima were killed and injured and only three of the city's 55 hospitals were usable after the attack.

Some time after the attack and Japan's subsequent surrender, Western reporters were able to travel to Hiroshima. Peter Burchett reported what he saw to readers of his newspaper, the London *Daily Mail*:

> In the hospitals, I found people who, when the bomb fell, suffered absolutely no injuries but are now dying from the uncanny side-effects. For no apparent reason, their health began to fail. They lost their appetite. Their hair fell out. Bluish spots appeared on their bodies. And then bleeding began to form in their ears, nose and mouth. At first the doctors … thought that these were the symptoms of general debility. They gave their patients Vitamin A injections. The results were horrible. The flesh started rotting away from the hole caused by the injection of the needle. And in every case the victim died.

Burchett was describing the symptoms of radiation sickness caused by direct and residual radiation released by the atomic detonation. By 1950, 200,000 people in the ruins of Hiroshima had died from these effects and a further 97,000 died from cancers associated with the 'Little Boy' explosion in the three decades of 1950–80.

President Truman issued a statement later on the day of the bombing:

> Sixteen hours ago, an American airplane dropped one bomb on Hiroshima, Japan and destroyed its usefulness to the enemy. That bomb

had more power than 20,000 tons* of TNT. It had more than two thousand times the blast power of the British Grand Slam, which is the largest bomb ever yet used in the history of warfare.

On August 9, three days later after the attack on Hiroshima, a B-29 named 'Bock's Car', carrying the more sophisticated 'Fat Man' plutonium bomb, arrived at its primary target, Kokura, at 9.44 a.m. The city was covered with smoke and haze and three bombing runs were unsuccessfully attempted. Because of the weather conditions, the pilot, Major Charles Sweeney, switched to his secondary target, Nagasaki. He found that was overcast too.

The city, with a population of around 173,000, was a major naval shipbuilding port and its buildings lay in two natural valleys divided by a mountain promontory. Its industries produced ordnance, munitions such as torpedoes and other military hardware. Again, with only two B-29s detected by radar, the Japanese believed the enemy aircraft were on a reconnaissance mission. No alert was sounded.

The bomb was released at 11.02 after just one run over the city to identify the aiming point through the clouds. It exploded at a height 1,660ft above a tennis court in Matsuyama-machi with a 21 kT yield.

The effects were similar to Hiroshima, although the local terrain – the mountain spur – provided some protection to some areas from heat and blast but in others exacerbated the effects. An area of 4.55 square miles was levelled by the blast; 11,574 homes were burnt down and a further 2,652 completely destroyed in the blast. The hillsides were scorched by the flash radiation. A total of 73,884 people were killed and another 74,909 injured. The terrible legacy of radiation sickness afterwards mirrored that experienced at Hiroshima.

The world had entered the atomic age.

Twenty-four hours later, on August 10, Japan asked that it be permitted to surrender.

Hiroshima and Nagasaki were the culmination of a highly secret project to develop nuclear weapons that began in 1941 and later in a former boys' school in the New Mexico desert that became the Los Alamos weapons laboratory from March 1943. It was a race against time, for it was known that atomic fission experiments by Otto Hahn and Fritz Strassmann had been successful in Germany in 1938 and

* Initial official estimates of the yield were too high

research work had continued there. The fear was that Germany would beat the Allies to the possession of atomic bombs, but in the event, these concerns proved groundless, as the project was starved of resources. Hitler failed to appreciate its strategic significance and was more interested in short-term projects for war-winning weapons. The Germans failed even to build a working nuclear reactor by 1945.

Unbeknown to the Western Allies, the Imperial Japanese Army was also working on atomic weapons at Kyoto, beginning in 1942 with plans to use them against the USA's west coast cities. Just before the war in Europe ended, a *Kriegsmarine* U-boat was captured, with a cargo of 1,200lbs of uranium oxide in ten cases, being shipped from Germany to the Imperial Japanese army. Two Japanese officers escorting the material committed suicide. But the programme was disrupted in April 1945 when a B-29 raid damaged a thermal diffusion separation plant and there was no completed weapon available to use by the time of the surrender. Immediately afterwards, US troops dumped five cyclotrons, used to separate fissile material from uranium, into Tokyo bay after smashing them.

The development of nuclear weapons by the USA and Britain came after the governments had been warned of the military significance of nuclear fission. Albert Einstein, ironically a pacifist, wrote to President Roosevelt, on August 2, 1939, warning him that research into nuclear chain reactions could lead to the construction of a new type of powerful bomb, probably carried by boat as 'such bombs may very well prove to be too heavy for transportation by air.' He urged an American research programme. But to Roosevelt and his advisers, such a weapon looked unlikely to be developed in time for use by US forces in any future conflict with Germany and the American research programme was accorded low priority.

In the UK, two refugee scientists from Nazi Germany, Otto Frisch and Rudolf Peierls, then Professor of Mathematic Physics at Birmingham University, wrote a memorandum in March 1940 to the British government on the properties of a radio-active 'super-bomb':

> The energy liberated in the explosion of such a super-bomb is about the same produced by the explosion of 1,000 tons of dynamite. This energy is liberated in a small volume in which it will, for an instant, produce a temperature comparable to that in the interior of the sun. The blast from such

an explosion would destroy life in a wide area, the size of this area is difficult to estimate, but it will probably cover the centre of a big city.

In addition, some part of the energy set free by the bomb goes to produce radioactive substances and these will emit very powerful and dangerous radiations. The effect of these radiations is greatest immediately after the explosion, but it decays only gradually and even for days after the explosion any person entering the affected area will be killed.

Their suggestions were investigated by a special British government technical group – the 'Maud' committee* – on the technical feasibility of such a weapon under Sir Henry Tizard. It reported positively in June and July 1940 and a British programme to develop atomic weapons was launched in September 1941. The devices were to be codenamed TUBE ALLOYS and were optimistically planned to be operational by the end of 1943.

The Maud committee's report, which was communicated to Washington, galvanised American attention. The MANHATTAN project was set up on December 6, 1941 and six months later Roosevelt proposed co-operation with the British.

A group of very distinguished scientists from both sides of the Atlantic were assembled for MANHATTAN. For example, the nuclear physicist Victor Weisskopf fled to the USA to create a new life shortly before the *Anschluss* in Austria. In 1939, while at the University of Rochester, he called for a code of voluntary secrecy on nuclear fission, to prevent the proliferation of weapons technology. In 1943, after becoming an American citizen, he became a group leader in the MANHATTAN Project, engaged in the theoretical design of the fission device. For him, like others, there were doubts about the morality of the project. Later he described his work at Los Alamos as 'a shadow over my life.'

MANHATTAN is estimated to have cost $20 billion up to August 1945, but this excludes the $76 million spent by the USAAF in modifying 49 B-29 bombers to carry atomic weapons, air and ground crew training and the logistic support on Tinian Island. To put this expenditure into context, during the Second World War, the USA spent $64 billion on tanks and $31.5 billion on airdropped ordnance, grenades and mines.

* Reportedly named after the former nanny of one of the members. Security is everything.

Just how does a nuclear weapon work? It's a matter of physics. Put simply, most elements occur in several different forms, called isotopes by scientists. They are identified by the number of neutrons within the element's central portion of the atom, the nucleus, which are orbited by protons and electrons. When the nuclei of the isotopes Uranium 235 and Plutonium 239 are struck by other neutrons they split into two equal portions. This is called fission and the process releases energy and more neutrons. The process is repeated again and again in a chain reaction amongst other nuclei and is enhanced when reflectors bounce back the neutrons into fission rather than let them escape. This is called becoming 'critical'.

The 'Fat Man' bomb used at Nagasaki used a large amount of explosive surrounding a sphere of uranium with a tungsten reflector and tamper to contain the fission process. This is called a gun-type detonator. Within the uranium sphere was a ball of 12 pounds of plutonium. Once detonated, the explosive implodes or compresses the fissile core and a neutron initiator releases neutrons that in turn trigger a fission chain reaction. The reflector pushing the escaping neutrons back into the process multiplies the reaction, and the tamper constrains the superheated core from expanding. The weapon detonates and is vaporised in the enormous release of energy – the nuclear explosion. The whole process takes about 0.00002 of a second.

Thermonuclear or hydrogen bombs work through fusion of two hydrogen isotopes called deuterium and tritium, initiated by an atomic chain reaction. The process begins with a shaped charge of high explosive triggering a fission chain reaction, as in an atomic bomb. But then neutrons from the fissile core transmute the atoms in an uranium-235 tamper and the fusion fuel, solid lithium-deuteride, is violently compressed, as is the so-called 'sparkplug' made up of fissile uranium 235 or plutonium, which explodes. The fusion fuel is now super-compressed and its nuclei collide and fuse, producing a huge energy release which vaporises the weapon in a giant explosion. It is the same process that happens within the Sun, producing the heat, light and warmth that provide the means for life on Earth, although we are protected by our planet's atmosphere from most of the harmful radiation.

But here mankind has harnessed these powerful forces for annihilation and destruction.

Nuclear explosions create five distinct physical effects. Fifty per cent of the energy is released as blast, 35% as thermal radiation and the remaining 15% as nuclear radiation. The temperatures formed at ground zero amount to tens of millions of degrees centigrade, instantaneously creating an awesome glowing fireball of air and vaporised weapon residues.

To examine the horrifying devastation of these effects, let's imagine that a 1 MT nuclear weapon has been detonated as an airburst above a target. This was planned as the normal method of attack on population centres in the 1950s–70s, but this size of weapon has been subsequently abandoned by most weapon designers, with the possible exception of the Chinese, because of the increasing accuracy of missiles. Instead, multiple lower-yield weapons, in the 50–100 kT range, would today be simultaneously exploded, causing similar levels of damage and casualties.

The diameter of the resulting superhot sphere of air and debris expands to 500ft within just one millisecond of the detonation of our 1 MT weapon, escalating to 7,000ft 10 seconds later. The fireball rockets skywards at a speed of 300ft a second, ever expanding and compressing the local atmosphere, creating a huge blast wave. As the fireball rapidly cools, a towering mushroom cloud forms from dust and debris that are contaminated by the radioactive isotopes and neutron radiation caused by the weapon's immense explosion. That mushroom cloud has become an icon of the 20th and 21st centuries – a symbol of the horrors of nuclear warfare.

The blast has the same characteristics as the detonation of conventional high explosive, but is of course, much, much larger. It causes 'static overpressures' and 'dynamic pressures', which are sudden and dramatic changes in local atmospheric conditions, triggered by the force of the explosion instantaneously pushing the air away from the immediate vicinity of the detonation. These either crush buildings, or the structures are literally blown away by the fierce, all-destroying wind of the dynamic pressure. These effects are measured in pounds per square inches (psi).

US studies show that a 1 MT nuclear warhead exploded above ground level would create a three-second overpressure of more than 5 psi or 180 tons on a two-storey house four miles away from the airburst, as well as triggering a 160mph wind. The detonation of a similar yield warhead 8,000ft above the surface would cause a peak overpressure of 20 psi on structures just under one mile from ground zero and

a wind that travels at a speed of 470mph. Reinforced concrete buildings would be levelled by the blast effects in these conditions. The blast
wave can be bent or distorted by obstacles in its path. At 15–20 psi, the
wind can hurl people through the air at more than 100mph to
become, horribly, themselves human missiles. Six miles out from the
detonation, the walls of steel framed buildings would be blown away
and people killed by debris and broken glass if they were caught in the
open by overpressures of 3 psi and 95mph winds. This psi value is high
enough to blow people out of modern office buildings. Our 1 MT
weapon would inflict destruction on 105 square miles at more than 3
psi.

The second effect is direct nuclear radiation, initially ionising radiation, mainly neutrons and gamma rays within 60 seconds of
detonation. As in the case of the so-called 'neutron bomb', this kills
people.

The third is direct thermal radiation, mostly visible light – the
'nuclear flash that turns night into day' – that precedes the blast shock
wave because of the faster speed of light. This is so powerful that it can
blind those unlucky enough to observe the nuclear flash, burn their
skin and ignite flammable material like some clothing at some distance from the explosion. At Hiroshima, the different protective
qualities of light and dark patterns on clothing was painfully etched
onto the skins of the victims. Possibly 50% of casualties caused by a
nuclear explosion would be suffering from severe burns.

The next effect is residual radiation, caused by the contamination of
dust and debris by the radioactive isotopes generated by the weapon.
This irradiated material spreads downwind of the explosion and falls
to earth as radioactive fallout.

The final is the electro-magnetic pulse (EMP) we met in the first
chapter – the electrical and magnetic energy released by the detonation – that can disrupt or destroy unprotected electrical or electronic
appliances and systems as well as distorting and degrading radio signals
for perhaps days or weeks afterwards. The effects are very similar to a
charge of lightning hitting a house and burning out its electrical
wiring circuits, destroying any appliances such as a television or freezer
that are plugged into the mains supply.

There are various types of nuclear detonations that are selected to
achieve specific military objectives.

We have already talked of an airburst when giving an example of the effects of a nuclear weapon's explosion. Airbursts are designed to inflict the maximum damage to a target area and variations in the height of detonation can be calculated to vary blast, thermal or radiation effects, or balance a combination of all three. The fallout is likely to be dispersed by winds over a very wide area. This kind of explosion would be used to destroy substantial unprotected military formations, the blast hurling tanks and armoured vehicles through the air like so much confetti, or against cities and their populations. High-yield weapons used in this way are also designed to trigger fires through thermal radiation, well beyond the area of structural blast damage they cause.

High-altitude bursts, above 15 miles up in the atmosphere, produce much bigger fireballs and the resultant ionising radiation and EMP would knock out communications, military command and control systems or destroy electronic equipment over a very wide area indeed. As well as interrupting an adversary's strategic command or control system, the fireball may also affect radar beams and satellite communications and so prevent detection of incoming missile re-entry vehicles carrying warheads as the main nuclear attack. As such, it is very much seen as a tactic to blind the enemy's defences against a surprise nuclear onslaught.

Ground bursts, where the explosion occurs right on top of a target or immediately above it, are designed to obliterate hardened targets like concrete military headquarters, or missile silos. The area devastated would be substantially less than an airburst would destroy but there would be deep cratering of the surface in the immediate vicinity. Ground bursts, because their fireballs suck up huge amounts of dust and debris, create a larger 'footprint' of fallout downwind of ground zero than an airburst. Their mushroom clouds are often brownish coloured because of the density of material gathered by the immensely strong updrafts caused by the fireball. Local effects of thermal radiation and ionising radiation are less than with an airburst.

A sub-surface burst is where a nuclear weapon penetrates the ground or ocean and explodes just below – again designed to attack hardened targets, or at sea, missile-firing submarines, for example. Cratering on land would be extensive and there will be substantial earthquake-like shocks as the blast waves rip through the ground or water. Local fallout levels would be intense.

By the time the first atomic weapons were dropped, there were tensions emerging between the Western allies who created their technology. The USA was unwilling to share information in continued development and in August 1946, the McMahon Act prohibited US administrations from any co-operation in the nuclear field, whether military or peaceful, with foreign states – including Britain and Canada – which had also taken an active role in MANHATTAN.

It was a bitter blow to London, already smarting over US attempts to keep the secrets of German ballistic missile technology in American hands. It was only too clear to most members of the new Labour government in Britain, headed by Clement Attlee, that to retain a seat at the negotiating tables of the world powers, nuclear weapons would have to arm its armed forces. There were others, concerned at the cost of post-war reconstruction in a failing and battered economy, who thought the price was just too high. The Foreign Secretary Ernest Bevin told GEN 75, a British Cabinet sub-committee on October 26, 1946:

> Our prestige in the world as well as our chances of securing American co-operation would both suffer if we did not exploit to the full a discovery in which we played a leading part at the outset.

These were the polite words of the official minute-taker. Those attending the meeting remember Bevin using much more direct language:

> We've got to have this thing over here, whatever it costs. We've got to have the bloody Union Jack on top of it.

Attlee set up another Cabinet sub-committee, GEN 163, deliberately made up of five ministers who were not opposed to nuclear weapons development. On January 8, 1947, the sub-committee approved plans for a British bomb. Bevin was characteristically blunt during the discussions:

> We could not afford to acquiesce in American monopoly of this new development. Other countries might well develop atomic weapons. Unless therefore an effective international system could be developed under which the production and use of the weapon could be prohibited, we must develop it ourselves.

Britain had already set up an atomic research establishment at Harwell, south of Oxford, and a production facility at Risley in Lancashire. In July 1947, the plutonium production site at Windscale on a remote site on the coast of Cumbria was announced, with the first reactor going critical in 1950. Operations began on February 25, 1952 and the first plutonium was produced just over a month later. The design for the first purely British plutonium weapon had begun the month before at Fort Halstead in Kent by a department known only as 'High Explosive Research' under the physicist Sir William Penney. Three years later the Atomic Weapons Research Establishment was created on a 670-acre former D-Day glider airfield at Aldermaston in Berkshire, 60 miles west of London. Another site, 270 acres, seven miles east of Aldermaston at Burghfield, was set up to manufacture British nuclear devices in 1954.

The first British test was of a 25 kT device, similar in design to 'Fat Man', in operation HURRICANE, at 9.29 a.m. on October 3, 1952 in Trimouille Island in the Monte Bello group, off Australia's north-west coast. No American observers were present. The plutonium implosion bomb was placed on a war-surplus 'River' class frigate, HMS *Plym*, to investigate the effects of a nuclear device exploding on board a ship that had entered a British harbour. It was anchored in 40ft of water, 400 yards offshore in the Bunsen Channel. The ship vaporised.

A British airdropped weapon, OR1001, based on the design tested in HURRICANE was supplied to RAF Wittering in November 1953 for delivery by its fleet of V-bombers. It was a massive weapon, code-named BLUE DANUBE, 23ft long, weighing 10,000lbs and with retractable tail fins to allow it to be fitted, in a tight squeeze, into the aircraft bomb bays. It had a yield of around 25 kTs. For safety reasons, the 17lbs of plutonium fissile material was not inserted into the weapon until just prior to the mission, using an in-flight loading system. The bomb probably became operational in mid-1955 and remained in service until 1961. Around 20 were produced at Burghfield by 1958, although plans called for an arsenal of 200 by 1957. Production of plutonium had to be expanded by adding two new MAGNOX reactors at Calder Hall. Embarrassingly, engineering drawings and specifications of BLUE DANUBE were inadvertently released to the Public Record Office in August 1994, leading to controversy about the possibility that this information could fall into the wrong hands.

Work continued simultaneously on a tactical nuclear weapon, codenamed RED BEARD, developed from 1954 as a freefall bomb to be delivered by RAF (80 bombs) and Royal Navy aircraft (30 bombs), such as the Buccaneer, between 1961 and 1971. Innovative work on the implosion system greatly reduced the size of the weapon, bringing the weight down to 1,750lbs and its length to 12ft. The 15 − 25 kT weapon was tested in the BUFFALO series of explosions at Maralinga in Australia in 1956. It was euphemistically or perhaps coyly termed a 'Target Marker' in operational orders, but Navy Scimitar jets armed with the weapon could not land on aircraft carriers because of concerns that the sudden shock of the arrester wire halting the aircraft could trigger an accidental detonation.

Elsewhere, fears that the secrets of atomic weapons could proliferate came all too true. Soviet scientists were involved in nuclear research during the Second World War from 1943 and purpose-built experimental physics laboratories were created in 1946 in a new city, Arzamas-16, in Nizhni Novograd, later renamed Kremlev and now Sarov. The site, quickly surrounded by miles of impenetrable barbed wire, was erased from maps of the Soviet Union. Well-placed Russian-paid spies in both the USA and Britain ensured that vital information about the design and construction of the weapons speeded development of a Soviet weapon. Design details of 'Fat Man' ended up on the desk of Lavrenti P. Beria, head of the Soviet secret police and the man in charge of the Soviet nuclear weapons programme, by October 1945, four months after the Nagasaki bombing. Unaware of the scale of success of the intense Russian intelligence offensive to win information about the atomic weapons, it was a considerable shock to the West when Moscow tested a plutonium device of 22 kT mounted on a tower at the Poligon site at Semipalatinsk, Kazakstan on August 29, 1949. It was an exact copy of 'Fat Man'.

Because of political pressure, the first test, codenamed *Pervaya Molniya,* or FIRST LIGHTNING, was a rushed job and more than two years elapsed before the second, on September 24, 1951, of a 38 kT improved plutonium implosion device, from a 100ft tower at Semipalatinsk.

The first tactical atomic freefall bomb was tested in an airburst with a yield of 28 kT on August 23, 1953. It entered service with the Soviet air force in 1954 and was operational until 1965.

In the USA, tests continued with a number of new weapons. The

CROSSROADS series, held in the Pacific Proving Ground, near the Bikini Atoll in the Marshall Islands, were of improved 'Fat Man' designs. The 'Baker' test on July 25, 1946, was of a 21 kT device submerged about 90ft deep in the Bikini lagoon. Two million tons of water were rocketed skywards in the explosion and two million square yards of sediment were removed from the seabed. A number of wartime hulks, together with captured warships were anchored near the detonation point. The heavily armoured ships withstood the blast remarkably well but overall, a total of nine ships were sunk.

By 1948, the American nuclear arsenal held about 50 weapons, the numbers restricted by limited plutonium production capacity.

At the same time, research was going on into fusion weapons – the so-called 'hydrogen bomb'. One test, 'George' on May 8, 1951, of 225 kT, in the GREENHOUSE series on the Enewetak Atoll in the Pacific, proved that such a weapon was technologically possible. After much debate within the scientific community and military planners on whether to mass-produce fission weapons or to create a hydrogen bomb to counter the emerging Soviet atomic threat, a design for the latter was finalised. It involved the cooling of the hydrogen fuel to a liquid state, near a temperature of absolute zero, and fusing the hydrogen nuclei into helium, using a fission weapon as a trigger.

The concept was tested in the 'Mike' shot in operation IVY in the Pacific on October 31, 1952. The 22ft long metal cylinder was detonated on Elugelah with a yield of 10.4 MTs. The island disappeared. Further H-bomb tests were held in the CASTLE series at Enewetak and Bikini atolls in the spring of 1954. The 'Bravo' shot on February 28 at Bikini yielded 15 MTs, the highest level in any US atmospheric test, mainly because a scientific miscalculation caused the yield to be double the planned size. Fallout was scattered over more than 7,000 square miles of ocean and islands, contaminating both US military personnel and those islanders who had earlier been moved to supposedly safe locations. Many received large amounts of radiation and suffered accordingly. One died from the effects. Compensation payments have amounted to hundreds of millions of dollars.

WIGWAM explored the use of atomic depth charges. A 30 kT device exploded in the ocean 500 miles southwest of San Diego, California, with a scaled-down submarine, moored beneath a floating barge, as a target. It disappeared.

There were other potential battlefields for nuclear weapons. Shot 'John' on July 19, 1957, in the PLUMBOB series at the Nevada proving ground tested the W-25 warhead on a Genie air-to-air missile. It had a yield of less than 1.5 kT and was in service from 1957. The idea of a nuclear weapon fired from one aircraft to destroy another seems to epitomise the popular notion of military 'overkill' but at one stage in the 1950s, the USAF saw this as a viable last-ditch defence against Soviet bombers, armed with high MT yield weapons, attacking US cities. Others were fitted to surface-to-air missiles like the Talos-W (armed with a warhead of less than 0.5 kT from 1959–74) and the Nike Hercules, fitted with a 2 kT weapon, in the late 1950s.

Washington was also keen to increase the striking power of its missiles. The Polaris A3 missile, operational from September 1964, was the first with multiple warheads fitted to a single rocket. This was just the beginning. If you had a number of warheads, why not develop a system where each one could hit a different target? The principle is called MIRVing: multiple independently targeted re-entry vehicles. The first MIRVed missile in the US inventory entered service in August 1970 as the silo-based Minuteman III.

The USA conducted 1,054 nuclear tests, beginning with the Trinity shot, 278 of them in the atmosphere, before this was outlawed by Treaty in August 1963.

During the Cold War, the USA deployed nuclear warheads with its forces based in 16 overseas countries, most being withdrawn in the 1970s. They remain in Belgium, Germany, Italy, Netherlands, Turkey and the United Kingdom.

In the 1950s, NATO, confronted by overwhelming superiority in conventional forces by the Soviet Union adopted a tough line on the use of nuclear weapons in Europe. This maintained that if Soviet forces ('just one soldier') crossed the Iron Curtain into Western Europe, there would be massive nuclear retaliation. This was later transformed into a policy of 'flexible response' allowing NATO commanders to seek political authority to use tactical nuclear weapons, if necessary, to match the threat they faced in specific circumstances and locations.

The Soviet Union, after stunning the West with its first atomic test before the end of the 1940s, was also moving down the thermonuclear route after receiving intelligence about US research in this area around 1948. The fifth Soviet test, on August 12, 1953, was of a device called the *sloika* or 'layer cake' design, involving the heating and compression of a fusion blanket surrounding a fission trigger. While not a true hydrogen bomb, the yield was increased to about 400 kTs.

Russian scientists moved on to a two-stage radiation implosion technology and the Soviet Union's first thermonuclear device was tested in an airdrop at Semipalatinsk on November 22, 1955, yielding 1.6 MTs. The blast was unexpectedly reflected downwards and killed three people in a house that was destroyed by the shock wave.

The largest nuclear device yet exploded was the Russian *tsar bomba* ('King of Bombs'), which exploded with a force of 50 MTs on October 30, 1961, at the Arctic test range on the island of Novaya Zemlya. Its design yield was 100 MTs but this was deliberately suppressed by eliminating fast fission by the fusion neutrons. It was designed for purely political purposes as its military value was next to useless: smaller yield weapons could achieve the same objectives. The 27-ton weapon was airdropped, fitted with retardant parachutes, from a Tupolev Tu-95 strategic bomber; the pilot A. E. Durnovtsev, not surprisingly, was later made a Hero of the Soviet Union.

In all, Moscow held 715 nuclear tests between the first, in 1949 and the last, on October 24, 1990, 177 of them atmospheric (before the Test Ban treaty came into force) and 445 related to weapons development.

Britain, now the proud possessor of atomic weapons, was faced with the prospect of having to develop thermonuclear weapons if she was to keep up with the Soviet and American growth in military might. In April 1954, a Cabinet sub-committee called GEN 464, under the Conservative Prime Minister Winston Churchill, agreed to purchase the raw materials necessary to develop a hydrogen bomb ahead of approval by the full government. At the end of the July, this was given and it was announced in the British Defence White Paper the following year.

Like the Russians, political impact was a key issue. The British struggled with a design for a true hydrogen bomb. The GRAPPLE test of a 720 kT device called ORANGE HERALD, on Christmas Island on May 31, 1957, was a hybrid, although it was called a thermonuclear device and the media was flown out to witness the triumph of British military technology. The bomb was dropped from a Valiant aircraft. The first true test was a 1.8 MT bomb, 'round C', again airdropped, on November 8, 1957.

An interim weapon was immediately deployed – VIOLET CLUB – possibly one of the most alarming (if that is an appropriate word) nuclear weapons ever to join any nation's arsenal. With some justice, one may claim it was rushed into service.

This Royal Air Force altimeter-fuzed 500 kT airdropped nuclear weapon, introduced into very brief service in late 1958, contained 155lbs of uranium-235, a high level of fissile material that increased the risk of accidental detonation. (The status-sensitive British counted its GREEN GRASS device as having a 1 MT yield, based on a hybrid fusion design that was planned to be tested in the GRAPPLE trials but never detonated.)

The RAF reported there was 'a risk of catastrophe' once the bomb was armed on board an aircraft by removing the 990lbs of steel balls that separated the two uranium masses that, combined, induced super-criticality. The design apparently did not allow the weapon to be de-armed. There are persistent reports of a near nuclear accident involving VIOLET CLUB in the Midlands but these have never been spoken about officially, let alone confirmed. Five of the weapons were deployed to RAF bases in Cambridgeshire, Lincolnshire and South Yorkshire until 1960.

The weapons were converted into 21ft-long Mk 1 YELLOW SUN devices, the first true British H bomb, with a yield in the 500 kT range. Again, only a few were deployed.

A new stronger relationship with the USA in nuclear matters was emerging after the disaster of the McMahon Act of 1946. On July 2, 1958 US President Dwight Eisenhower signed amendments to the 1954 Atomic Energy Act, which gave the green light, once again, to exchange of classified nuclear weapons design information between the two allies. The next day, he signed the Agreement for Co-operation on the Uses of Atomic Energy for Mutual Defense Purposes.

One of the first fruits of this dramatic change in relationship was the incorporation of some American technology in the Mk 2 version of the YELLOW SUN weapon which had a yield of 1 MT, very similar to Washington's Mk 28 warhead, codenamed RED SNOW by the British. The later version of these airdropped weapons armed RAF aircraft from 1961 to 1972, replacing the BLUE DANUBE. Around 120 were produced at Burghfield.

Britain moved on to the powered bomb BLUE STEEL for its RAF V-bombers, armed initially with a 200 kT fission warhead but later upgraded to a 1 MT thermonuclear device.

Concerns about the survivability of the bomber force against Soviet missile systems led London to cast around for other delivery platforms and after a number of expensive and perhaps embarrassing false starts, settled on the Polaris submarine-launched ballistic missile system. This required a new British warhead and Aldermaston designed a weapon, probably based on the American W-58 200 kT device, to be fitted, three apiece, to the Mk2 re-entry vehicles purchased from Washington.

It is understood that only a total of just over 144 British Polaris war-heads were manufactured at Burghfield from late 1966 or early 1967, enough to arm the 16 missiles in three of the four Royal Navy Polaris boats. A fourth submarine was always alongside for maintenance or refit at any given time, and as British strategic planning never envis-aged a nuclear war being fought toe-to-toe for any length of time, reloads were never required.

The painful and expensive CHEVALINE Polaris upgrade is discussed later in this book, but as this development was at last nearing comple-tion in the late 1970s, the British were confronted with the decision of whether to continue their independent nuclear deterrent and if so, what system to procure.

A number of options were considered. Cruise missiles, armed with nuclear warheads, as deployed to counter the threat of the Soviet SS-20s in Europe, were an attractive idea because of their terminal accuracy. But as they would almost certainly have had to be fired from submarine torpedo tubes, a bombardment of any credible size would have taken a long time to mount, given the limited number of boats the Royal Navy had at its disposal. Moreover, there were fears that the low-flying and relatively slow missiles could be shot down by Soviet air defences. 'It would have been like a grouse shoot', as one senior British official told me at the time.

Submarine-launched ballistic missiles remained the most viable answer. The British plumped for the American Trident C4 system, then entering service with the US Navy, shortly afterwards upgrading their purchase to the longer-range D5, providing them with the capa-bility of striking a target anywhere in the world from their patrolling submarines. Why go for second best?

Again, to preserve at least a veneer of independence, Aldermaston designed a British warhead for the new missiles, with remarkably similar characteristics to the American W-76 that arm the US Navy's Tridents. The development work was validated by nine underground nuclear tests at the US proving ground in Nevada. PHALANX ARMADA, the first on April 22, 1983, was almost certainly a test of the 20 kT fission trigger and the following seven detonations, in the 20 – 150 kT range, were probably proving trials of the thermonuclear device. The last two of this series, AQUEDUCT BARNWELL, on December 8, 1989 and SCULPIN HOUSTON, on November 14, 1990 were full-yield warhead tests.   Production of the warheads at Burghfield began in September 1992 and was completed in 1999, no doubt using recycled material from old Polaris weapons. They have variable yields, ranging down from 100 kT to 0.3 kT to conform with the British government's policy of using some Trident warheads as 'sub strategic' tactical weapons as successors to the WE-177 freefall bombs, the longest serving British nuclear weapon, now phased out of RAF service.

Aldermaston and Burghfield have designed and built an estimated 1,100 nuclear weapons for service with British armed forces, as a result of 51 development nuclear tests. The stockpile's peak megatonnage of 200 came in 1965, which included the BLUE STEEL strategic weapon. Today's inventory totals around 190 Trident D5 warheads with a combined yield of just 19 MT, the lowest level of the four established nuclear superpowers.

As we have seen, France was a late entrant to the superpower nuclear weapons club. She was fortunate to possess large domestic deposits of uranium, found near Limoges in the early 1950s, which could fuel the G-1 nuclear reactor at Marcoule that first went critical in 1956. This facility produced 30lbs of plutonium a year, suitable for the weapons programme, and enabled development of its first fission device, used in the AN-11 freefall bomb arming Mirage IVA bombers from October 1964. The 3,300lb plutonium implosion weapon, with a yield of around 65 kT, was designed for high altitude delivery against strategic targets. A live drop by a Mirage IVA with a 75 kT device was staged on July 19, 1966 in the TAMOURE shot at Fangataufa, French Polynesia. About 40 were manufactured before they were phased out in favour of the new AN-22 bomb in 1967. Modifications in service included fitting retardant parachutes to slow its descent to its airburst height, and reducing its weight by almost 50%. Additional safety features were also added. The weapon left the French inventory when the last Mirage IVA squadron retired in July 1998.

Paris then developed M-31 fission plutonium 120 kT warheads for its silo-based missiles in the Plateau d'Albion but was keen also to take its deterrent to sea. The MR-41 armed the M1 and M2 missiles that entered operational service in January 1972 on board the SSBN *Redoubtable*. These were lightweight boosted fission weapons with yields of 500 kTs and formed France's most powerful atomic weapons. About 35 warheads were built, beginning in 1969.

The first thermonuclear weapon was the TN-60, which began development in 1968 and experienced a lengthy gestation, involving 21 nuclear tests over eight years, including the first, CANOPUS, on August 24, 1968, with a yield of 2.6 MT. The improved TN-61 version, of which around 90 were produced, included penetration aids and was hardened against weapon effects likely to be thrown at it by the Soviet ballistic missile defences around Moscow. These two hydrogen bombs armed France's M4/M20 SLBMs as well as the S-3 silo-based missiles from early 1977 until 1996.

Development of multiple independently targeted warheads began in 1972 with the TN-70, six of which armed each M4A SLBM, the successor to the M1/M2s from 1985. A later version, the TN-75, arming the new M45 SLBM, was proved during France's much-criticised series of nuclear tests in the South Pacific and became operational in 1996. The MIRVed warhead is miniaturised and has built-in stealth characteristics to present a very small radar cross-section to evade Russian ABM radars. Six are fitted to each missile, each with a yield of 100 kT, and are hardened to withstand attack by ABM interceptors. Around 300 have been produced.

Altogether, France staged 211 nuclear weapon tests, 59 of them above ground. Her last atmospheric test was on September 15, 1974.

The final member of the acknowledged nuclear weapons club – until recently – was China. Beijing's nuclear research programme began in the 1950s with Russian assistance but this aid was cut off in 1960 after an ideological row with Moscow. China's progress has been rapid, with her first atomic test, of a uranium-235 implosion fission device, codenamed 596 with a yield of 22 kT, staged at the Lop Nor site in northern China on October 16, 1964. The USA staged a huge technical intelligence-gathering operation, gathering debris from the detonation at heights of around 30,000ft above Japan for subsequent analysis in 30 sorties flown by aircraft based at Yokota.

The first thermonuclear test followed less than three years later, on June 17, 1967, with an airdrop, from a H-6 bomber, of a 3.3 MT weapon, which exploded in an airburst nearly 10,000ft above Lop

Nor. This became a gravity bomb, deployed from 1967.

There seems little doubt that Chinese weapons development has profited considerably by the continuing theft of US nuclear technology, including the so-called 'neutron bomb', which got such a bad press in the West in the 1970s and early 1980s. This is more properly called a suppressed blast/enhanced radiation weapon and is a device that constricts the explosive power of a nuclear weapon but boosts the short-lived direct radiation levels of neutrons and gamma rays. Simply put, it kills people but causes minimal damage to buildings or infrastructure like bridges and railways. A Chinese newspaper, in March 2000, threatened the use of neutron weapons against Taiwan if it declared total independence from the Beijing regime. It is now an important part of the Chinese inventory of tactical nuclear weapons.

Certainly, some of the recent Chinese warheads have performances and characteristics remarkably similar to their American counterparts, particularly the W-88. However, the Chinese also take a pragmatic view in weapon design. Instead of the expensive high-tech ceramic oblative surfaces that coat Western warheads to protect them from the heat of re-entry into the Earth's atmosphere, the Chinese use red cedar wood. As one intelligence analyst pointed out to me: 'It works – and it's not as if they plan to use the warhead again.'

Main emphasis in Chinese research has been on missile development, with the first ICBM, 20 Dong Feng 5A deployed in hardened silos at two sites from August 1981, armed with a single warhead in the 4–5 MT range, indicating reliance on explosive power rather than accuracy to destroy targets in the USA. The Dong Feng 31 missile is MIRVed.

China has staged only 45 nuclear tests, 23 of them above ground. The last atmospheric test was a 450 kT explosion on October 16, 1980. Since the mid-1990s, Beijing has relied on computer simulation for its testing programme with software and technology reportedly purchased from Russia. Its stockpile of strategic nuclear weapons peaked in 2001, with 540 estimated to be in its arsenal with a combined yield of 530 MTs.

In the 1950s, other states, seeing the uncertain world situation developing around them, considered nuclear weapons as a deterrent to ensure their neutrality. Switzerland examined the issue of acquiring these weapons of mass destruction around 1957. Seven years later, the Swiss military estimated that a credible nuclear force would consist of about 100 airdropped bombs with yields up to 100 kT; 50 5 kT artillery shells and a number of missiles with 100 kT warheads, built at a production cost of about 750 million Swiss francs – on top of the 2,100 million price of development. Testing for the 15-year development programme could be held underground in 'uninhabited' areas of the country.

The plans were dropped during Switzerland's squeeze on defence spending in the 1960s and after it signed the NPT in November 1969.

Neutral Sweden also examined the issue for a decade from around 1955 and conducted independent research into nuclear weapons technology. By 1964, it had enough fissile material and the expertise to produce 20 kT atomic bombs. It decided not to.

Up to the mid-1990s when arms reduction measures began to really kick in as a result of the end of the Cold War, the four nuclear powers had built more than 137,000 nuclear warheads for use in an 'end-game' conflict. The USA's strategic stockpile alone peaked in 1967 with 32,500 weapons with a combined megatonnage of 20,500. By January 2000, total numbers among these four nations had declined to 35,810 with a total yield of 12,838 MTs – still more than enough to destroy human civilisation many times over. The START II reductions, from 2004, will reduce total strategic warheads still further, although the Chinese inventory will probably increase by 60.

Statistically, the trend looked hopeful, but from the late 1980s, other clouds were darkening the horizon of international peace and security.

Global attempts to prevent the spread of nuclear weapons read like an exotic itinerary for fortunate, sun-bronzed diplomats: the Rarotonga Treaty (South Pacific nuclear weapons free zone); the Tlatelolco Treaty (prohibition of nuclear weapons in South America); the Pelindaba Treaty (African nuclear weapons free zone); Missile Technology Control Regime, and, of course the Non-Proliferation Treaty (NPT) of 1970.

Despite all these treaties, a host of protocols, the best efforts of the International Atomic Energy Agency to verify compliance and, sadly, now obvious evidence of contraventions, there is a strange reluctance in the West to acknowledge that nuclear proliferation, like the spread of chemical or biological weapons, has destroyed the leak-proof seal around the technology of mass destruction. The metaphor 'burying one's head in the sand' quickly comes to mind – unless, of course, it's

Saddam Hussein, or North Korea, with the nuclear aspirations.

South Korea began a nuclear weapons research project in the early years of the 1970s but abandoned it after signing the NPT in 1975. Taiwan launched a similar programme at the same time, although it ratified the non-proliferation agreement in 1970. During the crisis of October 1995, when Beijing test-fired medium-range missiles across the Taiwanese Straits, the national assembly in Taipei was told by President Lee Teng-hui: 'We should restudy the question [of nuclear weapons] from a long term point of view. Everyone knows we had the plan before.' Much of this may be political posturing, and later he pledged that Taiwan would not develop nuclear weapons. Indeed, under American pressure, the republic has placed 187lbs of plutonium produced by its reactors under International Atomic Energy Agency safeguards and has shipped a further 174lbs to the USA.

Argentina, too, had nuclear ambitions, beginning a research programme in 1978 when it was governed by a military dictatorship. Progress was made in plutonium production capabilities but the plans were scrapped in the late 1980s and in 1991 Buenos Aires signed a bilateral agreement with Brazil governing the control of nuclear materials and later signed and ratified the regional treaty banning nuclear weapons in South America and the NPT.

There are persistent, but unconfirmed reports that after 1964, the Brazilian military began working on their own nuclear weapons under a programme codenamed Project SOLIMOES. As well as production of weapons-grade fissile material, it even involved the excavation of a deep underground shaft for warhead tests at a military base near Cachimbo, deep in the Amazon rainforest. The reports suggest that the Brazilian military built two weapons, one with a 12 kT yield, and the other of 20–30 kT, both designed to be airdropped. The project was abandoned when Brazil returned to a civilian administration in 1985.

Like Argentina, Brazil has now signed the relative treaties covering proliferation of nuclear weapons.

Other countries were not so easily dissuaded.

For years, Israel's development and deployment of nuclear weapons was an open secret in Washington, even though the emergence of the programme in the 1960s sent shock waves through the US Government. That reaction is surprising as most strategists realise that because of Israel's chronic lack of territory, it cannot afford to lose a single war with its Arab adversaries. Therefore, a nuclear arsenal at its disposal makes credible deterrent sense.

In developing nuclear weapons, what the Israeli government was annunciating was blunt and very straightforward to any bellicose neighbour that threatened its existence: 'Try to destroy us and, with our backs to the sea, we will destroy *you* with overwhelming power and might.' In Tel Aviv, it's called the SAMSON option – the plan to inflict massive nuclear retribution on any aggressor if and when Israeli cities are threatened with mass destruction.

The Israelis' repeated disingenuous statements that they would 'not be the first to introduce nuclear weapons into the Middle East' was a cosy blanket of assurance particularly for the USA officially to shelter beneath, in the hope the issue would just go away.

Underneath that blanket, things were different. France had helped construct a 24 MW nuclear reactor at Dimona, in the Negev desert, ostensibly for power generation. In reality, Tel Aviv planned that it would produce weapons-grade fissile material with the aid of an associated reprocessing plant. Its construction hoisted a clear signal of Israeli intentions for those who cared to see. Paris tried to force Israel to make the project public in May 1960 and allow international scientific inspection, even threatening to withhold the reactor fuel if they failed to agree. But then American U-2 spy aircraft photographs produced incontestable evidence and the secret was out. The US president of the time, John F. Kennedy, secretly wrote to the Israeli Prime Minister Levi Eshkol soon after his appointment, bluntly telling him that American support of his country 'could be seriously jeopardised' if Washington did not obtain reliable information about any Israeli nuclear weapons programme, 'a subject ... vital to peace.' He insisted on visits by American scientists to Dimona at regular intervals to check what was going on.* They were granted with American inspectors making seven visits in the 1960s, but the Israelis were not to be dissuaded from possessing their own nuclear deterrent.

The first Israeli nuclear weapons were swiftly produced by 1968 and in the early 1970s, they manufactured a number of airdropped nuclear weapons, 175 and 203mm artillery shells and a version of the 'neutron bomb'. This weapon is particularly useful, in military terms, to neu-

---

* Preserved in the JFK Library, national security files section, University of Boston, Massachusetts.

tralise large concentrations of armoured vehicles and so has obvious appeal as a weapon to the Israelis, potentially faced by huge Arab tank fleets.

Possession of nuclear weapons has certain advantages beyond their final terrible, irrevocable use. In 1973, during the Yom Kippur war, the Israeli air force went on nuclear alert as Arab ground forces rapidly advanced on three fronts. It was a deliberate decision by the Israeli government, not necessarily linked to their intention to use these weapons. They knew that American and Russian signals intelligence (SIGINT) would pick up the text of the order, decode it and fearful of the consequences, Moscow would restrain their Arab allies in their attacks and the USA would take a more active role in support of the Jewish state. In the event, the Russians did urgently signal the Egyptian High Command in Cairo, informing them that Israel had loaded three nuclear weapons onto their F-4 Phantom aircraft and was preparing to arm them. SIGINT to this day is a handy way of signalling bluff and counterbluff in any military posturing to avoid escalation to nuclear conflict.

During DESERT STORM, Israel's forces also went on nuclear alert to reinforce Tel Aviv's message to Saddam Hussein that a chemical weapons strike on Israeli population centres would immediately call down an overwhelming nuclear retaliatory attack upon his towns and cities.

By 1995, Israel's nuclear arsenal had grown to just over 100 air-dropped low-yield bombs, plus another 80 to 100 other types of devices such as ADMs (with yields of 0.1 kTs) and neutron weapons, together with the warheads arming Jericho ballistic missiles. A year later the first plutonium-based weapons appeared in the stockpile together with more warheads for the Jericho force. Today Israel's nuclear weapons total perhaps 400, including thermonuclear devices, with an estimated combined yield of around 50 MTs – more than the UK. It has not signed the non-proliferation treaty.

Tel Aviv is also keen to prevent potential enemies from acquiring these weapons. In 1981, Israeli air force aircraft bombed the Iraqi nuclear reactor at Osirak to prevent production of weapons-grade fissile material.

Elsewhere, covert projects to develop and build these weapons of mass destruction were also underway, including South Africa, where nuclear weapons were developed by the white regime with Israeli assistance, partly in return for supplying 300 tons of uranium. This programme began in the mid-1970s after intervention in southern Africa by Cuban expeditionary forces in support of Marxist regimes in the region led to increasing fears in Pretoria about communist domination of its near neighbours.

Three years after approval to build a gun-assembly nuclear device was given by the then South African president John Vorster in 1974, a US satellite spotted construction work on a nuclear test site in the Kalahari Desert. Washington brought diplomatic pressure to bear on the South Africans to halt the preparations and the site was abandoned but the nuclear weapon development continued, with the assembly of a prototype device, codenamed MELBA.

Another US satellite picked up a brief brilliant flash in the southern Indian Ocean on September 29, 1979 that looked suspiciously like a nuclear detonation. At the time it was believed to be a South African test, but MELBA was not completed until November and it is more likely to have been a trial of an Israeli weapon, using South African naval resources.

Another two prototypes were constructed before the first deliverable air-dropped bomb, with a yield of 18 kT, was produced in August 1987, using 121lbs of Highly Enriched Uranium. It measured 6ft in length and weighed 2,200lbs. A further three bombs were assembled before the programme was terminated in 1990. All devices were subsequently destroyed before July 10, 1991, when South Africa signed the NPT. With the end of the Cold War and the collapse of communism, the motivation to possess such weapons of mass destruction faded into history.

Of far greater concern is the Indian sub-continent where two nuclear powers with a history of bitter border and religious wars now confront each other: India and Pakistan.

India, with ambitions for regional superpower status and fearful of the nuclear weapons deployed by China and now Pakistan to the north and west, built a Canadian-designed nuclear reactor in 1960 and began separating plutonium, with French technology, in 1966. Its first test, codenamed SMILING BUDDHA, was of a 15 kT fission device on May 18, 1974 at its Pokhara range in the Rajasthan desert. This was developed into an airdropped weapon, which entered service in 1980. India also needed more effective means of delivering its weapons and like everyone else turned to the development of ballistic missiles, pur-

chasing three liquid-fuelled rocket engines and the associated technology from Russia in 1992.

This was the basis for India's ambitious missile programme, with the
short-range Privthi entering service in the mid-1990s and the longer-
range Agni later. A series of tests at Pokhara in the SHAKTI series in the
later 1990s confirmed the missile warhead designs.

New Delhi now has an arsenal of about 165 nuclear devices with a
total combined yield of about 8 MTs. It has the plutonium production
capacity of between 165 and 400lbs per year, enough for about 65
atomic weapons. India also has ambitions for a submarine-launched
missile and intends to deploy the Surya ICBM by 2010. A former
nuclear scientist who presided over the Indian nuclear tests in 1998,
Avil J. P. Abdul Kalam, known as 'Missile Man' to the Indian media,
has become the next President of India.

Pakistan's capacity for nuclear weapons production is more limited
by cash constraints, but is nonetheless very active. In a stunning intelligence *coup*, India apparently first learned of Pakistan's programmes by
analysing the hair samples snatched from the floors of barber shops
near the Pakistani nuclear research facility at Kahuta. India's external
intelligence agency, the Research and Analysis Wing, sent the samples
to New Delhi's Bhabha Atomic Research Centre, which discovered
clear indications from analysis of the hair, that Pakistan had developed
the ability to enrich uranium to weapons-grade quality.

Pakistan began research in 1976 and is now estimated to have
between 220 and 500lbs of weapons-grade uranium available for
weapons production. Its first fission test came on May 25, 1998, with
the underground explosion of a 32 kT device. Considerable assistance
from China has been provided, some under the guise of supplies of
missile designs and components supplied by North Korea.

Pakistan now has about 23 warheads in its arsenal, with a total yield
of just under 1 MT. Production rate is estimated at about two or three
a year.

Nuclear proliferation has not stopped with the Indian sub-
continent.

It is now confirmed that North Korea possesses two plutonium-
based nuclear bombs − the first acknowledgement that one of the
USA's 'rogue states' − now called 'the axis of evil' by President George
W. Bush, has developed nuclear weapons. North Korea initially denied
the claim but later confirmed it. The US assessment was based on

above: Dawn of the Nuclear Age. A 19kT device is exploded from atop a tower at Alamogordo, New Mexico, on July 16, 1945 in TRINITY, the first atomic explosion. *US Department of Energy*

right: Hiroshima, Japan: the mushroom cloud created by the first use of an atomic bomb in war on August 6, 1945. *PA Photos*

The CROSSROADS-BAKER explosion at Bikini Atoll in the Pacific Marshall Islands on July 25, 1946. The 21kT explosion, using a 'Fat Man' device similar to that which destroyed Nagasaki, deployed at a depth of 90ft, threw more than two million tons of seawater into the air. Nine ships were sunk in tests to establish the ability of warships to withstand nuclear attack. *US Department of Energy*

A German V-2 rocket attack wreaks havoc on houses and factories in the London area, 1945. In seven months a total of 517 V-2s hit London, killing over 2,700 people. *PA Photos*

left: A V-2 rocket stands on its launch pad at the US Army's White Sands missile test range in New Mexico. The German missile was the ancestor of all modern intercontinental ballistic missiles. *US Army*

below: The IVY MIKE test at Enewetak in the Pacific on October 31, 1952 was the first explosion of an experimental thermonuclear device. *US Department of Energy*

left: Overkill? The US deployed a number of nuclear-armed missiles to shoot down aircraft in the late 1950s and 60s. The 1.5kT JOHN shot on July 19, 1957 tested an air-to-air missile nuclear warhead. *US Department of Energy*

below: The GRABLE shot on May 25, 1953 at the Nevada test si was a 15kT explosion from a shell fired by a US Army 280mm 'atomic cannon' – the only nuclear artillery blast recorded, so fa *US Department of Energy*

25 OCTOBER 1962

MRBM LAUNCH SITE 1
SAN CRISTOBAL, CUBA
22-40N 83-18W

OXIDIZER TRAILERS

FUEL TRAILERS

MISSILE TRANSPORTER & PRIME MOVER

MISSILE SHELTER T

FIRING TABLE

MAINSTAND FOR ERECTOR

MISSILE TRANSPORTERS

bove: A low-flying USAF Voodoo reconnaissance aircraft ook this photograph of the an Cristóbal site in Cuba on October 25, 1962. Detection f preparations to base Soviet S-4 medium range missiles here, eleven days earlier, had riggered the Cuban missile risis. *US Department of Defense*

ight: Polaris was the first submarine-launched ballistic missle and joined the USA's nuclear triad from 1961. These underwater photographs how an A1 missile launching om the *Theodore Roosevelt* n March 1963, beneath the urface of the Atlantic off the oast of Florida. *US Navy*

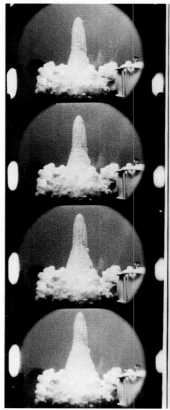
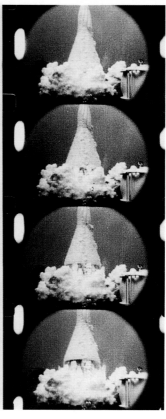

above: Dummy warhead re-entry vehicles enter the Earth's atmosphere over the Kwajalein missile range in the Pacific in October 1984. This is what an attack from a single missile's multiple, independently targeted warheads would look like a few seconds before impact. *USAF*

The Soviet Union's SS-20 'Saber' missile was intended by the Kremlin to be a NATO-busting weapon, designed to de-couple the USA from her European allies. *US Department of Defense*

he US Army's deployment in Europe of the highly
·curate Pershing II mobile missile, in answer to the
·-20, sent a shock wave through the Soviet leader-
·ip, who realised that their national command head-
·uarters was now vulnerable to attack – with little
·arning. *US Army, Aberdeen Proving Ground*

After the collapse of the Soviet Union,
some former Soviet Republics found
themselves with ICBMs on their hands.
Here, men from the Ukrainian 43rd
Rocket Army ease a Soviet SS-19 ICBM
from its silo at Pervomaysk in the
Ukraine, before its destruction. The nose
cone, with its six MIRVed warheads, had
been removed earlier and shipped to
Russia. *US Department of Defense*

UN weapons inspectors check Iraqi
chemical warheads in the aftermath of
the 1991 Gulf War. *Reuters*

Dr Hans Blix, chief UN weapons inspector, in charge of the 2003 operation to discover whether Iraq has any remaining weapons of mass destruction, photographed at a press conference in Brussels on January 16, 2003. *PA Photos*

A civilian chemical/biological warfare exercise under way in the UK. Firefighters, police, paramedics and hospital staff joined in to test contingency planning. *PA Photos, Tony Harris*

A Black Brandt XII sounding rocket of the type that inadvertently triggered a Russian nuclear alert in 1995. *NASA/Goddard Space Flight Center* intelligence studies that showed the country had foreign assistance in creating its uranium enrichment programme – almost certainly from Pakistan, which dates back to at least 1994. In November 2002, a CIA study detailed covert co-operation between the two countries, reporting, for example, satellite evidence of a Pakistani military aircraft flying into North Korea to pick up components for Islamabad's force of medium-range ballistic missiles, notably the Ghauri, which bears a strange resemblance to North Korea's No-Dong. Ironically, the Pakistani aircraft was a US-supplied C-130 Hercules.

In 1994, North Korea agreed to halt its nuclear weapons project in return for the annual delivery of 500,000 tons of heavy fuel oil and the building of two light water nuclear reactors by an international consortium led by the USA to help meet its energy needs. It was a clumsy, naive agreement, almost certain to fail as it had grave shortcomings in verification procedures. It did. It is now clear that Pyongyang has reneged on this agreement, as well as contravening the Non Proliferation Treaty (by secretly building weapons) and has misled the International Atomic Energy Agency in its declarations on its nuclear infrastructure.

The problem for Washington and the whole international non-proliferation movement is that North Korea's now publicly acknowledged possession of nuclear weapons may well put pressure on neighbouring countries such as South Korea and Japan to develop their own nuclear arsenal. Japan is already paranoiac about the threat to its homeland islands posed by North Korea's No-Dong and Taep'o Dong 1 missiles.

The world has other pressing problems of proliferation: Iraq for one. Baghdad initiated its research during the war with Iran in the late 1980s with focus on the production of enriched uranium using gas centrifuges to separate out fissile material. The aim was to produce a simple implosion device with a yield of around 20 kTs to arm its missiles. During the second Gulf War in 1990–91 it launched a crash programme to build a single nuclear weapon as a political and diplomatic weapon to use against the Western-led coalition forces, possibly as an ADM. The plan was frozen when the USA and her allies launched their ground offensive.

It was restarted after the departure of the UN weapons inspectors in 1998. The computer used for weapon design reportedly remains in a hospital in Saddam City on the outskirts of Baghdad. Other assets have been dispersed into small units with exactly mirrored back-up facilities that are hard to detect by the new UN team. Iraq has made substantial efforts to acquire dual-use technology to use in its nuclear weapons programme including attempts to purchase vacuum pumps and specialist aluminium tubes, both necessary in the gas centrifuge process.

With the knowledge and expertise Iraq has gained, British intelligence believes it could assemble a nuclear weapon within two to five years – if it could acquire enough fissile material and the right components from outside the country.

But can the spectre of an Iraqi nuclear weapon ever be completely exorcised? There are unconfirmed reports that Iraqi scientists involved in the programme have been sent to Libya and Syria to escape the attentions of the new UN inspection team. Other reports suggest that parallel development programmes have been running in these two countries for some time, under contracts signed with Baghdad.

So the poison of nuclear proliferation spreads. There are unconfirmed reports that Saudi Arabia has begun active efforts to acquire nuclear weapons in the last two years, possibly involving approaches to North Korea and China. It is perhaps significant that a Saudi prince was guest of honour at a test-firing of Pakistan's Ghauri missile in 2002. Engineers from North Korea also attended.

Across the Persian Gulf, Iran is also reported to be pursuing a nuclear weapons programme, claims that are repeatedly denied by the Teheran government. But US intelligence believes it will be capable of deploying such a weapon within three to ten years, possibly as warheads for its expanding ballistic missile capability. Israel believes it will not take so long. Algeria is also reported to be working on a nuclear weapons programme.

At the superpower level, pressure remains to reduce the nuclear stockpile, although much of it is more smoke and mirrors than reality. The agreement signed between Moscow and Washington in 2002 commits each side to reduce the number of its deployed strategic warheads to between 1,700 and 2,200 by 2012, a deal hailed by President George W. Bush as 'liquidating the legacy of the Cold War'. Each side will decide either to destroy the excess warheads or merely store them – and whether they will reduce the number of the delivery missiles. As such, the agreement is another ineffective compromise, done for effect rather than substance. In truth, Russia cannot afford to maintain its current level of strategic nuclear weapons but has already decided to retain its MIRVed missile capability until 2016. It cannot afford not to.

No, the true issue of nuclear confrontation lies elsewhere. As the former British Defence Secretary Francis Pym pointed out in the early 1980s, nuclear weapons cannot be disinvented. This is particularly pertinent today as the number of countries possessing such weapons grows inexorably. The knowledge of how to make these horrific weapons will remain in the minds of scientists, threatening and destabilising, despite all the military action in the world being summoned to destroy perceived 'illegal' facilities or stocks of fissile material. Bombs cannot target expertise or physics.

Nuclear weapons, sadly, will always be with us – as will be the constant threat of proliferation into hands of those we would rather not have armed with these weapons of mass destruction. To pretend otherwise is the action of a fool.

CHAPTER 5
DELIVERING THE HAND OF GOD

THE AWESOME POWER of nuclear weapons make them a breed apart in the military arsenals of the world. They are treated very differently from run-of-the-mill bombs or artillery shells. In all countries, the strictest security is maintained around their underground storage depots by squads of armed guards with orders to shoot to kill any intruder who approaches, precautions backed up by dense thickets of alarmed razor wire. The fuzing and arming devices are stored separately.

The terrible consequences of nuclear weapons' use have ensured that special arrangements have also been made for their political control and deployment. In every country that possesses such devices, the order to release them comes from the very top – in US parlance 'the national command authority' (NCA) – a president or prime minister, be they elected democratically, or otherwise. Elaborate failsafe procedures have been put in place not only to ensure the order to fire gets through to their delivery platforms, such as the Russian 'Perimetr' system, but also to safeguard against the nightmare of accidental detonation, or worst still, deliberate release by deranged or evil-mind individuals lower down the command chain, à la frightening satirical plot of *Dr Strangelove*. Disappointingly, from the dramatic point of view perhaps, a national leader does not, nor ever did, have a red-painted nuclear button to press. There are also arrangements to ensure that in authorising a nuclear release, the 'national command authority' has not had some kind of brainstorm. These vary from country to country but are likely to be effective.

In the USA, considerable levels of redundancy are built into the system to ensure that properly authenticated orders to launch nuclear weapons are speedily transmitted, even while under the stress of attack. For 29 years from 1961, the USAF's Stregic Command's airborne command post, codenamed LOOKING GLASS, was in the air, 24 hours a day, ready to relay coded launch orders to manned bombers and silo-based missiles. These were EC-135 aircraft, manned by a specially trained battle staff who clocked up more than 280,000 flying hours in this lonely, apocalyptic role. At the same time, the US Navy operated a similar system, codenamed TACAMO (for 'take charge and move out') on EC-130Q aircraft to relay, by extra low frequency radio signals transmitted from a long trailing wire, firing orders to its ballistic missile submarines around the world.

The US now provides the E-4B National Airborne Operations Centre (NAOC) for the President and the Secretary of Defense, who would join the aircraft in the tense hours and minutes before an imminent massive attack on America. It was used in the immediate confusing aftermath of the terrorist attacks on New York and Washington on September 11, 2001. The aircraft, a converted Boeing 748 Jumbo jet, is capable of 12 hours' flying before being refuelled in flight. Its main deck is divided into a command and operations areas, conference room and briefing rooms and comfortable rest quarters and can accommodate up to 114 people. Advanced satellite links provide a worldwide communications capability. The aircraft is protected against the effects of an electromagnetic pulse triggered by a nuclear explosion and heat and other radiation effects. It is also fitted with electronic jammers to confuse and evade attacking missiles. The Air Force operates four of these $223 million aircraft, with at least one kept on 24-hour alert in the vicinity of the President, or in the event of his/her incapacity, the Vice President. During the transition to nuclear war, both may well be airborne in separate aircraft, in case one is lost through enemy action or accident, flying long circuits well away from likely targets and protected by relays of fighter aircraft.

The E-6B Mercury aircraft, a converted Boeing 707, transmits the presidential orders to US strategic and tactical nuclear forces worldwide, based in two squadrons at Tinker air force base in Oklahoma. It is fitted with the so-called airborne launch control system (ALCS) to fire Minuteman and Peacekeeper silo-based ICBMs, as well as authorising submarine launches.

Aside from the network of heavily protected command bunkers, in the event of very limited time being available for the fateful decision, a military officer always accompanies the US President with a briefcase containing the nuclear launch codes. Sophisticated and secure communication links are always available nearby, together with elaborate technical and human procedures to authenticate the launch orders.

Russia inherited the ageing 'nuclear football' system of decision-making from the Soviet Union. These are, in reality, suitcases containing portable dedicated Kazbek communications and the ability to issue launch codes. They are constantly carried alongside the Russian president, defence minister and chief of the general staff. The 'go codes' are transmitted directly to the general staff central command post at Chekhov where the launch order is extracted from a safe in the war room, drawn up and forwarded to the missile forces. Two separate combinations, held by different senior officers, protect that safe. The launch order includes special codes to unlock security devices as well as the approval for weapons firing. As we explored earlier, the Perimetr system can authorise silo-based launches after attack, if a number of tightly defined conditions are met, including disruption of communications between the Russian president and the nuclear retaliatory forces, to protect against decapitating strikes on the national command authority.

Britain has a less defined system. Shortly after appointment as Prime Minister, the new incumbent is always briefed on the UK's nuclear forces and command and control system by his or her chief military advisor, the Chief of the Defence Staff, a job that traditionally rotates between the three armed forces. It is important to realise that the British system is based on political *authorisation* rather than detailed *instructions* to attack. The launch and targeting details, regularly reviewed and updated, would have already been worked out by the Defence Ministry's strategic planners and are held in the safes in the cabins of the Royal Navy Trident missile boat commanders. You may think these are the most secret documents within the British military establishment. In reality, much of the information is pure common sense, which could be gleaned from a map of the world by anyone with even a rudimentary knowledge of military affairs. Even Britain's potential adversaries know the targets: after all they are sitting on them. What they don't know is the targeting priorities.

Because of the possibly limited time available to take a decision to authorise a British retaliatory nuclear strike, a failsafe system has operated for the last three decades, since the end of the RAF's V-bomber force in the early 1970s, requiring each new prime minister to write down, in pen and ink, personal detailed instructions, which are sealed in envelopes and given to the commanders of each of the four Royal Navy Trident submarines before their departure on patrol. These boats, at least one of which is always stationed in the icy ocean wastes of the North Atlantic, can receive radio messages, but cannot transmit any requests for authentification or verification, for fear of disclosing its exact position and thus risking swift destruction.

According to my old colleague Peter Hennessy, that assiduous and authoritative delver into the innermost secrets of Whitehall, who first revealed them, the instructions cover the eventuality of Britain being unexpectedly destroyed by a pre-emptive nuclear strike and the authorisation to launch thus prevented from transmission. There would sit a Trident boat, armed with 16 missiles, all carrying horrendous powers of annihilation, cut off from instructions from the political authority. There would only be silence.

The orders include a number of tests to determine whether Britain was still functioning, including, apparently, one instruction to listen into BBC Radio Four broadcasts of the daily news and current affairs programme *Today*, transmitted each and every weekday morning. If there is continual silence over a lengthy period from the BBC transmitters and the other tests draw a blank, Britain would reasonably be regarded as existing no more. The authorisation to launch from the Prime Minister, contained in the envelope, becomes a message from the grave of British government.

The instructions, says Hennessy, can include a number of options, beginning with placing the submarine under command of surviving US strategic forces. As Britain has always maintained that its nuclear forces are a contribution to NATO's strategic weapons' arsenal, the Royal Navy must be clearly briefed on the US Navy command and control arrangements to enable synchronised attacks, in case Britain is knocked out. This option, I understand, has been fed into Washington's nuclear war targeting document, called the *Single Integrated Operational Plan*. An alternative is sailing to Australia, a rather touching reflection of Whitehall's view of the remaining importance of the Commonwealth, or more starkly, launching the nuclear weapons at the attacker's capital city on the commander's own authority. This has traditionally been regarded as Moscow, although some cynics in the Royal Navy have always asserted it could be Paris. With today's proliferation of nuclear weapons and the conversion of some British warheads into a 'sub-strategic' role, other more exotic targets in hotter climes may be on the Prime Minister's list. Finally, the Trident commander could be offered the unenviable responsibility of using his own judgement, a true Armageddon option and a decision we would all dread having to take.

If there is more time in the run-up to nuclear war, the Prime Minister and selected members of the government, together with appropriate military and civil service staffs, would decamp to a prepared government command bunker with secure communications and from there issue the authority for a British nuclear strike. After September 11, a review of British nuclear command and control systems was carried out, in case the Prime Minister was killed in a terrorist attack. His or her authority has now also been devolved to a nominated minister or group of ministers, in case the top political authority becomes decapitated.

There's nothing new in this concept.

A group of British senior civil servants reviewed the UK Government's arrangements to launch retaliatory nuclear strikes in the early 1960s. Documents in the Public Record Office in London, once top secret, but now released to public view, provide a graphic picture of the decision-making involved in such apocalyptic circumstances, involving some processes current to this day.

The working party, in drawing up its conclusions, based its report in 1961 on a number of grim assumptions:

Warning time – Then, the British government would have about three and a half minutes warning time of nuclear attack, provided by the ballistic missile early warning system base at Fylingdales in North Yorkshire, but this was increased to nearly five minutes when MIDAS, the missile defence alarm system, became operational in 1964–5.

Government operations –   The apparatus of government, including the prime minister, would remain in Whitehall during the 'precautionary period', the official description of the seven days when international tension creates a situation which could trigger a global nuclear exchange. During this period, the then so-called alternative seat of government, a huge secret bunker codenamed STOCKWELL, then BURLINGTON and later TURNSTILE (situated underneath old quarry workings between Bath and Corsham, Wiltshire), would have been 'manned by selected Ministers and officials'. Two deputies to the British Premier would have been appointed in peacetime, one always available 'to act as the Prime Minister's deputy for purposes of nuclear retaliation during any period, however short, when the Prime Minister was not immediately available'.

Scale of Russian attack on the UK – A combined initial attack with both bombers and missiles, the aircraft first penetrating allied radar screens at the moment of impact of the missiles. The papers add:

> There is evidence that the Soviet Government has devoted effort to the training of saboteurs. There are certain targets, such as vital communication links in the governmental and nuclear strike control systems which it would pay the enemy greatly to have put out of action at the outbreak of hostilities; and it must be assumed that the Russians would do their best to strike at these, by treachery or sabotage, should they find the means to do so without prejudice to surprise.

In the early 1960s, the British strategic nuclear deterrent rested in the capable hands of the RAF's V-bombers, armed with the Blue Steel stand-off nuclear missile, which could scramble into the air around 150 seconds after receiving the order to go from Bomber Command. They would need a further three minutes to be certain of getting clear of the danger area from nuclear bursts over their home airfields. Under what the British called the 'positive control procedure' the bombers, en route to their Soviet targets and on the attack start line in the Baltic, would not complete their mission unless they received orders authorising them to do so. Without those orders, the aircraft would automatically return to base after a set period. The Cabinet papers emphasise:

> The reliability of communications between Bomber Command and the aircraft is therefore vital to the certainty of nuclear retaliation and hence to the effectiveness of the nuclear deterrent. There has been duplication and re-duplication of the channels of communication and of the necessary telephone, telegraph and wireless installations on which they rely. The Air Ministry are re-examining these communications and considering if any improvements can be made. Consideration is also being given to providing an airborne headquarters.

Authorisation for a retaliatory strike by the V-bomber force could come only from the Prime Minister, his (in those days) designated deputy, or, as we shall see, the Commander in Chief of Bomber Command in certain circumstances. A British nuclear strike 'is subject only to the general agreement about consultation between the Prime Minister and the [US] President,' say the papers. 'It could, if necessary, be committed without specific agreement with the President.' The British *did* have an independent nuclear deterrent.

In those days, the British also operated medium-range Thor ballistic missiles on British bases in eastern England, which could be held at 15 minutes' operational readiness for prolonged periods but at 90 seconds for only about two hours. To launch these weapons, American approval had to be gained – indeed an American officer, acting under orders from the USAF Strategic Air Command, together with his British counterpart, had to insert his own key to unlock the launching mechanism.

The nuclear bombs arming RAF Valiant bomber squadrons assigned to NATO, under the control of the Supreme Allied Commander Europe (SACEUR) were normally held in store and guarded by American military personnel.

> If bombs had to be taken from store, the arming of all the aircraft could take up to 12 hours in the present situation when all the aircraft are concentrated at one station. Proposals for a dispersal scheme are under consideration; if these are implemented rather more flexible arrangements would have to be made with the Americans for the removal of bombs from store.

The topics to be discussed between the Prime Minister and the US President in deciding on a nuclear strike are detailed in a revealing annexe to the report. These included:

- A general decision whether to launch strategic nuclear forces, both British and American.
- Operational use by US forces of British bases, including Strategic Air Command airfields and the (then) US Navy Polaris submarine base at Holy Loch.
- Launch of Bomber Command's Thor missiles.
- Clearance for operational use of US tactical nuclear armed aircraft

based in Britain, assigned to SACEUR.
* Declaration of 'R-hour' – 'the time at which nuclear weapons may be released.'

The working group believed that 'normal discussion of all these items would be too slow a process in the face of the current threat from missiles. A revised procedure is therefore required for the conduct of discussions between the President and the Prime Minister during a period of international tension; by this means all preliminaries could be cleared in advance leaving only the final decision to order nuclear retaliation to be taken.'

Communications with the US President then would be over a secure submarine telephone line, via France or Transatlantic Cable No. 1, via England, or two insecure telephone circuits via the HQs of the 3rd USAF at Ruislip, in Middlesex. A secure telegraph was to be made available in 1962.

If Soviet missiles hit British targets in a 'bolt from the blue' attack, the Commander-in-Chief RAF Bomber Command had been granted certain powers. The documents define a 'bolt from the blue' as 'a tactical warning with no preceding period of strategic warning that a nuclear attack is imminent' – a true surprise strike – or an attack 'actually having been received (i.e. nuclear bombs having burst) in this country before any authority has been given to a nuclear force to retaliate.'

He was authorised by the Prime Minister to order 'all his bombers under positive control' and to try to contact the British Premier or his deputy in London or at BURLINGTON and if possible the United States authority responsible for launching United States strategic nuclear weapons' from the UK.

In the last resort, 'When he has confirmed that a nuclear attack has actually landed on this country, [he is authorised] to order on his own responsibility nuclear retaliation by all means at his disposal.'

The civil servants were clearly concerned at the problems of communicating with the Prime Minister (Harold Macmillan, later Earl of Stockton) when he was away from his desk at No. 10 Downing Street, or the Admiralty.

It is most important that reliable communications should be available to ensure that the Prime Minister can be recalled to London at any time.

> Normal communications will suffice in most circumstances, except for
> periods when the Prime Minister is travelling by car or rail. In either case
> it should be possible to intercept him through police or railway channels
> but the Working Group recommend that consideration should be given to
> providing a radio link in the Prime Minister's car.

The then Chief of the Defence Staff, Lord Mountbatten, was keen on
a radio link. He noted that he had 'a radio link in my car when I was in
SE Asia in 1943–6' and communications technology had improved
since then.   Accordingly, Major General L. de M. Thuiller of the
Cabinet Office was authorised to initiate action with the Treasury and
the Automobile Association to provide a radio link to and from the
Prime Minister's car.

There is something very British about all this. The American and
Russian Presidents may well have their nuclear launch codes held by a
military officer and the means to deliver them 24 hours a day. The
British, in 1962, relied on an organisation that provided roadside assistance to motorists whose vehicles had broken down, presumably
because the AA had the only national radio network in those days.
One can conjure up a mental picture, if the radio link broke down, of
an AA patrolman, on his motorcycle, waving down the Prime Minis-
terial car, saluting smartly and telling him of an imminent devastating
Russian nuclear strike on Britain. Presumably, as customer service was
and is part and parcel of the AA code, he also checked the prime min-
isterial tyres and water afterwards. No wonder that the AA's marketing
slogan is the 'fourth emergency service.'

The Royal Navy at the time also proposed a floating national
command centre based on a Royal Fleet auxiliary but this plan was
turned down.

The British plans were timely. In October 1962, the world teetered
on the edge of nuclear conflict during the 13-day Cuban missile crisis,
triggered by the medium-range SS-4 missiles covertly deployed by
Moscow to two sites on the Caribbean island, just 100 miles from
American soil. On Saturday October 27, the British prime minister,
still Harold Macmillan, authorised the RAF V-bomber force to be
placed on Alert Condition Three, the so-called Quick Reaction Alert
at the end of their runways, at 15 minutes' notice to take-off for their
nuclear attack. Five days earlier, the US Strategic Air Command instituted an alert for its B-52 heavy bombers, guaranteeing that at least an

eighth of the force was airborne at any one time. It also dispersed its 183 B-47 bombers, armed with nuclear freefall bombs to 33 civilian and military airfields.

US reconnaissance flights over communist Cuba had begun in the summer of 1962 and one early morning mission, by a U-2 flying north–south over the west of the island on October 14, produced the first hard evidence of a SS-4 medium range ballistic missile site at San Cristóbal, together with the uncrating of Iluyshin IL-28 light bombers, ready for re-assembly. Sixteen missile launchers were then considered operational with missiles capable of being fired within eight hours of a decision to launch. Another site at Sagua la Grande also became operational later in the crisis. A nuclear warhead storage bunker in Cuba was also identified.

After considering 'surgical air strikes' against the sites, the Kennedy administration decided instead to impose a naval blockade from October 23 to 'quarantine' Cuba and prevent more Soviet medium-range missiles being delivered by ship. Intelligence reports suggested that any form of action against Cuba would result in greater chances of Soviet military retaliation and suggested there was

> a possibility that the Soviets, under great pressure to respond, would again miscalculate and respond in a way which, through a series of actions and reactions could lead to a general war.

Air strikes, whilst strongly urged by some powerful members of the administration, became a hollow reed when it was realised that there could be no 100% guarantee that all the missiles could be destroyed by US air attacks.

On the evening of Friday October 26, an emotional telex message from the Russian leader Nikita Khrushchev arrived in Washington, via the US embassy in Moscow. It was six or seven feet long and was clearly dictated by an individual under great emotional stress. It included this phrase:

> If war should break out, it would not be in our power to stop it. War ends when it has rolled through cities and villages, everywhere sowing death and destruction.

Tension mounted. During the blockade on October 27, an American destroyer detected a submerged Russian submarine and dropped exercise depth charges near it to force it to the surface. Within the submarine, the commander had earlier been given clear rules of engagement by the Soviet naval high command: he was allowed to return fire if fired upon, but three officers all had to agree to launch its weapons – a nuclear-armed torpedo. A conference on the crisis, held in Havana in October 2002 was told that the three Russians, one presumably the political officer, had a fierce debate about whether to open fire, with two agreeing and the third vetoing the decision. One of the conference co-hosts, Thomas Blanton, of Georgetown University, told the *Washington Post*: 'A guy named Arkhipov saved the world.'

On the same day, a routine U-2 reconnaissance flight from a Strategic Air Command base in Alaska strayed into Soviet airspace over the Chukotski peninsula as a result of a navigational error. During an agonising 45 minutes, a number of American F-102 interceptors, apparently armed with Genie nuclear-tipped air-to-air missiles, were scrambled from Alaska to protect the spy plane, as Russian MiG fighters took off from a base near Wrangel Island. The second nuclear confrontation of the day had occurred, but again, peace was happily maintained and the U-2 returned safely with no shots fired. Later that day, however, another U-2 was shot down by a Soviet surface-to-air missile as it flew over Cuba in a decision made by local Russian commanders without reference to Moscow.

The end of the crisis was heralded just after noon on October 28 when Soviet military forces in Cuba received orders from Moscow to begin dismantling the missile sites. The world could breathe again.

The upshot of the crisis was an American promise not to invade Cuba and, to the fury of the government in Ankara, dismantle the Jupiter intermediate-range missiles stationed in Turkey, in the Soviet Union's backyard. The Russian SS-4 missiles were disassembled and shipped back home. Another outcome was the establishment of the so-called 'hot line' between Washington and Moscow; in reality, up to the 1980s, a slow, clattering teleprinter deep in the basement of the Pentagon, rather incongruously located near a staff restaurant.

There have been other scares connected with nuclear weapons, but not linked with international tension.

A frighteningly large number of accidents have involved such devices since their first deployment. Secrecy surrounds much of what happened, but at least there seems good grounds to believe that there has never been even a 'fizzle' – the chilling jargon for a partial detonation of a nuclear weapon. But some have been completely lost and others destroyed.

The Pentagon has acknowledged there have been 32 such incidents in the three decades from 1950. The first occurred on February 13, 1950 when a B-36 bomber en route between Eielson airfield, Alaska and Carswell airbase in Fort Worth, Texas, developed serious mechanical difficulties. The crew diverted the flight over the Pacific and dropped the atomic bomb from a height of 8,000ft off the coast of British Columbia. The HE detonator exploded as the bomb hit the surface of the sea but no nuclear explosion occurred. It is understood that the weapon is still on the seabed.

Worse was to come. A B-47 bomber from 307th Bombardment Wing was making a touch-and-go landing at the USAF airfield at RAF Lakenheath, Suffolk on July 7, 1956 when it careered out of control off the runway and hit a nuclear weapons storage bunker, called an igloo by the Air Force. The aircraft burst into flames. Within the bunker were three Mk 6 airdropped atomic bombs fitted with TNT as triggers. Fire-fighters from the base put the blaze out, but the four-man crew of the aircraft was killed. General James Walsh signalled Strategic Air Command that

> the B-47 tore apart the igloo and knocked about 3 mark sixes. Aircraft then exploded, showering burning fuel overall. Crew perished ... preliminary exam by bomb disposal officer says a miracle that one mark six with exposed detonators sheared didn't go ...

Other accidents followed hard on the heels of Lakenheath. On May 22 1957, a B-36 transporting a large-yield atomic weapon from Biggs air force base in Texas to Kirkland, accidentally dropped it on a fortunately uninhabited area of the desert near Albuquerque, New Mexico. Again, the detonator exploded on impact, creating a 12ft wide crater, but the bomb failed to go off because the fission capsule was not fitted. It was recovered by the Air Force.

Just two months later, on July 28, a C-124 Globemaster transport aircraft carrying atomic weapons accidentally jettisoned two of them into the Atlantic 100 miles south-east of New Jersey. Both sank without trace.

Other accidental jettisoning of nuclear weapons occurred over the Savannah River in Georgia, in February 1958 and Florence, South Carolina, just over a month later in March 1958. In the last incident, the nuclear weapon ended up in the garden of the home of a Mr Walter Gregg in Mars Bluff and the HE detonation seriously damaged his home, as well as inflicting minor injuries on him and five other members of his family.

Two fires on board B-47 aircraft carrying nuclear weapons occurred later in 1958 in Texas and Louisiana causing minor radioactive contamination. In this aspect, the worst accident came in January 1966 when a B-52 bomber, carrying four thermonuclear weapons, collided with a KC-135 air-to-air refuelling tanker over the coast of Spain, both crashing near Palomares. Two bombs were recovered, one from the sea at a depth of 2,500ft, but the HE detonators of the remaining two exploded on impact with the ground. Around 1,750 tons of radiation-contaminated soil was shipped to a dump at Aiken, South Carolina.

Finally on January 22, 1968 another B-52, again carrying four hydrogen bombs, crashed seven miles south-west of Thule air force base in Greenland, scattering fragments of the weapons over the ice. Another huge clean-up operation was mounted, with 237,000 cubic feet of contaminated ice, snow and water removed to the United States for storage.

Other nuclear nations have suffered accidents, like the Soviet Union's total loss of at least four submarines, one of them a 'Yankee' class SSBN, off Bermuda in October 1986, but few details are known of these.

Safety measures have now been substantially improved and some of the more hazardous activities such as Strategic Air Command's airborne alert force have been stood down.

The dangers have not, however, gone away. Concerns about nuclear weapons' safety have, as we shall see later, now been replaced by an even more fearful danger – that some may fall into the hands of terrorists.

CHAPTER 6
MISSILE PROLIFERATION

WITH THE BENEFIT of hindsight, it is now obvious to us that it was only a matter of time before the technology to inflict mass destruction on an enemy would leak out from the superpower guardians of the secrets of ballistic and cruise missiles. The world, preoccupied with the dangers of the Cold War, failed to notice that another nation, desperate to create its own deterrent, would develop such means for self-protection – or as a method of power projection in its perilous region.

That country was Israel. We have already seen how this tiny Mediterranean state developed its own nuclear capability in answer to the threat of the overwhelming Arab conventional forces that surrounded its borders – the so-called SAMSON option, designed, as a final resort, to protect the populations of its teeming towns and cities if they faced imminent annihilation. It now needed the platforms to deliver these weapons, if necessary, to targets belonging to those enemies who had pledged the ultimate destruction of the Jewish state.

Israel believed that the Soviet Union would always support its Arab enemies in any war they fought against it. Therefore, targets in the southern areas of the USSR were considered fair game for the military planners in Tel Aviv, as well as sites in Syria, Iraq and elsewhere in the Arab world. But how could Israeli aircraft reach these long-range targets? The acquisition of 50 American F-4 Phantom ground-attack aircraft in 1968 provided the first viable platform, with air-to-air refuelling, capable of dropping freefall nuclear weapons on objectives as far away as southern Russia. But airdropped bombs, whilst a temporary solution, did not provide the complete answer to the pressing strategic need to strike at enemies further away if such an end game came to be played out. There was always the nagging fear that modern battlefield anti-aircraft defences were so concentrated and powerful that no longer could the bomber be guaranteed always to get through. Moreover, because of geography, Israel lacks any defence in depth and fears pre-emptive strikes on its airfields before its own attack aircraft can take off. Israel is a narrow country, less than 50 miles wide at one point and is only the size of New Jersey. Every inch of it is in range of aircraft taking off from perhaps hostile neighbours. Their targets could be reached in a matter of minutes. Wags maintain that the tall, prominent and ugly skyscraper of the Defence Ministry in Tel Aviv would be an aiming point for such hostile aircraft. No wonder, during times of tension, that almost every Israeli, at home and in the factories and offices, constantly tunes into the regular radio and television news bulletins.

Israel's military strategy's prime objective is designed to hold the nation's territory at all costs and deny enemy forces possession of its land. They have no choice: they have nowhere to withdraw to – except the sea. Hence, the decision to deploy and detonate nuclear weapons may be an easier one for the Israeli High Command than for all other nations. The stakes are that much higher and time may be very limited for the decision makers. After the shock of being caught wrong-footed in the early stages of the 1973 Yom Kippur war, three batteries of 175mm self-propelled ordnance were later deployed in the north of the country, armed with a reported 108 nuclear shells with yields in the 2–5 kT range, to use in a last-ditch defence of Israel. And after the massed tank onslaughts of 1973 that nearly broke through their defences in the Golan Heights, the Israeli Defence Force also deployed a number of atomic demolition munitions in the area in the late 1970s to delay any new Syrian armoured offensive from the north-east. No doubt they still remain – as does the threat.

In an almost biblical philosophy, Israeli military doctrine also dictates that the devastation of war should always be taken right into the enemy's own backyard. Like the USAF, the Russian Air Force and the RAF before them, Israel decided that the ballistic missile provided the only credible way to deliver its weapons of mass destruction to such high-value targets.

In 1962, development began of a short-range missile, later called 'Jericho 1' in the West, based on a French design called the MD-620.

The Israelis called the weapon 'Luz' and designated it the YA-1. First test-firing came in 1965 with a further 15 following up to 1968. Ten of these launches were considered successful. Jericho 1 is a two-stage solid-propellant missile, armed with a 1,000lb HE warhead, although American intelligence reports suggest it was also sometimes fitted with a nuclear device in the 20 kT range, or a chemical weapon (probably a nerve agent) warhead. Fourteen missiles were manufactured in France before production began at Israeli Aircraft Industries, near Ben Gurion airport, where 50 more were manufactured during 1971–8. The rocket systems division of Israel Military Industries built the motors. An upgraded version, possibly designated YA-2, was produced in the late 1970s, with a larger, more powerful warhead. Between 50 and 100 were deployed in underground bunkers in the Golan Heights in the north of Israel, against Syrian targets and in the Negev desert in the south in 1973 to counter the threat of an Egyptian advance through Sinai, but all are now believed to have been withdrawn from operational service.

Jericho 1 had a range of only 310 miles and that was clearly inadequate to provide the reach necessary to attack all of Israel's potential enemies with a killer punch. A longer-range weapon was needed and this came in the form of the YA-3, or 'Jericho 2', which began development in 1977, almost certainly partially funded by Iranian cash, for the then Shah of Persia had his own interests in developing a potent weapon for use in cowering his enemies. The swift and sudden collapse of the imperial regime in Teheran ended that co-operation and Israel looked around for possible partners to continue their vital strategic programme. South Africa proved the ideal candidate, as it was by then developing its own ballistic missile, the 'Arniston.' Unconfirmed reports in 1989 said that a missile, similar in appearance to a Jericho 2, had been seen positioned on a launch site north of Cape Town in South Africa, suggesting that launches were being staged to test the full range of the weapon.

Jericho 2, with a range of up to 2,200 miles, is a two-stage missile armed with a thermonuclear warhead in the 1 MT range or with a conventional 2,000lb HE weapon. Its re-entry vehicle may have a system to match radar images of its target with pre-programmed information for additional accuracy in the terminal phase of flight. Test flights were conducted both in South Africa and from the Palmahim facility, south of Tel Aviv, beginning in 1986. The missile is now operational, with 90 stored in specially excavated caves at the heavily defended Zacharia site, south-east of Tel Aviv. Commercial land resource satellite images of the site do not indicate any launch silos and it seems likely that the missile is road-mobile on a wheeled transporter-erector-launcher vehicle or may be moved around on railway flatbed trucks.

A third missile, the Jericho 3, with a range of 3,000 miles, will provide Israel with a near ICBM capability. This may be a three- or four-stage missile with a smaller-yield nuclear warhead but with improved accuracy. Development is reported nearing completion and this new weapon may be deployed very soon.

To be effective, accurate targeting information is vital for any successful ballistic missile strike. In 1979 Washington agreed to supply Israel with high-resolution KH-11 spy satellite imagery of potential targets among its neighbours. It is understood that this agreement also provided access to images of some areas of south-west Russia, although this was perhaps not the USA's original intention. The USA also provides satellite 24-hour early warning data on possible hostile launches in the region to Israel, although a new Israeli photoreconnaissance satellite may ensure this vital information is firmly in Tel Aviv's hands.

Elsewhere, ballistic missiles were also under development during the decades from the mid-1970s to provide a strike capability for numerous ambitious regimes. Mainly, these were (and still are) based on an old design for a theatre missile originally deployed in the Soviet Union from 1955. This is the ubiquitous R-11, codenamed 'Scud' by NATO, which became notorious for raining death and destruction from the skies during the 'war of the cities' in the first Gulf War from 1985 onwards and later in the Iraqi attacks on Saudi Arabia and Israel during the DESERT STORM conflict in 1991.* The name 'Scud' has become synonymous with the global problem of missile proliferation in the last decade of the 20th century and into the next.

The missile was designed by our old friend Sergei Korolyev's design bureau, based on the German V-2 and was carried on an eight-wheeled all-terrain vehicle for erecting and launching. Various

---

* The attack on an US barracks at Dhahran air base in Saudi Arabia on February 25 – 24 hours after the Coalition ground forces attacked Iraqi positions – killed 28 American soldiers and wounded a further 98, the single greatest US loss of life during the campaign.

warheads were carried – HE, chemical or nuclear - on successive versions in Soviet service with a maximum range of 300 miles. As many as 7,000 were produced in Russia and a considerable number of the 'B' version were subsequently exported to 21 client states in the Middle and Far East and Soviet satellite countries in Eastern Europe.

A small number, armed with HE warheads, were fired against Israeli targets by Egypt in the 1973 war with little effect, but in March and June 1985, Scuds were first used by Iran against Baghdad, with the Defence Ministry there as an aiming point, in retaliation for Iraqi air raids on 30 Iranian towns and cities.

Iran obtained 20 of the missiles from Libya under a secret supply and training agreement signed with Tripoli in 1983. The weapons were shipped in by Boeing 747 cargo aircraft or by sea to Turkey and then transported covertly overland to Iran in January and February 1985. Fourteen were fired against Baghdad, some hitting their targets and killing a total of several hundred people, before the Soviet Union insisted that Libya stop the missile transfers to Iran. With dubious Libyan logic, Tripoli asked the Iranians for all the missiles back, as, they told the Russians, they had been only lent to the Teheran regime. Undeterred, Iran bought 10 more Scuds from Syria for $15 million in 1986 in a deal linked to the supply of oil and embarked on a longer-term co-operative development programme for the Scud B with North Korea, called the 'Hwasong 5'. It soon afterwards launched a single missile at the Iraqi petroleum refinery at Dowra, but missed, hitting a nearby suburban settlement as well as mounting further strikes later that year against Baghdad, one of which killed 48 civilians and injured a further 52 when an apartment block was demolished in a direct hit. More missile strikes on Baghdad and Basra followed in January 1987, with 11 hitting the Iraqi capital. Although the Iranian missile attacks were not strategically important and caused relatively slight damage, their political symbolism in being able to strike deep inside Iraqi territory and the impact on civilian morale was a lesson that was not lost on the Iraqi leadership.

Nor was this the only conflict in which this missile was used. A small number of Scud B missiles were also used in anger during the civil war in Yemen in 1994 and up to 2,000 were fired by both sides in the wars in Afghanistan in the 1980s and 1990s.

Perhaps the most strategically important deployment came in April 1986, when USAF and Navy ground-attack aircraft attacked what were called 'terrorist-related targets' in Libya, in retaliation for a terror bombing of a Berlin disco in which an American soldier was killed. In turn, Libya launched two Scud B missiles armed with HE warheads the following day at US naval facilities on the Italian island of Lampedusa, south of Sicily. Operating at extreme range, both fell in the sea three miles short of the island. The Libyan leader, Colonel Ghadaffi, had considered using them to attack two US military bases in Crete and these targets might have been attainable had the missiles been launched from a position east of Benghazi. In the event, Lampedusa was selected because the Libyans did not want to antagonise Greece and, Ghadaffi claimed, civilian casualties would have been minimised there.

The attacks, whilst militarily a complete failure, awakened political fears in southern Europe about the threat of ballistic missiles against targets nearer home than the remote battered cities of Iraq. And across the Mediterranean, in Ghadaffi's mind, like that of Iraq's leader, Saddam Hussein, there was now a clear understanding of the psychological value of these weapons. 'If the world enjoys the missiles and bombs, we must be able to enter this game ... We therefore must have this force so that the Americans and others would not think to attack us once again,' as the Libyan leader said after the US air attacks on Tripoli. Some time afterwards, he mused: 'If we had a deterrent force of missiles able to reach New York, we would have directed them at that very moment.' The stark motivation behind the proliferation of ballistic missile technology was revealed.

This is one of the most worrying factors behind the issue of the international spread of weapons of mass destruction in the 21st century. The inexorable spread of nuclear, chemical and biological weapons is bad enough, but many nations now also seek and are acquiring the means to develop and deploy them, creating one of the greatest threats to international stability and constituting a root cause of the USA's desire to build a national missile defence shield.

The belief that the secrets of missile design and development were safely locked up for all time within the security vaults of the superpowers has become illusory. International co-operation between what once seemed unlikely alliances of countries has pooled expertise and designs to create a new generation of powerful delivery vehicles. Details of the numerous projects now underway around the world are difficult to discover and evaluate, as development naturally remains highly secretive. At the heart of this very complex web of relationships and co-operation lie China, North Korea, Iran and, perhaps, Libya. Sometimes the motivation is pure politics and diplomatic advantage. Mostly, it's about hard cash.

One of the earliest examples was the sale by China of Dong Feng-3 or CSS-2 missiles to Saudi Arabia in 1987, under a deal signed in July 1985 for a price variously estimated at between $1 billion to $3.5 billion. The missile, now belatedly being removed from Chinese operational service, was developed by Beijing to attack US bases in Japan, the Philippines and South Korea.

Between 50 and 60 of these 1,700-mile-range missiles were supplied to the Saudis, fitted with HE warheads instead of the 1 to 3 MT nuclear devices carried by the Chinese rockets. There are unconfirmed reports that chemical warheads were later developed, although Saudi Arabia ratified the chemical weapons treaty in September 1996 and King Fahd has stressed that the missiles will not be armed with unconventional weapons. The Reagan administration in Washington was assured about this in writing by the Saudi government in 1988. Certainly, the missile's notorious inaccuracy – it has a CEP of more than one and a half miles – makes a HE warhead look less than a credible military weapon, except as one of terror against civilian populations. (The original massive 'rubble-bouncing' Chinese single multi-MT warhead made the question of accuracy merely academic because of its explosive power.)

Western intelligence was caught off-guard. The first the USA learnt of the transfer was when its spy satellite pictures showed the missiles on the decks of ships being unloaded in Saudi Arabia. They are now deployed at two Royal Saudi Air Force sites in the desert, al-Sulayel and al-Joffer, 311 miles and 62 miles south of Riyadh respectively, with four to six concrete launch pads, together with around 30 support buildings, at each location. The missiles are within easy range of Israeli targets, although Saudi sources firmly maintained they were targeted on Teheran and other Iranian cities. But they also have the range to strike most areas of the Middle East and some parts of eastern India. The missiles are low-technology, first-generation weapons and took until 1990 to become fully operational in Saudi service for reasons that remain unclear. Chinese personnel may well be resident in Saudi Arabia to maintain and fuel these weapons, which could now be declining in effectiveness because of the corrosive nature of their liquid fuel and the effects of the desert climate and dust. There have been no reported flight tests, which again casts doubts on their operational status.

Nor were missiles fired against Iraq during DESERT STORM, although Iraqi forces were threatening Saudi Arabia's territory. Saddam clearly was aware of the missiles' lack of readiness and gambled that the House of Saud would not launch them. Their deterrent value had diminished only months after they entered service. Defence Minister Prince Bandar bin Sultan said afterwards that:

> King Fahd ruled out that option because of the fact that you cannot control it [the missiles] accurately. Our problem was that our war was not with the Iraqi people, it was with Saddam Hussein and his clique.

This is a tacit acknowledgment of the problems with the DF-2's accuracy and its likelihood to cause civilian casualties. It is believed that the Middle Eastern nation is now examining the possibility of purchasing the Chinese Dong Feng DF-31 as a replacement for these elderly and unreliable weapons, although its greater range may rule it out as a candidate and anyway, Saudi Arabia may go to other supplier states such as Pakistan.

China has played other roles in the proliferation of missile technology – despite repeated official denials. She is believed to have provided assistance to North Korea with development of Pyongyang's No Dong missile, beginning in 1988: certainly earlier collaboration with Beijing on a weapon in the Dong Feng series is apparent in the final shape and performance of the No Dong. North Korea's missile developments are born out of its paranoia about its survival and the desire to reunify the Korean peninsula. It maintains a standing army of just under one million men, plus reserves totalling a further three million strong, 3,800 tanks and the highest concentration of artillery in the world – 11,200 separate guns, most self-propelled or towed, positioned within 60 miles of the demilitarised zone separating North and South. The missiles are an extension to this military might, providing longer reach to strike at targets in South Korea and at American bases in Japan. They also took on the mantle of a financial bonus – earning desperately needed foreign currency, through exports overseas.

The Scud C and D missiles were the baseline for North Korean upgraded designs for its Hwasong 6 and 7 missiles, beginning in 1984, with ranges of between 300 and 400 miles, armed with chemical and HE warheads. Around 60 each were sold to Iran and Syria in 1991 and some of the Scud C technologies were also purchased by Egypt and Libya. Sudan was offered assistance to build a Scud C assembly plant in 1999, with Iranian aid and some complete missiles have been reportedly sold to Vietnam. But North Korea was aware of its own requirements and those of its burgeoning customer list for longer-range weapons.

The answer, the No Dong 1 missile, is a larger version of the C variant of the Scud missile with a 1,600lb warhead, probably HE or chemical. One warhead may also include 100 sub-munitions that explode at various times after impact to effectively knock out operations at enemy airfields. After a difficult test flight programme, it entered production at the No. 26 General Plant at Kanggye in 1994. Range is estimated at more than 810 miles.

In the early 1990s, North Korea began to develop a longer-range version, at just under 1,000 miles, with a smaller warhead and greater terminal accuracy. This is the No Dong 2, destined to become the base design for two other new missiles – Iran's Shahab 3 and Pakistan's Ghauri 1 or Hatf 5 rocket. Both versions are now in operational service with up to 100 missiles deployed on 18 transporter-erector-launcher vehicles (TELs) at four sites, Mayang-do, Myongchon, Chunggang and Okpyang.

North Korea's ambitions did not end with the No Dong. What really set the cat amongst the international pigeons was the development of the Taep'o Dong 1 missile, beginning in 1990 and using a No Dong rocket as the first stage. It remains unclear whether the initial motivation was simply to create a satellite launch vehicle, for reasons of national prestige, or a new long-range weapon. Certainly, it has all the characteristics of an embryo ICBM. What increased suspicions were the use of decoy mock-ups to confuse and mislead US and Russian satellite surveillance, and much of the development and subsequent production was conducted in specially built underground facilities at Hwadaegun and Doksang to hide progress on the project.

The missile has a range of at least 1,250 miles, although in a test flight in August 1998, from Hwadaegun, the third stage reached nearly 2,500 miles. It was watched by Iranian and Pakistani engineers. The development caused an international furore with Japan particularly vocal in its condemnation, realising that it was now firmly in the sights of the Pyongyang regime. As a result, North Korea declared a moratorium on missile tests until 2003. US intelligence believes that between 10 and 20 Taep'o Dong 1 missiles are now operational, armed again with a HE or chemical warhead, and mounted on TEL vehicles recycled from tank chassis. There are unconfirmed reports that Libya is providing at least some of the cash to fund this project.

North Korea is also working on an extended-range version, the Taep'o Dong 2, with a reach of 3,750 miles, based on technologies evolved in the development of missiles by client states such as Pakistan and Iran. If the moratorium on testing is lifted, the first trials could begin around 2005 and with the known North Korean desire to deploy operationally very speedily, the first missiles could enter service as early as 2005–6.

As we have seen, Libya is keen to acquire ballistic missile capability. In the early 1980s, Ghadaffi launched a project to build or acquire a number of different delivery systems, codenamed ITTISALAT. Prime project was the Al Fatah missile, armed with a chemical warhead, that apparently progressed with the assistance of Chinese technicians. The strict international trade embargo on Libya, and discoveries of consignments of contraband components and technology, constantly stymied progress and only a few test flights from the Gawat missile facility, 450 miles south of Tripoli, have been reported. Only three prototypes are believed to have been manufactured.

Thus thwarted in indigenous development, Ghadaffi decided to go down an easier route and to buy in the technology. Talks to purchase China's Dong Feng 15 or M-9 medium-range missile collapsed in early 1989 without a deal. The following June, the Libyan government purchased 140 of North Korea's Hwasong 6 development of the original Russian Scud C missile at a cost of $170 million, of which 80 were generously paid for and supplied to Syria, the remainder to Tripoli. First shipments of disassembled missiles arrived during 1993 via Tanzania and Zimbabwe and a total of almost 100 now equip Libyan forces. This 310-mile range missile is reportedly being equipped with chemical warheads with the possibility of biological weapons being developed in the future.

Ghadaffi also wanted a longer-range missile and began negotiations to purchase North Korea's No Dong missile in 1991 with Libya perhaps providing the cash for Pyongyang to continue the project.

The final $200 million deal, struck in 1999, provided 50 missiles, seven TEL launchers, training and maintenance, with the first rockets reportedly arriving in July 2000 and deployed along the Mediterranean coast, threatening, once operational, areas of southern Europe, Israel and wide swathes of North Africa.

Iran, which, as we have seen, used ballistic missiles in anger for the first time since the Germans V-2s in the Second World War against Iraq in the 1980s, is also now pursuing an aggressive programme to develop ballistic missiles with North Korean and Russian assistance. Iranian engineers were reported in Libya in 1996 swapping information and providing technology and missile components.

Iran's Shahab 3 programme is based on North Korea's No Dong 1 missile, of which Teheran purchased components for about 150 in the mid-1990s and began assembly. After Pyongyang quit the Iranian programme in 1995 because of international pressure, Iran went it alone and began test flights of the Shahab 3, only to have deliveries secretly resume from North Korea in 1997. The rocket's performance is similar. Work on a successor programme, the Shahab 4, is believed to be based on the old Soviet intermediate-range SS-4 'Sandel' missile, although Russia denied providing assistance. Finally, Teheran is also developing another version with a range of 2,500 miles, the Shahab 5, as both an ICBM and a satellite launch vehicle, based on the Taep'o Dong 1.

Its old adversary, Iraq, having learnt a hard lesson in the 'war of the cities' in the 1980s, was not slow in seeking its own ballistic missiles. Whilst surrounded by states with current or evolving weapons of mass destruction and the means to deliver them, Iraq is the only one, ironically, that has been threatened with military action to neutralise its arsenal.

The first project was the so-called Al Abbas missile, based yet again on the Scud B, with a first flight in April 1988. Bigger fuel tanks and a smaller HE warhead increased the range of its Soviet origin technology out to 560 miles. But work stopped because of stability problems just before the invasion of Kuwait in 1990 and none were fired during hostilities with the Western-led coalition forces.

Saddam Hussein had better luck with the Al Hussein missile – another design based on the Scud B, of which nearly 1,000 were acquired from Russia during the 1980s. Al Husseins were fired during DESERT STORM and the headline-grabbing threat they posed to

Baghdad's enemies led to a dramatic and frantic hunt for the mobile TELs by American and British unmanned air vehicles and their special forces deep behind Iraqi lines. A total of 43 missiles were successfully fired at targets in Saudi Arabia and 39 at Israel in salvoes of up to five rockets at a time in an attempt to defeat the defending American Patriot SAM batteries in both countries. Another 11 launches were failures.

Al Hussein has a range of up to 400 miles and may be armed with HE, chemical and biological agent warheads. At the end of the second Gulf War, Iraq declared it had 51 missiles remaining and 23 HE and 30 chemical warheads for the Al Hussein. Although 122 were destroyed, the UN inspection teams estimated, before their ejection from Iraq in 1998, that 50 Al Hussein missiles had been hidden, together with 20 TEL vehicles. Western intelligence estimates that at least 20 remain capable of firing and would be able to strike targets in Cyprus, Turkey, Saudi Arabia, Iran and Israel.

Iraq also sought even longer-range missiles. The Al Abid was a multi-stage satellite launch vehicle, partially based on Scud technology. The Badr-2000, a 440– 650-mile range missile, originated in Iraqi research completed during the now abandoned joint project with Argentina and Egypt in the 1980s to build the 'Condor' missile. Both projects faltered and died under the UN inspectors' scrutiny after the second Gulf War. Now, British intelligence believes Iraq is working on weapons with ranges of more than 700 miles for deployment before 2007 with focus on new rocket motors and improved guidance systems to boost warhead accuracy.

Across the Indian Ocean, India, surrounded by her sworn enemies in Pakistan and China to the north and with ambitions to achieve regional superpower status, also began development of ballistic missiles in 1979 as vehicles to carry its projected nuclear warheads. After a number of false starts, the fat, stumpy short-range Prithvi ('earth') missile series emerged, beginning with the Prithvi 1, first tested in February 1988, with a range of just under 100 miles, and now operated by the Indian Army. The longer-range Prithvi 2, in service with the air force, can hit targets up to 155 miles from the launch site. A ship-launched version, called the Dhanush, was unsuccessfully tested in April 2000 from the offshore patrol vessel *Subhadra* in the Bay of Bengal but now looks likely to evolve into a submarine-launched weapon, given the Indian military leadership's publicly expressed desire for a strategic nuclear triad on the lines operated by the USA – although not, of course, on the same scale. All they need now are submarines capable of launching the weapon and this problem may be solved by the reported leasing of nuclear-powered 'Akula' submarines from cash-starved Russia.

Around 130 Prithvi 1 missiles have been produced and are operated from 35 TEL vehicles. The second version entered service in 1999 and a total of 70 will be manufactured. Both are armed with nuclear weapons in the low kT range, HE warheads or fuel-air explosive – similar to napalm.

India was also seeking a delivery system eventually capable of reaching Beijing and the slim, elegant Agni missile looks like fitting the bill with four versions in service or under development, culminating in Agni 4, called Surya, planned as an ICBM for possible military service after 2010. Only 10 Agni 1 missiles, with a range of more than 1,500 miles, have been built and are kept in storage as the focus has switched to the 1,865-mile Agni 2, of which five became operational in the autumn of 2000, armed with 200 kT warheads.

Pakistan, also now a nuclear power, and in frequent military confrontation if not open conflict with India, also has embarked on a ballistic missile programme, beginning in the early 1980s with the Hatf series, developed with Chinese assistance, including delivery of 30 of Beijing's M-11 (or DF-11) missiles, later designated the Hatf 2A which were copied and placed into production locally. An upgraded and larger version became the 375-mile-range Hatf 4 or Shaheen 1 missile.

The quantum jump in Pakistani ballistic missile capability came with the Ghauri 1 and 2 missiles, look-alikes for the North Korean No Dong and with similarities to the Iranian Shahab 4. Ranges are between 950 and 1,400 miles. Ghauri 1 is armed with a single chemical or nuclear warhead with a 15-35 kT yield, the latter also arming Ghauri 2.

The more rational among us may wonder why nations with terrible problems of poverty and starvation embark on such expensive military programmes to build weapons of mass destruction. It is not just a matter of political clout: national pride comes into play too. Drive around some of the Pakistani cities and look at the full-scale mock-ups of the Ghauri missiles that stand menacingly in the centre of some road roundabouts, surrounded incongruously by attractive flowers and gardens.

There's a stark message here and one we would all do well to learn. Possession of such weapons provides membership of a very exclusive club: a group of nations able to inflict terrible annihilation on an enemy perhaps hundreds or now thousands of miles away – just by pressing a launch button. It signifies not only status but also something of a coming of age in nationhood in the eyes of those who pay for such an arsenal of destruction.

Military apologists for NATO's military expenditure during the Cold War used to point to the huge conventional and nuclear capability of the opposing Soviet Union and stressed that the size and strength of such an arsenal could not quickly change, but the intention to use it could – almost overnight.

The same is unfortunately true of today's ballistic missiles that arm an increasing number of sometimes volatile nations in very unstable regions of the world. But are the same checks and balances in place as they were (and are) among the experienced higher echelons of command in Washington, Moscow, Paris and London?

Sadly for the world, the realist must answer 'No' and that makes for some uneasy nights for those on the current or potential target list for this new generation of missiles, armed with the same horrific weapons as their Cold War ancestors. In truth, the world is a yet more dangerous place in which to live in the first decade of the 21st century.

CHAPTER 7
THE LAST DITCH DEFENCE

THROUGHOUT HISTORY, man's ingenuity has created new, powerful weapons – and then sought the defences necessary to negate them. Military technology has never stood still. In the Middle Ages, ever more complex armour was designed to protect the knight against the thrusts of lances and the furious cuts of swords in battle, but was eventually rendered useless by the development of gunpowder and increasingly powerful and accurate guns. So it was in the 20th century with ballistic missiles and their nuclear, chemical or biological warheads. Once the ability to deliver these weapons of mass destruction directly onto a target was demonstrated, it was inevitable that research would be pursued to enable defenders to neutralise the attack in an attempt to survive a nuclear attack – and retaliate in kind. Anti-ballistic missiles (ABMs) systems became a holy grail for super-power defence technology.

One of the first nations to seriously contemplate this was Britain, with bitter memories of the World War Two German attacks on London and southern England by V-1 cruise and V-2 ballistic missiles still fresh in the mind of strategic planners. In 1954, the Ministry of Supply placed contracts with two defence companies, English Electric and Marconi, to study the development of a ballistic missile defence (BMD) system under the RAF's Air Staff Target AST 1135, codenamed VIOLET FRIEND, for operational deployment in 1963. Main development work, later involving Ferranti and Bristol Aircraft, began in 1957. Few details of the once top-secret project have emerged into the public domain.

The plan was to intercept and shoot down warheads carried by medium-range Soviet R-5 missiles, codenamed SS-3 Shyster by

NATO, which from 1956 were based in forward positions in East Germany, or the intermediate-range, single-stage R-12 (SS-4 Sandel) fired from the western Soviet Union. It was known by British intelligence that some of the East German-based weapons had chemical warheads targeted on London, while the R-12s, deployed from 1959, were nuclear-armed, with powerful 1.3 or 2.3 MT warheads.

The problem the British had in designing a viable defence was the very short reaction times available to them from the moment of detection of an enemy launch as the missile rose above the RAF's radar horizon. There were just minutes to spare. The attacking warheads would also present very small, head-on radar cross-sections to identify and intercept. Bound by Treasury constraints on funding, the British government also wanted a system on the cheap – utilising batteries of the high-altitude surface-to-air missiles (SAMs) then under development, the Bristol Bloodhound I and English Electric Thunderbird I, although the former was eventually selected as the 'kill vehicle'. At least using existing or projected equipment could speed up deployment and reduce costs.

The design stipulated that the system should be able to handle up to six missile engagements simultaneously with fast reloading times to tackle follow-on salvoes. VIOLET FRIEND was unlikely ever to be able to provide 100% protection and almost certainly only had the objective of trying to shield RAF V-bomber bases in East Anglia and other military strategic assets, rather than defending urban population centres.

Any such engagement would each involve four separate radar systems. The early warning radar was the Type 85 BLUE YEOMAN, to be based at RAF Watton, Norfolk. The missile booster and warhead tracking radars were the Marconi AN/FPS-16, a few of which are still operational today in the UK and USA serving as instrumentation radars. The Type 83 YELLOW RIVER radar would illuminate targets for the Bloodhound SAM system and guide it to its target. Two warhead trackers, looking east, were to be sited in the Netherlands, at Terneuzen and on the island of Terschelling, to provide targeting information for the missile interceptors. The boost tracking radars, which would detect the separation of warhead from re-entry vehicle, were to be based at RAF Coltishall, Norfolk; Felixstowe, Suffolk and Strubby, Lincolnshire, where the missile batteries were co-located.

The attacking Soviet missile re-entry vehicles would be engaged by the Bloodhound missile at a height of between 30,000 and 40,000ft, initially relying on a high-explosive warhead, fitted with a proximity fuze. The aim was to knock out the nuclear warhead before it was armed. There must have been growing doubts about the terminal accuracy of the interceptor, as later on there seemed fewer concerns about the effects of a nuclear explosion high over Britain's friends and allies. The Series 2 Mk2 Bloodhound was later intended to carry a lightweight 6 kT nuclear warhead such as INDIGO HAMMER, (formerly BLUE FOX) under concurrent development, or the cosily codenamed GWEN small warhead.

In the event, VIOLET FRIEND never became operational and the project was cancelled in 1962.

Across the great European divide of the Iron Curtain, Russian strategic planners had not missed the significance of ballistic missile defence and the strong card it provided in the grim poker game of nuclear war. In the early 1950s they began work on a primitive system that would offer a quick fix – some limited protection against NATO short- and medium-range missile attacks across the western borders of the Soviet Union. It was based on the two-stage RZ-25 or V-1000 missile, codenamed 'Griffon' by Western intelligence.

Development work was begun by the Grushin design bureau and flight tests against warheads carried by the R-5 (SS-3 Shyster) and R-12 Sandel were staged in 1956. The first successful intercept was in March 1961 at a height of 15 miles. The Griffon was armed with a HE blast fragmentation warhead literally to shred the target warhead, although some recent Russian reports suggest it was operationally nuclear-tipped. Although the missile was not seen until the 1963 Moscow May Day parade, it had begun deployment around the Estonian capital of Tallinn with 30 launchers also positioned to protect Leningrad (now St Petersburg) in 1961–2.

The system, however, was soon abandoned because the missile was slow, inaccurate, and required data transmitted from a number of radars to provide any hope of a successful engagement.

Work on a larger and much more ambitious BMD had been under-way concurrently since 1954 to protect Moscow against missile attack. The aim was not primarily to defend the Soviet capital's population but to safeguard the national command authority – the Russian leadership – from nuclear oblivion. In the parlance of strategic nuclear war, the system would create a 'sanctuary' for the members of the

Communist Party Central Committee, although up to 1967 it was by no means certain that the system would not be deployed around other Soviet cities.

The system was based on the A35ozh, again designed by the Grushin bureau, a liquid-propelled two-stage missile with four solid boosters wrapped around the based of its fuselage. NATO called the rocket SH-01 'Galosh', another of the Western Alliance's more bizarre codenames. It was designed to engage incoming warheads at a range of 220 miles, well outside the Earth's atmosphere, destroying a number of them with a single nuclear warhead of 2–3 MTs. All the Muscovites would have known of the drama way out in space would have been a single bright flash in the sky, followed by the distant roar of the explosion. The Russians built a firing trials site for the Galosh at Sary-Shagan from 1956 and used a test site in present-day Kazakhstan to simulate the battle management techniques. Three radars were constructed around the site to track both incoming and defending missiles and generate radar commands to the interceptors. A full-scale trial was mounted in 1961 when a Galosh HE warhead destroyed a SS-4 Sandel target re-entry vehicle hurtling through space at more than two miles a second. The Russians then tested an infra-red seeker to enable the interceptor to home in on the heat generated by the attacking missile but this proved unsuccessful.

The missile first appeared in public at the traditional May Day Parade in Moscow in 1964. It trundled through Red Square, hidden inside a huge cylindrical container and towed by a powerful tractor-trailer, causing a sensation within Western military circles. However, the missile did not begin deployment until 1969–70 and only became operational in 1971. Galosh was held in above-ground reloadable launchers at four sites to the north-west and west of Moscow, at Novo-Petrovskoye, Klin, Verena and Aleksandrov, although initially eight were planned and work began on six. A total of 64 missiles were ready for firing at any given time, with another 80 held at the sites as reloads. However, their UDMH liquid propellant (which could not be stored within the missile's main fuel tanks) counted against fast reaction times in a crisis. The command headquarters was located at Kubinka, 43 miles from the Russian capital, near a huge 'Dog House' battle management radar site. Further proving test flights were held in 1972 and 1974. The Russians had become the first with a workable BMD system, although it was probably designed to neutralise an attack by only six to eight ICBMs. Their defences would have been overwhelmed by a saturation attack by enemy missiles, particularly so with the development of American multiple, independently targeted re-entry vehicles (MIRVs).

Across the Atlantic, during the 1950s, the US Army also sought approval and funding to build a missile shield around the continental USA, based on the Nike-Hercules and Nike-Ajax anti-aircraft missile systems, but using a modified medium-range interceptor, the Nike-Zeus, armed with a W-31 20 kT nuclear warhead. The missile successfully intercepted a target dummy warhead launched by an Atlas ICBM from 4,500 miles away in 1962,* but the project had some fundamentally serious flaws: the guidance radar was turned mechanically, limiting the system's ability to tracking only one enemy warhead or missile at a time and the interceptor itself was slow.

Unsurprisingly perhaps, some in Congress looked favourably on the plan, seeing it as a way to provide protection for their voters. Anything, they maintained, was better than nothing. But the Army and the Joint Chiefs of Staff met considerable resistance from the Eisenhower and later the Kennedy administrations who felt that the project would be costly, technically difficult and largely ineffective against the new Soviet ICBMs. Bowing to political pressure, the 1963 US Defense Budget provided funding for research on a new anti-ballistic missile system, the Nike-X, designed to knock out attacking warheads as they re-entered the Earth's atmosphere about 100 miles above the surface, after their brief sojourn in space. At this point, many of the 'penetration aids' (or 'penaids' in the language of nuclear deterrence) such as balloons, designed to fool a defending force into shooting at decoy warheads, would be stripped away by the heat generated by re-entry into the upper layers of the atmosphere, so allowing a BMD system a better chance of interception.

The Nike-X eventually included two new missiles. Spartan was designed to attack incoming warheads at ranges of nearly 500 miles at heights averaging around 300 miles out in space. It was armed with a single W-71 massive 5 MT warhead that would generate intense X-ray bombardment of several re-entry vehicles at a time to knock them out. Development of this area defence weapon began in 1965. The

* A version of the Nike-Hercules was deployed as an anti-satellite weapon on Kwajalein atoll in the Pacific in 1964 for two years before being replaced by the Thor anti-satellite missile.

sleek cone-shaped Sprint two-stage missile was a very short-range, high-speed interceptor, fitted with a W-66 10 kT warhead, which could engage enemy warheads at altitudes of between 82,000 and 112,000ft. It was very much a last-ditch weapon, designed to pick off those warheads that had escaped Spartan's powerful radiation weapon. By the end of 1966, Congress voted cash to deploy the two missiles, fully in the teeth of administration objections, with Sprint planned to defend 25 US cities, increasing to 52 in the long term.

It was not to be, at least not how Congress planned it. All too reluctantly, Defense Secretary Robert McNamara announced in September 1967 the decision to deploy a 'light' or partial BMD system, codenamed SENTINEL, but only able to provide a shield against what was becoming a Chinese ICBM threat and against an accidental Soviet launch. It would no longer provide protection for the US civil population. Prophetically, it heralded Washington's concerns of recent years over 'rogue states' armed with ballistic missiles, as what was planned was a system capable of countering only 'light' nuclear attacks. McNamara pointed out:

> The Soviets are now deploying an anti-ballistic missile system. If we react to this deployment intelligently, we have no reason for alarm ... This is not in any sense a new issue. We have both the technical possibility and the strategic desirability of an American ABM deployment under constant review since the late 1950s ... In point of fact, we already initiated offensive weapons programs costing several billions in order to offset the small present Soviet ABM deployment. We will be forced to continue that effort over the next few years if the evidence is that the Soviets intend to turn what is now a light and modest ABM deployment into a massive one.

McNamara was at some pains to differentiate between a full BMD system that shielded civilian populations and the US planned version that would offer protection against any future 'irrational behaviour' of a Chinese missile strike against America. He warned that the 'danger in developing this relatively light and reliable Chinese-orientated ABM system is that pressures will develop to expand it into a heavy Soviet-orientated ABM system. We must resist this temptation firmly.'

His words were not only aimed at a domestic audience. They were also directed straight at the America-watchers in the Kremlin.

Why was the US government so dead set against a full-scale BMD system? The State Department had tried repeatedly to win Soviet approval to limit *their* anti-ballistic missile defences, maintaining that these would deny important targets to Western strategic nuclear planners and this would threaten the deterrence and stability provided by the nuclear balance of power between the USA and the Soviet Union – both would no longer face necessarily mutual assured destruction. Vice-versa, of course, the same was true for a US BMD system. But the Americans failed to convince Moscow of the wisdom of their argument. Washington was also convinced that a costly BMD system could soon be weakened by less costly countermeasures installed in their weapons by Soviet missile engineers. SENTINEL had almost built-in obsolescence against an overwhelming Russian ICBM nuclear attack.

The Russians were steadfast in maintaining that an anti-ballistic missile defence system was not provocative in relations between the two superpowers. At a June 1967 summit meeting, the Soviet Union's Premier Alexei Kosygin angrily told US President Lyndon Johnson:

> Defence is moral. Aggression is immoral. Which weapons would be regarded as a tension factor – offensive or defensive weapons? I think that a defensive system, which prevents attack, is not a cause of the arms race but represents a factor preventing the death of people .... Which is cheaper, to have offensive weapons that can destroy cities or entire states or to have weapons that can prevent this destruction? An anti-missile system may cost more than an offensive one, but it is intended not for killing people but for saving human lives.

Conversely, there were some in Washington who argued that the defensive ring of missiles around Moscow fitted in with a perceived Soviet firm belief that they could fight and *win* a nuclear war with the USA.

After launching a pre-emptive ICBM attack on US nuclear assets, the consequent losses to their population and infrastructure from a weakened American retaliatory strike would be acceptable to the Russian leadership, safe in their sanctuary. Certainly, for decades, the Soviet leadership had invested hundreds of millions of roubles in technology and construction work, in addition to active defensive measures, to ensure *their* survival in a nuclear exchange. Protected command posts, hundreds of feet below the surface, and even secret dedicated underground rail systems had been built beneath Moscow and other major cities. These could accommodate thousands of people. The Pentagon commented in 1989:

> The provision of leadership protection facilities for Party and state officials having no responsibilities for the conduct of military operations indicates that a major program goal is support of post-strike societal and economic reconstitution efforts.

The US deployment of SENTINEL was postponed after the Nixon administration took office in January 1969 to allow a thorough review of the BMD project to be undertaken. The project reappeared three months later, on March 14, from beneath the Pentagon paper mountain, disguised under the name SAFEGUARD, to provide, in the words of President Nixon:

> Protection of our land-based retaliatory forces against a direct attack by the Soviet Union. Defense of the American people against the kind of nuclear attack which Communist China is likely to be able to mount within the decade. Protection against the possibility of accidental attacks from any source ... By approving this system, it is possible to reduce US fatalities to a minimum level in the event of a Chinese nuclear attack in the 1970s or in an accidental attack from any source.

In reality, then, no change. There was little thought of civilian protection, or at least only against very small levels of attack indeed. The system was designed to shield the US Minuteman ICBM silo fields, no more, despite Nixon's bland words. After much havering over the choice of operational locations, Congress eventually approved a dramatically scaled-down plan to deploy a single SAFEGUARD site at the Minuteman ICBM base at Grand Forks, North Dakota. Seventy Sprint and 30 Spartan were held in protective underground silos, becoming operational in 1975.

Pentagon documents compiled in 1972, recently declassified under the US Freedom of Information Act, disclose a belief that even four SAFEGUARD sites might be insufficient to counter a mass attack by the Soviet ICBM force of SS-9s and SS-11s; the US DoD wanted 12 bases.

> Analysis of the latest projections concerning Soviet capabilities indicates that, if the most severe of the postulated SS-9 and SS-11 type missile forces

were directed at Minuteman, the Minuteman force (assuming that the silos are undefended but are upgraded, as scheduled to 1,000 psi) could be drawn down to 300 survivors or less as early as 1975.

A new military requirement also emerged in 1972 for another SAFE-GUARD site to protect the National Command Authority (NCA) – the euphemism for the President and his senior political colleagues – in Washington by 1979.

> This will provide substantial protection of our NCA and its attendant command/control against a small or accidental attack and above all afford additional valuable time for decision-making in the event of a mass attack on Washington. In particular, this deployment will counter submarine-launched ballistic missiles off our coast with very short time of flight. More specifically, such defense will discourage what could otherwise result in a situation whereby the NCA could be destroyed in a surprise attack, perhaps with a small expenditure of enemy resources, e.g. one 'Y'[ankee] class [SSBN] submarine and its missiles.

The Pentagon's fears did not resonate around Capitol Hill. Congress turned down a funding request for the Washington SAFEGUARD site in 1973. But events were overtaking the American BMD system. At long last, some progress was being made between the superpowers towards limiting their means to destroy the world. In May 1972, the texts of the Strategic Arms Limitation Talks (SALT 1) were agreed by the USA and Soviet Union in Helsinki, which included a treaty limiting BMD systems. The agreement banned missile defences covering an entire nation or an individual region and limited anti-ballistic missile launchers to a total of 100 within 90 miles of each country's capital and a further 100 inside a 90-mile radius of each superpower's main ICBM silo field. The deal conveniently allowed Moscow to keep its defences and the Americans to continue the SAFEGUARD deployment at Grand Forks.

Afterwards, Washington decided against keeping its single BMD site that offered only limited protection at very high cost. It decommissioned the Sprint and Spartan missiles in 1976, just a year after they became operational. The missiles were held in store and finally destroyed in 1983.

The Soviets had no such doubts. BMD development remained a

high priority for the Soviet Ministry of Defence throughout the 1970s, with substantial funding and resources continually made available. New Russian intelligence estimates of American nuclear war plans indicated the probability that Moscow could be targeted by at least 60 warheads with yields in the 1 MT range. Therefore, an updated version of the Galosh was introduced in the mid-1970s, fitted with a restartable liquid-fuelled third stage to implement improvements to targeting after launch. There were also enhancements to radar surveillance, with the introduction of a 'Cat House' phased-array battle-management radar, south of Moscow, to cover any possible launch against the Soviet capital from China, or from US submarines in the Pacific. The Grushin design bureau also developed a new prototype 'last chance' interceptor to take out warheads within the Earth's atmosphere just moments before impact, but this project never came to fruition. It was abandoned in favour of another short-range missile that became operational in the late 1980s.

The upgrades to Moscow's strategic defences posed a particularly difficult dilemma for the British with their 'independent nuclear deterrent' based, in the 1960s–80s, on the 16 Polaris A3 missiles carried in each of four Royal Navy SSBN submarines, at least one of which was always on patrol in the icy waters of the North Atlantic and Barents Sea. The British government was aware of the Soviet research work and likely future deployment of a BMD system even as the first British Polaris submarines entered service in the mid-1960s. As the three 200 kT warheads fitted to each of the British missiles would travel fairly closely together in a triangular formation, there were clear dangers that the Galosh interceptor's massive 2–3 MT weapon could neutralise a significant proportion of the attacking British-designed and built warheads, moments before they could re-enter the Earth's atmosphere on the final descent to their targets. The existence of the Soviet BMD defences forced the British into a high-risk and astonishingly expensive secret programme to maintain the integrity of their nuclear weapons. 'We could not allow a sanctuary to be created by the Soviet Union,' one British official told me later – although he was careful to stress that this did not imply that Moscow was the sole British nuclear target.

The USA had already decided to pursue the MIRV route as a solution by adopting the Poseidon submarine-launched ballistic missile with 10 W-76 warheads, although it could carry a maximum of 14. It is believed that US President Richard Nixon offered Poseidon to the British Prime Minister of the time, Sir Edward Heath, in 1970, but the offer was declined with polite thanks, for a number of political, cost and technical reasons.

Instead, a Conservative Cabinet sub-committee decided secretly in 1973 to develop a complex system of penetration aids to defeat the Soviet BMD defences and any upgrades envisaged until the late 1980s. This was an extraordinary decision considering that Britain had quit any involvement in strategic systems research or development, with the demise of the Blue Streak liquid-fuelled medium-range ballistic missile in 1960 and space research had a very low government priority when it came to handing out funding. But the British were aware of an earlier US project, codenamed ANTELOPE, for agile warheads with penetration aids, considered for their Polaris missiles but discarded because the Pentagon believed the best decoy was simply another live warhead and that saturation of BMD defences was the only way to defeat the ring of interceptors around Moscow. Washington provided technical details of the project to London in 1967. A variant of this seemed the best solution for the British to adopt.

The project was codenamed CHEVALINE, apparently after a French mountain goat, capable of death-defying leaps from rock to rock in the foothills of the Juras. Work began at the closely-guarded British Atomic Weapons Research Establishment at Aldermaston, Berkshire, whose scientists were confronted with the considerable technical problem of squeezing a new small space craft into the already confined area of the Polaris nose cone carrying the three warheads.

The cost, hidden under 'Other Research & Development' in successive defence budgets, escalated dramatically from the autumn 1972 hopelessly optimistic estimates of £175 million to £495 million (on the same price base) at the time of the Labour government's 1976 Defence Review. All difficult projects present hard choices for those in charge: can you really take the painful decision to stop the haemorrhage on your budget, or is it easier to carry on, in the Micawber-like hope that things will get better? The Cabinet sub-committee repeatedly reviewed the project in the late 1970s and each time ruefully decided to press ahead as cancellation would not only waste considerable sums but also tacitly acknowledge that the British nuclear arsenal would no longer constitute a true deterrent. After 1976, the Defence Ministry Procurement Executive took on the project's management and greater industrial participation was sought. In the end, CHEVALINE cost the British taxpayer, in blissful ignorance, over £1 billion at 1980 prices.

The system was based on a new liquid-fuelled penetration aids carrier (PAC), the British version of the American warhead post-boost bus, capable of manoeuvring in space, fitted with a new powerful on-board computer and a range of sensors to determine orientation and direction. Its design caused a great deal of creative tension between the Royal Navy and the weapon systems scientists. Liquid fuel presents grave problems in storage as well as safety, but naval objections to its use, rather than solid propellant, were eventually overruled.

The PAC, euphemistically known as the 'front end', would be deployed from the Polaris missile at speeds of around 12,000mph in space. Each would dispense two warheads and 'a variety of penetration aids' – four dummy warheads and a large number of decoy balloons, together with large quantities of chaff, thin strips of metal fired from flapped tubes – to blind and confuse the Soviet ABM radars. The plan was that the Russian defences would be unable to distinguish between dummy and real warheads and must expend 'significant numbers' of interceptor missiles to be sure of eliminating the threat. This in turn would saturate and overwhelm Moscow's defences in the same way as a MIRV attack by American missiles.

The modified warheads were apparently designated KH 793, origi-nally codenamed SUPER ANTELOPE. Each would re-enter the Earth's atmosphere at even faster speeds – around 3.5 miles per second – posing, in a typically British understatement, what was termed 'an interesting fire control problem' for the enemy BMD commanders. The warheads also had additional protection – hardened against the effects of EMP and explosive blast and coated with an ablative sub-stance that melted down to a ceramic-like skin to provide a shield against high re-entry temperatures. During the last moments of flight, each warhead was capable of a planned skip through the atmosphere, like a stone skimmed across a pond, as a further measure to fool the defences. Hence the name CHEVALINE. Each A3-TK missile's three new warheads had a 'footprint' – the separation between impact points – of about 43 miles.

Trials began in September 1977 with launches from flatpads in the USA. In November 1980, launches down the American missile range off the Florida coast revealed 'unsuspected problems in separation' of dummy warheads from a test PAC vehicle, called the CQ941 FAL-STAFF, but these were overcome and the development phase ended in February 1982 with a number of 'highly successful' launches from the Royal Navy SSBN *Renown*. Out of six submerged launches from the sister boat *Revenge* in 1983, one was aborted for range safety reasons. The first warheads entered the British stockpile in 1980 and the system went on operational patrol for the first time on board *Renown* in mid-1982. Around 100 of the new CHEVALINE warheads were produced at Burghfield between 1979 and 1982. Deployment ended in 1996. A CHEVALINE PAC is on display at the Bristol Collection at Kemble, Gloucestershire.

The British Defence Secretary Francis Pym publicly disclosed the existence of CHEVALINE on January 24, 1980. Deterrence has no effect or value unless the other side has some knowledge of your military capabilities, although it is somewhat naïve to believe the Soviets were completely unaware of the work to upgrade the British Polaris force, such was (and remains) the reach of the *Glavnoye Razvedyvatelnoye Upravlenie,* the Russian Defence Ministry intelligence agency.

The British had secured the integrity of their deterrent and believed that sufficient warheads could now penetrate the Moscow defences to achieve a credible threat. Or so they thought. They discovered, at the end of the 1970s, that the motors of the three stages of the A3 missile had problems of shelf life. The solid fuel degenerated in storage. There was corrosion in some of the components. However, the Lockheed production line had long since closed down – as the US Navy had only anticipated a life of three years for each motor, but this had been extended as the Polaris programme continued. But the British models had been around for nearly two decades. After all the agony and expense of CHEVALINE, it was galling that the missile propulsion might not work on the day. The awful spectre of dud missiles confronted the British government.

The missiles were late 1950s' rocket science. Technology had moved on a long way. The Royal Navy could not use new state-of-the-art components, as these would cause impossible interface problems with the missiles. They had to recreate the technology of 20 years before – at a cost of a further £300 million-plus. Lockheed brought some of its experts out of retirement and re-started the production line for the first-stage propulsion units. The US contractors Aerojet and Hercules worked on the motors for the second and third stages. The missiles, with new engines, were re-designated A3-R (for replica). Happily, for the British government (and taxpayer), they worked.

The Soviets continued their development of the Moscow BMD system, beginning in 1967, in response to the introduction of American MIRVed missiles. They upgraded the number of ABM launchers from 64 to 100, as permitted under treaty, and replaced the ageing Galosh missiles with a two-tiered system, reminiscent of the USA's SAFEGUARD, but at least a generation ahead in technology terms. The Soviet Council of Ministers approved plans for the new generation ABM system in June 1975 and deployment began in 1984. It became fully operational in 1989.

It consists of two types of missiles, both now launched from within underground hardened silos to remove vulnerability to pre-emptive strikes. Each missile is loaded in a disposable canister. The SH-11 'Gorgon' (called the Baton/A-50 by the Russians) replaced the Galosh missiles as the frontline weapon against attacking warheads. Its battlefield is again on the fringes of space, outside the Earth's atmosphere. It was hardened against the effects of nuclear radiation.

The Gorgon has a range of 220 miles, with a solid-fuel first stage and liquid propellant for the second, or possibly a third. Each silo is fitted with a fast-moving hatch for quick response, and the missile is 'cold-launched' – that is, its first stage motors only fire after it has risen 100ft above the mouth of the silo. This prevents heat damage to the launch site and allows the silo to be reloaded. The missile has high acceleration and relies on increased accuracy to knock out enemy warheads, as its single AA84 nuclear warhead is reported to have a yield of only 10 kTs.

Thirty-six Gorgon launchers are deployed on an outer ring of launch sites, used by the old Galosh interceptors.

The cone-shaped Gazelle has a range of just 50 miles and originally was armed with the same nuclear warhead as the Gorgon. Now, it is understood, it has been fitted with an HE blast fragmentation warhead, probably directed right onto the target by command from the 'Flat Twin' phased-array engagement radar, although terminal guidance may also be by infra-red seeker. The missile's solid-fuel motor enables it to power up to two miles a second, or 10 times the speed of sound. Immediately after launch, the missile would make an abrupt turn to meet the warhead target in the minimum distance. Sixty-four Gazelles are based on silos on Moscow's new inner ring of defences at sites at Schodna, Mervskino, Kaliningrad and Lytkarino.

The BMD system is activated by notification of an enemy ballistic missile launch from the Russian Prognoz early warning satellites, fitted with infra-red sensors, direct to its command centre. As we saw in Chapter One, there are cash problems affecting the maintenance of this vital satellite network, which must cast a shadow over the efficiency of the system.

Even though a proving test flight in 1999 demonstrated the Gazelle missile has a further decade of operational life ahead of it, there are reports that the Russian government had developed further improvements to the Moscow BMD system, but had not deployed them, presumably for financial reasons.

In 1991, the Russian President, Mikhail Gorbachev withdrew some of the interceptor's nuclear warheads to central storage facilities, although the missiles remained in their silos. After controversy in the Russian media in the mid-1990s about the collateral damage that ABM nuclear warheads would cause to the Moscow population they were supposed to be defending, a number of missiles were stood down. The then Defence Minister, Igor Sergeyev, said in February 1998 that he was 'deeply convinced that the larger the umbrella we try to deploy over Moscow, the more warheads could ultimately be targeted on it.'

The Moscow ABM defences are now at low combat readiness and are likely to continue to decay in operational capability, with its battle management radar at Sofrino, 19 miles north-east of the city, turned on with only intermittent frequency, and problems in early warning coverage blinding the system. Shortage of cash is blunting its teeth.

Another legacy of the Soviet Union is a plethora of mobile SAM systems that could be deployed to attack short- or medium-range attacking missiles in defence of military operations in a specific theatre. These include the mobile SA-12 or S-300V Antev missile, called Gladiator/Giant by NATO, developed specifically to defend against the USA's now obsolete Lance and Pershing missiles. Latest is the S-400 Trieumf, ('triumph') mounted on a transporter/erector/launcher vehicle, which is designed to counter cruise missiles and short-range ballistic missiles. Western observers first saw the system in 1998, when it was offered for export.

Missile defence did not go away in the USA with the demise of SAFEGUARD. In the 1970s, concurrent with its BMD developments, the

Soviet Union added new missiles to its inventory, all with increasing accuracy, in addition to MIRV capability. The Pentagon became uneasy that American static land-based ICBMs were facing a growing risk of devastation through a pre-emptive strike launched by Moscow, with some estimates putting around 90% of the US missiles in jeopardy from an unexpected counterforce attack. Something had to be done, if the US President was not going to be forced to rely solely on any surviving bombers and submarine-launched ballistic missiles to provide America's retaliatory strike, probably only against Soviet cities, in such horrendous circumstances.

The US Army developed the Low Altitude Defense System (LoADS) as a successor to the Sprint high-speed atmospheric interceptor in the 1970s and early 1980s, as well as the Homing Overlay Experiment (HOE) that relied on physically hitting enemy warheads to destroy them, ('hit to kill'), demonstrated in 1984. By now developments in technology had enabled radar and optical sensors to pinpoint objects very precisely in space, as well as providing improved guidance systems for 'killer' satellites to be stationed in orbit, waiting to destroy missiles or re-entry vehicles by high-powered laser particle beam. It all seemed like improbable science fiction, and appropriately, formed part of President Reagan's much-vaunted 'Star Wars' system of national missile defence (NMD) that threatened to eat up billions of defence dollars to provide what could never be an 100% watertight shield against missile attack. But certainly, new technology, researched by both the USA and Soviet Union, has the potential to knock out enemy warheads, particularly direct-energy weapons like lasers, mounted on aircraft, or on the ground protecting strategic, high-value assets.

The Soviet programme, which began in the early 1980s, also envisaged space-based weaponry that was not only targeting enemy ballistic missiles but additionally planned to destroy Western satellites or space vehicles in orbit, triggered by Russian suspicions that the NASA Space Shuttle had a covert military role, possibly delivering weapons from space. Plans in the waggishly termed 'Red Star Wars' included missile- or laser-armed space stations, as well as ground-based directed-energy weapons. In October 1984, during the USA's 13th Challenger mission, the Space Shuttle was tracked in orbit by the Russian Terra-3 laser at Sary Shagan, operating at low power. The beam caused malfunctions in the Shuttle's electronic systems and distress to its crew and drew formal US diplomatic protests.

Successive reductions in strategic nuclear weapons through international treaty and the end of the Cold War killed off the wizardry of Star Wars. But with the apparent end of confrontation between the superpowers, concerns about the proliferation of ballistic missiles, particularly among so-called 'rogue nations' led to fresh preoccupations with missile defence.

Although future weapons programmes in countries such as Iraq, Iran and North Korea are the stated rationale for the USA's new $60 billion NMD shield, this threat lies largely in the future, and it is more likely that the new shield for the American homeland, armed with 'hit to kill' (HTK) interceptors, is more concerned with fending off the small bombardment that Communist China could mount.

One test of the system in July 2001 used a Minuteman ICBM fitted with a mock warhead launched from Vandenberg air force base in California. The prototype interceptor was fired 29 minutes later, 4,800 miles away on Kwajalein Atoll in the Pacific. The HTK weapon separated from its rocket booster while still more than 1,400 miles from the target warhead and used its on-board infra-red sensors, supplemented by radar data transmitted from the ground, to locate and track its quarry, ignoring a nearby large balloon decoy. The intercept occurred 10 minutes after the prototype was launched at a closing speed of 15,000mph, 140 miles above the Earth.

Work on the first missile silos at Fort Greely, near Delta Junction, Alaska, began in June 2002 a few days after the USA unilaterally pulled out of the 1972 ABM treaty. President George W. Bush said the world was no longer living in the Cold War for which the ABM treaty was designed. 'We now face new threats from terrorists who seek to destroy our civilisation by any means available to rogue states armed with weapons of mass destruction and long-range missiles.'

It is not a giant leap of logic to understand that the more likely nuclear threat to America comes from an anonymous device hidden in a suitcase or in a freight container, rather than delivered, very publicly, by a ballistic missile. The latter form of attack would inevitably result in massive retaliation by US strategic forces. The former poses the problem to Washington: whom do we strike in revenge?

Of course, the new NMD cannot detect or defend against such unconventional delivery means — that is purely a very basic law-enforcement role, rather than having to employ interceptors, expensive phased-array radars or battle-management systems.

Defences against short- and medium-range missiles, so-called 'theatre ballistic missiles' (TBM), are also flavour of the moment for the military, following experiences in the 1991 Gulf War against Iraq. During that conflict, Baghdad fired 39 modified Soviet-era Scud missiles against Israel over a six-week period, as well as more against coalition bases in Saudi Arabia. Although the missiles were armed with high explosive, there were fears that the Iraqis would deploy the chemical or biological warheads they were known to possess. (Diplomatic reports at the time suggested that Baghdad was deterred from this course by US threats of immediate retaliatory nuclear strikes.) The missiles were ineffective and inaccurate but caused terror amongst Israel's urban population – just like the V-2 launches against London nearly 50 years before.

Patriot SAMs were hurriedly pressed into service as ABM defences that were only partially successful in countering that threat.*

Today, Israel perceives a growing and menacing threat from theatre ballistic missiles. In September 2001, their radar tracked the test of a Syrian Scud-B missile launched from Haleb in northern Syria and impacting 186 miles away in the south of the country. It carried a simulated chemical warhead, possibly indicated by an airburst at altitude to disseminate the agent over a wide area. The Jewish nation also faces threats from Iraqi and Iranian missiles with ever-increasing range, targeting not only its population, but also its own three squadrons of Jericho nuclear-armed missiles based at Sedot Mickha, 28 miles south of Tel Aviv.

With the USA sharing the costs, Israel's IAI developed the two-stage Chetz (Arrow) 2 interceptor, armed with an HE fragmentation warhead, with the first operational missile entering service in March 2000 in a battery with four to eight launchers, at the Palmahim air base, 12 miles south of Tel Aviv, defending the major population centres in the centre and south of the country (as well as the Jericho base) from missile attack. A second battery was assembled at Ein Shemer, near Hadera, to protect Haifa and the north of Israel. A third battery is expected to be operational before the end of 2005 to cover southern Israel. Range of each missile is just over 60 miles.

Arrow 2 has an indigenously developed command and control

---

* Taiwan successfully used an upgraded version of the Patriot in tests against a tactical ballistic missile target in 2001 at the Chiu Peng range in the southern region of the country.

system capable of detecting hostile missile launches and computing their flight paths and targets only seconds after launch. The system has reportedly been successful in monitoring of both Syrian and Iranian missile tests. The Israeli Defence Force ordered development of the unnamed system in 1998 by a classified air force unit known as *Mamdas*, or 'operational engineering systems'. This has provided an early warning capability of a precious seven minutes, compared with between two and four previously. It also removes Israel's reliance on information provided by US satellites.

There are unconfirmed reports that India, Japan, South Korea and Taiwan have expressed interest in acquiring the Arrow 2 – an indication of the global spread of the threat posed by theatre ballistic missiles in the 21st century.

CHAPTER 8

AWAKENING FROM THE NUCLEAR NIGHTMARE

COME THE END of the Cold War, triggered by the collapse of communism and the institutional demise of the Soviet Union in 1989, there was almost an audible global sigh of relief that the bad old days of mutually assured destruction, megatons and nuclear deterrence had wonderfully, miraculously, gone for ever. 'Peace in our time!' was enthusiastically and universally proclaimed – *this time*, at least.

In the ever more expensive East–West battle to maintain and enhance military capability, the wheezy and creaking centralised economy of the Soviet Union had finally collapsed into rusty bankruptcy, utterly crushed and defeated by the forces of capitalism and high-inflation technology. The guys wearing the white hats had won, using free market dollars to overcome President Ronald Reagan's 'evil empire', *spending* their way to a clean, bloodless victory. As night follows day, it was inevitable that Western politicians, particularly in finance ministries, immediately sharpened and honed their budgetary axes, seeking to slash military spending and divert the huge savings achieved into vote-winning social programmes: education, welfare, new hospitals and other forms of medical care. 'Where's the threat?' was their strident cry. 'Whom are our expensive armed forces defending us against *now*?' The much-trumpeted (but always illusory) 'Peace Dividend' appeared, mirage-like, at the top of the political agenda in the Western democracies.

But peace and international stability remained elusive. In reality, the world has become a more uncertain and more dangerous place – no doubt, much to the chagrin of many opportunistic and disingenuous politicians across Europe. International diplomacy and geopolitics has no real resemblance to a Hollywood epic where the hero rides off into the golden sunset, leaving peace, prosperity and goodwill behind him (or her) before the closing credits roll.

The rosy-glow illusion permeating Western capitals was steadily diffused by emerging fears about the threat of proliferation of weapons of mass destruction among so-called 'rogue states' first in the Middle East, later in the Far East. Initially, there was little real sense of urgency or even disquiet among many military planners or intelligence staffs. Some in Western Europe, perhaps driven by their political masters, were even in a state of denial. According to them, no such domestic threat existed or would exist; all such talk was mere posturing by the US military-industrial complex, a vain attempt to preserve defence budgets – or to maintain Washington's influence in European diplomacy.   Subconsciously, there was a rather smug underlying feeling that at least these existing or potential weapons represented only *regional* threats and Western targets were incapable of being attacked for at least a decade, maybe 15 years. The problem, it was firmly pointed out, was not in *our* backyard. And Micawber-like, there was a belief that 'something would turn up' to avert any future threat to national targets. The bluebirds would remain flying over the white cliffs of Dover.

There was little realisation that the poison of proliferation was spreading quickly and insidiously through the global veins, injected and accelerated by common strategic interests, political expediency or even simple, naked commercial advantage – mere cash in the bank. Inconveniently, WMD weapons systems, their technology and the associated expertise were (and are) being transferred from country to country in defiance of the mountains of paper prohibitions created by international treaties, conventions or diplomatic accords. Even the ignominious departure of the hard-pressed and diligent team of United Nations personnel that investigated the banned Iraqi nuclear, chemical, biological and ballistic missile programmes, (which conclusively demonstrated the bluntness of the verification sword as a weapon against proliferation), failed to push many panic buttons. That writing on the wall has yet to dry.

Concurrently, came a rash of brushfire wars, disfiguring Continental Europe and Africa – involving large-scale peacekeeping and humanitarian operations by cash-starved Western forces, operating in environments far removed from the plains and forests of Northern Europe that they were trained or equipped to fight in.* International peace and stability, begotten after decades of Cold War fear, suddenly looked a very sickly child indeed, even to politicians. The entrenched stability of confrontation between Eastern and Western power *blocs* was looked on with nostalgia by the military. As one heavily medalled Russian general told me: 'At least in the Cold War, we knew who the enemy was.'

Ironically, it was the collapse of the Soviet Union that created the most perceptible and immediate clear and present danger to Western populations and infrastructure, although again, there was little political will to act swiftly and effectively.

Suddenly, a new raft of countries, former republics within the Soviet Union became nuclear powers, legatees of Moscow's nuclear warheads stranded on their soil. Only concerted international persuasion and effort neutralised these weapons or had them returned to the Russian military. By the end of 1996, the last of the Soviet strategic nuclear warheads had been removed from Kazakstan, Ukraine and Belarus.

The very worst was yet to come: the unauthorised leakage of fissile material from the many weapon facilities within the old Soviet Union, to exchange for black market dollars and a potential brain drain of scientists equipped with the knowledge of nuclear weapons technology. The end of communist rule, economic and political chaos, and the cataclysmic decline of Moscow's armed forces brought anarchy to much of the institutional structure of the old empire. Quickly, assets, *any assets*, became targets for cash conversion. Crime, both organised and casual, mushroomed and prospered. Government failed to protect sensitive nuclear material because of funding shortages. Guards protecting facilities worth perhaps hundreds of millions of dollars are still paid the equivalent of just $70–$200 a month – and these are the officers. For them, the temptation must be great to resort to theft, despite the hazardous nature of the substances involved. The need to feed your family is a strong motivation and outweighs many risks unacceptable to those of us who are not starving, or constantly cold.

---

* Tanks, for example, are of little use militarily, except against other tanks, or over-running field fortifications. Counter-insurgency operations against nimble, shadowy targets on foot are *not* what they were designed for.

V. N. Obarevich, head of Russia's Nuclear Weapons Security Inspectorate, warned the Russian Duma (or parliament) in October 1996: 'I really can't imagine how people who work with nuclear weapons are managing to live, especially at the Ministry of Defence. People have no money. They do not have the means to live. A major who is going to be doing technical maintenance on nuclear munitions tomorrow is fainting from hunger today.' Despite some improvements in paying personnel, the temptations persist.   In 2000, Moscow's counter-intelligence directorate, the Federal Security Service (FSS), increased attempts to recruit informants inside the organisation responsible for nuclear weapons security and logistics, the 12th Main Directorate of the Ministry of Defence, GUMO (*Glavnoye upravleniye Ministerstvo oborony*). In 1997, the 12th GUMO closed a nuclear weapons facility because of hunger strikes by the workers. The CIA rates housing for the Directorate's personnel as 'of poor quality or non-existent'. The 12th GUMO's Chief of Staff says the organisation has 9,500 homeless active duty or retired officers.

Even today, many nuclear facilities in Russia have no detector system or security cameras to warn of the theft of weapons-grade uranium and plutonium – or of the weapons themselves. Around 70% of security devices at weapon facilities were reported worn out in 1999 and 20% had been working, unserviced, for two or three years. At other sites, in the recent past, alarm systems were non-operational because electricity supplies had been severed due to non-payment of bills.

Washington tried to tackle the problem through the ambitious Co-operative Threat Reduction Program, pouring dollars into Russia to improve security at nuclear installations. The Russians earmarked a total of 123 nuclear weapons and material storage sites for improvements to security. However, as of mid-2002, only work on 60 locations has been completed. The task is enormous.

No surprise then, that there have been a number of confirmed thefts of small quantities – up to 2½lbs each time – of weapons-grade material in the former Soviet Union which has an estimated 1,200 tons of excess Highly Enriched Uranium (HEU) and 170 tons of weapons-grade plutonium. The US National Intelligence Council reported in 2002 that 23 attempts to steal fissile material had been discovered and frustrated by Russian security forces during 1991–9.

In August 1994, 1¼lbs of MOX (used as fuel in light water reactors) was found on an airliner in Munich that had flown in from Moscow. It contained 12oz of plutonium probably produced in a Russian reprocessing plant. A tiny sample of 99% plutonium 239 was found near Konstanz on the Swiss border; more highly enriched than normally found in nuclear weapons, it probably originated in a Russian weapons research centre. Four years later, there was a conspiracy at part of the Chelyabinsk-65 complex (one of Russia's largest nuclear weapons production facilities) to steal more than 44lbs of HEU. The plant re-processes nuclear materials for weapons and also handles spent nuclear fuel. According to some reports, FSS agents arrested the thieves before they left the plant. Other sources say the material *was* stolen. Viktor Yeratsov, chief of the Ministry of Atomic Energy's Nuclear Materials Accounting and Control Department, is reported as saying that the amount lost was 'quite sufficient to produce an atomic bomb', although this seems unlikely with this quantity alone. The then Russian president, Boris Yeltsin, ordered a radical overhaul of security at the site, where more than 30 tons of weapons grade uranium is stored.

Add to this military nuclear material, the potential black-market value of radioactive devices used in industry or medicine, and a new, lucrative trans-national criminal trade emerges. In July 2002, Portuguese police arrested a man on charges of belonging to an international criminal syndicate engaged in the smuggling of HEU from eastern Europe, following a tip-off from French intelligence.

Who are the potential purchasers for this dangerous contraband?

Terrorists.

Or those states anxious to leapfrog the most difficult stages in the development of a crude nuclear weapon: acquisition of suitable fissile material.

The terrorists' reasoning is simple. Remember the fear of nuclear exchanges in the Cold War. Remember the environmental fears concerning nuclear power station safety. Nuclear material commands its own demonology in the public mind. There is a familiar lexicon of fear: radiation sickness; radioactive fallout; nuclear half-lives, denying life, occupation and prosperity to contaminated land for decades. We've all inherited these fearsome mantras from the days of the Cold War. Terrorists can harness and utilise the demoralising power of those old, chilling folk memories to further their objectives. Deploying fissile material provides a terrorist group or a small country with the ability to punch well above their weight and instantly achieve their desired horrific headlines or vastly increased political clout.

In November 2001, a Russian general reported two unsuccessful attempts by terrorist groups to break into military nuclear storage facilities. These incidents are not confined just to Russia: in Columbia, a small consignment of 66% enriched weapons-grade uranium was seized in 2001.

This all sounds alarmist, the stuff of nightmares. But it is clear that terrorists intend to use nuclear material to further their aims sometime in the future.

A US bipartisan panel warned in 2002: 'The most urgent unmet national security threat to the United States today is the danger that weapons of mass destruction of weapons-usable material in Russia could be stolen and sold to terrorists or hostile nation states.'

America's CIA, in February 2002, reported to Congress that Russian facilities housing nuclear weapons material 'typically receive low funding, lack trained security personnel, and do not have sufficient equipment for securely storing such material.'

The report said of thefts from Russian nuclear research institutions: 'We assess that undetected smuggling has occurred, although we do not know the magnitude of such thefts. Nevertheless we are concerned about the total amount of material that could have been diverted over the last 10 years.'

And of nuclear weapons facilities, the CIA told Congress: 'To secure their weapons, the Russians employ a multi-layered approach that includes physical, procedural and technical measures. The security system was designed in the Soviet era to protect weapons primarily against a threat from outside the country and may not be sufficient to meet today's challenge of a knowledgeable insider, collaborating with a criminal or terrorist group.'

Just 50 out of an estimated 650 tons of stockpiled nuclear materials have been safeguarded after more than a decade of Washington-sponsored programmes in Russia. The problem will get worse: as Moscow dismantles 2,000 strategic nuclear weapons each year from the current 7,000 level, the stockpile, however insecure, will grow ever greater. On top of this, as we have seen, the Soviet Union has accumulated HEU and plutonium to manufacture new nuclear weapons – enough for about 20,000 devices. More than 80lbs of weapons-grade material has been stolen over the last 10 years, although much of this has

happily been recovered, as in Tbilisi in October 2001, when the Geor-
gian State Security Ministry foiled a shipment of 23 containers of
stolen plutonium, valued at $65,000 to the smugglers. With money-
laundering, crime, narcotics, and donations amply supplying the ready
cash, many terrorist groups would be prepared to pay a large multiple
of this figure to get their hands on such a potent weapon.

One of the major problems is the determination of just how much
nuclear material is held. A nuclear worker in Podolsk managed to steal
3lbs of HEU over a protracted period because the amounts involved
fell within Moscow's approved 'acceptable' levels of loss or wastage –
so the missing fissile material initially went unnoticed. In 1994, the
USA removed 900lbs of HEU from Kazakstan in operation SAPPHIRE
but discovered this amount was 4% *above* declared inventory levels,
simply because the Soviet system routinely inflated holdings to cover
losses during processing.

So the international community can work together to make safe
nuclear material. In August 2002, a joint operation by the USA and
the Russian Federation secured 100lbs of HEU from the Vinca Institute of Nuclear Sciences in Belgrade, Yugoslavia. After more than a
year of negotiations with the Yugoslav government, the 6,000 ingots
were flown to Dimitrovgrad, 525 miles south-east of Moscow for
reprocessing into reactor fuel. Large areas of the Yugoslav capital were
sealed off by 1,200 armed troops as a convoy of three trucks shipped
the HEU the 22 miles from the Institute to the airport. Two of the
lorries were empty decoys. Police wearing gasmasks and carrying
automatic weapons guarded crossroads as the convoy drove through. A
senior Serbian police official said: 'We were vigilant and ready to cope
with any potential assailant.' The Yugoslav government commented:
'By disposing of the hazardous material, Vinca is no longer a potential
target for possible terrorist attempts to get hold of this fuel.' Hopefully, we shall see more of these multi-national operations to remove
the risk of nuclear material falling into the wrong hands.

According to US intelligence sources, the al-Qa'eda leader Osama
bin Laden's interest in acquiring the technology to build a crude
nuclear weapon dates back to the early 1990s. One of the four al-
Qa'eda members who bombed the US embassies in Kenya and
Tanzania in November 1998 claimed to have been paid $10,000 to
buy uranium from a former Sudanese army officer. Where this officer
obtained the material and whether it was weapons-grade remains

speculative and the report seems to carry little veracity.

What seems certain are bin Laden's ambitions to acquire nuclear weapons. In the summer of 2000, he allegedly had extensive discussions in Kabul with two Pakistani scientists (who had resigned from Islamabad's nuclear programme the year before), about nuclear, biological and chemical weaponry. Bin Laden apparently told them that he had access to radiological material acquired for him by the Islamic Movement of Uzbekistan, but the al-Qa'eda leader was told this could not be used to construct even a crude nuclear weapon. A few months later, a Russian Security Council official confirmed that a Taliban attempt to recruit a former Soviet nuclear weapons expert 'from a Central Asian state' had been foiled.

In October 2001, bin Laden told a Pakistani journalist: 'If America used chemical or nuclear weapons against us, then we may retort with chemical and nuclear weapons. We have the weapons as a deterrent.' He clearly understands the nuances of the language of deterrence, even if he has apparently failed to acquire or manufacture a nuclear weapon.

The world's arsenal of nuclear weapons remains large, even more than a decade after the Cold War ended. There are around 30,000 warheads or bombs held by the 'nuclear club' of the USA, Russia, China, the UK, France, Israel, Pakistan and India. A further 20,000 decommissioned tactical nuclear warheads are held by Russia in component form. In addition, stockpiles of separated plutonium and HEU – the essential building blocks of nuclear weapons – total around 450 tons of plutonium and more than 1,700 tons of HEU globally. On top of that there is more than three tons of HEU in research reactors in 43 nations. Reactor-grade plutonium is good enough to build crude but reliable explosive devices.

The only comforting thought is the level of expertise required to create a primitive nuclear weapon. You would need around 60lbs of highly enriched uranium or 19lbs of plutonium, as well as knowledge of quite complex physics, and sophisticated equipment, to trigger criticality and thus a nuclear explosion. Mohamed El Baradei, Director General of the United Nations' nuclear watchdog, the International Atomic Energy Authority (IAEA), says: 'While we cannot exclude the possibility that terrorists could get hold of some nuclear material, it is highly unlikely they could use it to manufacture and successfully detonate a nuclear bomb.' He adds, chillingly: 'Still, no scenario is impossible.'

Easier then, at least, from the technical point of view, is the theft of a ready-to-use nuclear weapon. Whilst it is the stuff of countless thriller novels and movies, this unfortunately, is not as far-fetched as it sounds.

There are disturbing but unsubstantiated reports of missing nuclear weapons from Russia, including the unresolved mystery of the lost 84 suitcase bombs disclosed by Alexander Lebed, one-time national security adviser under Boris Yeltsin, and the two tactical nuclear artillery shells with explosive power in the low-kiloton range that reportedly were sold by criminals to Iran in the early 1990s. In addition, there remain persistent reports of 23 low-yield nuclear warheads that went missing from a storage site at Komsomolskna-Amure in Siberia in March, 1992 and a further 12 nuclear artillery shells based with Soviet forces in the former East Germany, that were not located during the withdrawal of all such weapons from the Warsaw Pact nations in eastern Europe. The KGB, the Soviet era intelligence agency, is also believed to have held an unspecified number of tactical nuclear weapons, each weighing less than 100lbs, that were excluded from post-Cold War inventories of Moscow's nuclear arsenal. Just where are they now?

Russian officialdom strongly denies the *theft* of nuclear weapons. Since September 11, there has been a concerted public campaign by Moscow to offer reassurances about the security of Russian nuclear weapons and that terrorists have not acquired such weapons from Russian sources. General-Colonel Igor Valynkin, chief of the 12th GUMO, describes such allegations as 'barking mad'. He reiterated that nuclear warhead security personnel were subject to psychological, lie detector, drug and alcohol abuse testing. The Russian President, Vladimir Putin, said in November 2001 that he was 'absolutely confident' that terrorists in Afghanistan do not possess Soviet or Russian weapons of mass destruction. What are we to believe?

Outside Russia, in June 2002, there were unconfirmed reports of a Palestinian attempt to break into the Israeli nuclear weapons store two miles from Kefar Zecharia, a small village west of Jerusalem. This was not a plan to steal a warhead but for a suicide bomber to blow himself up outside the protective bunkers – a direct attack on Israeli military prestige. Winning headlines again.

The threat, while remaining remote, is being taken seriously. In the USA, the Defense Threat Reduction Agency launched a $20 million, one-year programme to evaluate commercial technology that can be used to detect or prevent 'unconventional attacks' against America. Despite the political furore over missile defence of the continental USA, the more immediate threat may come hidden in a freight container, or broken down in component parts in suitcases, ready for reassembly in some seedy apartment in the Bronx.

A more likely threat is the use by terrorists of nuclear waste material to stage a high-profile attack – with an impact far beyond the cost or difficulty of mounting the operation. Whilst by no means weapons of mass destruction, the impact of so-called 'dirty bombs' on public morale and confidence and government policy is wildly disproportionate to the small bang they would create.

The idea is chillingly simple. There is no need to master the complex physics of nuclear chain reaction. Merely wrap radioactive waste material around a conventional high explosive. Large quantities of both are not necessary. Hide the device within a high-profile target to achieve maximum effect. Detonation, by radio control, simple electric or clockwork timer, or booby-trap, scatters the radioactive material over the immediate area, not only denying it temporarily to the target's use – but also sowing demoralising panic among the population and creating maximum disruption to commercial and political life. Imagine the economic impact if such a device were to be exploded in or near the New York Stock Exchange. It is on these valuable and vital intangibles of life in a Western democracy that the effects of such a small device mimic the lethality of weapons of mass destruction.

The threat of 'dirty bombs' has already become very real. Chechen terrorists planted a canister of radioactive caesium 137 (used for calibration in the detection of flawed surfaces) strapped to a stick of dynamite in Moscow's Izmailovo Park in November 1995 as a 'demonstration shot' of their capability to disrupt life in the Russian capital. The device was not detonated and posed no public health risk as radiation levels were only between 10 and 50 millicuries. But the incident inevitably met its objective of hitting the headlines and provided no guarantees that more radioactive material could not be used in anger, in the future. The Iraqi dictator Saddam Hussein is claimed by US intelligence sources to have authorised experiments on this class of weapon in 1987, with three subsequent but unsuccessful tests of such devices. No doubt further development work by Baghdad has continued.

The concept of *radiological dispersal devices* is nothing new. It was well known to weapons developers in the 1940s. The MANHATTAN Project, for example, is believed to have investigated 'dirty' bombs as well as producing the atomic weapons dropped on the two Japanese cities. Up to 1954, the US Joint Chiefs toyed with the notion of using radiological weapons as an integral part of the defence of Western Europe, before finally discarding the idea.

For today's terrorist, the tactic is low-cost, low-risk and not difficult to achieve. Dirty bomb incidents should therefore be expected.

There was a great deal of officially generated excitement in the summer of 2002 over reports that the Islamic fundamentalist group al-Qa'eda were in the early stages of plans to explode a 'dirty' bomb in an American city, probably Washington DC, based, partly, on papers captured in Afghanistan after the Coalition war against the Taliban. US Attorney General John Ashcroft told reporters that the law enforcement agencies had 'disrupted an unfolding terrorist plot to attack the United States by exploding a radioactive dirty bomb.'

Although the briefings smacked more of the need to reawaken the American public to the continuing dangers of terrorist attack rather than a real threat, there seems little doubt that al-Qa'eda plans to build and deploy such a device, as a cheap and effective psychological weapon. According to CIA reports, bin Laden was present during a meeting in Afghanistan in early 2001, when a metal canister was produced, containing what was claimed to be radioactive material.

In the case publicised by the Bush administration, none of the radioactive material necessary to create the terror weapon had been obtained, intelligence sources suggest. US Defense Secretary Donald Rumsfeld claimed that a search of caves near the airport of the southern Afghan city of Kandahar, in December, had revealed material associated with weapons of mass destruction. There were unconfirmed reports of traces of non-weapons grade uranium 238 being found in a complex network of deep tunnels in the nearby Turnak Farms area.

Although it is believed al-Qa'eda *has* obtained small quantities of radioactive waste from Uzbekistan, one of the republics bordering Afghanistan, there would have been no need to take the risk of smuggling the radioactive waste into the USA – as this is already available inside the country.

The US's Nuclear Regulatory Commission (NRC) licenses 21,000 organisations in the USA that use 'millions' of radioactive devices for a host of legitimate purposes in industry, healthcare or for research purposes. It says that an average of 300 such radiation sources are lost, abandoned or stolen in America each year. The most common to go missing are isotopes of caesium, americium, iridium and cobalt, used in radiotherapy, and a host of industrial and agricultural processes. Each would be ideal for use in a terrorist dirty bomb.

According to the IAEA there have been 175 cases of trafficking in nuclear material since 1993 and 201 instances of smuggling other radioactive sources. Of these, just 18 have involved small amounts of HEU or plutonium – insufficient to make a nuclear device. A dedicated IAEA database, involving 69 countries, logged 63 cases in 2000, of which 75% involved criminal activity. It should be stressed that these figures relate to *seizures* or foiled attempts and provide little indication of the true size of the illicit trade. There seems little doubt that the business is increasing every year.

Of the total number of radiological material seizures, 16 have been made on Turkish soil. Turkey has become a focal point of the nuclear smuggling network, as it is positioned at the crossroads between Western Europe and the republics of the former Soviet Union – Georgia, Azerbaijan, Kazakstan and Russia – where much of the contraband originates. Most of the arrested smugglers prove to be amateurs, uncertain both of the potential market and the nature of the substances they are smuggling. Much of the material is passed on to dealers in Istanbul, who, using the city's reputation as an international trading centre, canvass prospective purchasers. Some seized by Turkish customs has proved to be red mercury – osmium – as part of a fraud, frequently perpetrated on the smugglers themselves.

Material stolen in Kazakstan is brought to Turkey by sea from Romania and Bulgaria for onward shipment, also probably by boat. The USA has provided radiation detection equipment and training to border guards in how to find and identify hidden nuclear material. Turkey has installed 14 radiation detection systems at six land border gates and one airport and 55 hand-hand detectors have been distributed to other border posts in the east and south-east of the country, but this is clearly not enough by itself to defeat the smugglers.

Guarding radioactive material is a daunting task – just because of the sheer scale of the problem. There has been a six-fold increase in the amount of nuclear material, used for peaceful purposes such as power generation, since 1970. The IAEA estimates there are 438 nuclear power reactors and 651 others used for research purposes, of which 284 are operational. There are also 250 fuel cycle plants, including uranium mills and plants that convert, enrich, store and process nuclear material. On top of all this, of course, are the tens, perhaps hundreds of thousands of radiation sources used in everyday life. These are not subject to the same levels of security as found in military facilities or nuclear power stations. Abel Gonzalez, IAEA Director of Radiation and Waste Security, says: 'There are few security precautions on radiotherapy equipment and a large source could be removed quite easily, especially if those involved have no regard for their own security. Moreover, in many countries, the regulatory oversight of radiation sources is weak. As a result, an undetermined number of radioactive sources has become orphaned of regulatory control and their location is unknown.'

He adds: 'Certainly the effect of a dirty bomb would not be devastating in terms of human life, but contamination in even small quantities could have major psychological and economic effects.'

A study, published in the *Journal of the Federation of American Scientists,* investigated three imaginary scenarios involving radiological dispersal devices against American civilian targets. The first theoretical weapon was exploded in downtown Washington, using a stolen medical measurement device containing caesium, jacketed by 10lbs of TNT. Whilst the radioactive material would have proved relatively harmless immediately, there was a longer-term effect of increased cancer risks to those in the vicinity, if the area was not properly decontaminated.

The second envisaged using cobalt stolen from a food irradiation plant in a dirty bomb exploded in Manhattan, eventually scattering a footprint of radioactive material perhaps 600 square miles in extent, depending on wind strengths and other weather conditions. The study predicted that residents could have an extra one in 100 chance of suffering some form of cancer through this residual radiation.

The third scenario involved the use of an isotope of americium used by oil exploration companies in prospecting in a bomb detonated by just 1lb of TNT. Here, a mile-long strip of buildings would have to be evacuated within just half an hour. The US National Council on Radiation and Protection and Measurements says the contamination in such attacks would be 'catastrophic but manageable'.

A graphic real-life illustration of the potential effects of a terrorist dirty bomb incident occurred accidentally in September 1987, in the major Brazilian city of Goiânia. Scavengers broke into an abandoned radiology clinic and stole a caesium 137 source. Junkyard workers broke open the casing and cut up the 20-gram capsule of radioactive material into pieces for resale as scrap metal. They distributed their loot among friends and families throughout Goiânia. The result? Fourteen people were overexposed to radiation and 249 contaminated. Four subsequently died. More than 110,000 people had to be continuously monitored. The clean-up operation involved filling 125,000 drums and 1,470 boxes with contaminated material – clothing, furniture and soil – and burying it safely. Eighty-five houses had to be demolished.

This was an accident, caused by desperate poverty and blind ignorance. But the IAEA's Gonzalez warns that the September 11 attack on US targets demonstrated that terrorists no longer prize survival in planning and mounting attacks. 'The deadliness of handling intensely radioactive material can no longer be seen as an effective deterrent.' Martyrdom continues to appeal to the true fanatic.

IAEA experts believe the primary risks to nuclear power plants involve theft or diversion of nuclear material from the facility, or, just as frightening, a physical attack or act of sabotage designed to cause an uncontrollable release of radioactivity to the environment. The US NRC has calculated that in a worst-case scenario, sabotage of a nuclear plant could cause more than 100,000 deaths from dispersal of intensely radioactive material.

Western nuclear power stations are designed to be robust, able to withstand earthquakes, tornado-force winds and accidental crashes by *light* aircraft on top of the reactor. But the September 11 attacks on the World Trade Center and the Pentagon dramatically changed officialdom's perception of potential threat. The extent of damage caused by the deliberate crash of a large, fully fuelled airliner into a reactor or other nuclear facilities is still being analysed by experts in the world's atomic energy authorities. Designs differ from country to country: some would be able to withstand such an onslaught better than others. Security measures to protect such facilities also vary: the French government, for example, has positioned mobile Crotale surface-to-air missile batteries outside the perimeter of its Cogema nuclear site at La Hague, near Cherbourg. In Russia, heavily armed Interior Ministry troops patrol the perimeter of nuclear power stations.

However, the terrorist threat to nuclear power stations does not require the sophisticated planning and execution of a reprise of the September 11 attacks. In the USA, the NRC requires that the 104 operational nuclear power plants should be protected against three types of terrorist attacks under its so-called Design Basis Threat – by a small highly trained group, assisted by information provided by an accomplice within the complex; by a single insider acting alone, or finally, by using a four-wheel drive vehicle packed with explosives – the 'truck bomb'.

Defences are tested once every eight years at each US site, using a force of mock intruders. According to the pressure group, Union of Concerned Scientists, before 1998, at 27 out of 57 sites examined, there were 'significant weaknesses' in security that would have put the nuclear reactor in jeopardy in a real attack. Similar tests in 2000–2001 have seen the simulated disabling of enough equipment to damage reactors at six out of 11 site evaluations. Remedial action has now been taken at all these sites.

At least in the USA and in most Western European countries, armed guards protect the power plants. This is not the case in Japan and some other countries where response by civilian armed police within 10–15 minutes is seen as adequate protection. In an IAEA research project, not one out of six unnamed countries responded had plans for countering a 'truck bomb' attack on a nuclear power station or for dealing with widespread radioactive contamination outside the installation's immediate area. Four nations, however, ranked 'armed attack by outlaw, terrorist or military unit' as the most likely sabotage threat to their nuclear plants.

Yet, terrorist threats or attempts to damage or penetrate nuclear reactors have been reported to the IAEA, in Western Europe, in Argentina, Lithuania, South Korea and South Africa. In 1998, Italian police detained criminals trying to sell 19.9% enriched uranium, apparently stolen from a reactor in the Republic of the Congo.

After all this, it comes as no surprise then, that some governments are belatedly building contingency plans for disasters involving nuclear accidents or incidents triggered by terrorists. In Britain, a nuclear police force, the Civil Nuclear Constabulary has been pro-posed, particularly to guard shipments of nuclear waste. Currently, the armed UK Atomic Energy Authority Constabulary is responsible for security of civilian nuclear materials and sites and new anti-terrorist legislation, introduced in the wake of September 11, enables them to mount patrols and stop-and-search operations up to three miles from nuclear sites as well as to arrest terrorists who have snatched nuclear materials at ports and airports. In case the worst happens in the UK, government stockpiles of anti-radiation pills have been hurriedly increased – but these potassium iodate tablets only protect the thyroid gland from the effects of radioactive iodine if taken within four hours of contamination.

The G8 nations agreed at their summit in Alberta, Canada, in June 2002 to assign $20 billion for the disposal of Russian weapons-grade uranium and plutonium over the next decade to minimise the proliferation problem or prevent such material falling into terrorist hands. Concurrently, Washington has agreed to buy 500 tons of Russian HEU for $12 billion over the same period through the USA Enrichment Corporation. A US-funded computer system to handle reporting of nuclear material inventory for the Russian Ministry of Atomic Energy has become operational to help track movement or check holdings. The USA has also paid for a new state-of-the-art fissile material storage facility at Mayak in the southern Ural mountains to hold 66 tons of plutonium and HEU from dismantled nuclear weapons. A second, similar site is being considered.

Is this all too little, too late? Despite the Convention of Physical Protection of Nuclear Material (which came into force on February 8, 1987, and is now signed by 81 countries) and a myriad of other agreements and international initiatives, there seems little reason to be optimistic that terrorist groups have not or will not get their hands on some kind of nuclear material to use as a primitive weapon, or at the least destructive end of the scale, a dirty bomb. There also remains the very real possibility of deliberate sabotage of a nuclear facility and the risk, subsequently, of some measure of radioactive contamination.

Some Western intelligence analysts believe it is entirely plausible that coupled with the potential growth of nuclear weapon capability among the so-called rogue states, this unhappy situation of leakage of fissile material, predominantly from nations of the former Soviet Union, may well result in the detonation of a small nuclear or radioactive device in Europe or the USA some time within the next decade. The prospect is horrific but must be confronted.

Of course, such an event is difficult to predict precisely as to timing or location or, indeed, who would be responsible. As Sir Stephen Lander, until recently director general of Britain's Security Service, MI5, says: 'Intelligence is about security information others wish to keep secret — 100% success is never achieved.' He adds: 'If you expect 100% success, you are living in cloud cuckoo land.' Those who believe intelligence should be able to stop every terrorist attack 'hadn't been paying attention'.

The nuclear genie cannot be squeezed back in the regulatory bottle. Only a feeble-minded politician would think otherwise. Today's reality is, in many ways, more frightening than the old East–West nuclear confrontation. Those who may arm themselves with the weapon of radioactivity today have radically different and more unpredictable motives than the member states of the 'nuclear club', who have developed their own nuclear weapons and are bound by some, at least, of the accepted diplomatic and political conventions.

Despite all our best hopes, the end of the nuclear nightmare was mere illusion. It should now loom larger in our daylight fears than ever it did in the latter, stable, days of the Cold War.

CHAPTER 9
MAN'S INHUMANITY TO MAN –
CHEMICAL WEAPONS

AROUND FIVE O'CLOCK ON the evening of April 22, 1915
French soldiers and their colonial brothers-in-arms, the
Zouave and Turco troops of the Algerian Division, were
manning their muddy trenches in the Ypres salient, between Lange-
marck and Bixschoote in Belgium. Their sentries saw a strange dense
green, almost iridescent, cloud silently emerge from the German positions facing them and roll inexorably across the short distance of no
man's land between the frontlines. Some believed the enemy trenches
had caught fire. The solution to the mystery was all too quick to
follow.

Moments later, the curiosity of the watching soldiers, huddled
below their firing step, instantly changed to an unbearable suffering,
coupled with a terror and panic unknown to war. The French trenches
were suddenly full of soldiers collapsing in violent spasms, coughing
blood, their lungs burning as the linings of these organs were ruthlessly stripped away. Some drowned, froth-mouthed, in the fluid
created in their lungs. Others suffered uncontrollable vomiting as the
thick cloud of acrid gas crept further into the defences and settled low
in the dugout shelters. Those still able, staggered away.

Behind the deadly green fog advanced a mass of armed men, their
faces obscured by gauze or cotton masks, their rifles, with bayonets
fixed, held at the ready, or even casually slung over their shoulders. The
German officers belaboured the backs of some of their men with the
flat edge of their sword blades, urging ever more speed in the advance
across the Allied positions. They met no resistance. There were few left
alive in the frontline to offer any. On the first day of the dreadful

second battle of Ypres, chemical warfare had been added to the daily, brutal horrors of the First World War's Western Front.

The German's 35th Pioneer Regiment, wearing miners' Draeger breathing sets, improvised as gas masks, had spannered open the valves of 5,730 large and small cylinders of chlorine stacked along the parapets of their trenches, releasing 168 tons of the gas in just six to eight minutes, allowing the fresh north wind that evening to blow death and suffering briskly towards the French lines. With Teutonic efficiency, the release was codenamed DISINFECTION, and it certainly and cruelly cleansed their enemy's trenches of any opposition.

An eye-witness testified:

> No human courage could face such a peril ... There staggered into our midst French soldiers, blinded, coughing, chests heaving, faces an ugly purple colour, lips speechless with agony and behind them in the gas-soaked trenches, we learned that they had left hundreds of dead and dying comrades. It was the most fiendish, wicked thing I have ever seen.

Chlorine asphyxiates its victims, inducing chronic bronchitis and suffocation from the mucous and watery fluid the afflicted lungs create. Many of those gassed subsequently died from pneumonia. Will Irwin, the *New York Tribune*'s correspondent on the Western Front, wrote on April 25:

> The effects of the noxious trench gas seems to be slow in wearing away. The men come out of their nausea in a state of utter collapse. Some of the rescued have already died from the after-effects. How many of the men left unconscious in the trenches when the French broke died from the fumes it is impossible to say, since those trenches were at once occupied by the Germans.

But company roll calls after the survivors painfully regrouped indicated that around 5,000 French and Algerian soldiers had died, with similar numbers rendered feeble casualties by the gas. Two thousand more were taken prisoner. More than 50 guns were captured. But although they had smashed the Allies' frontline along a four-mile wide strip of trenches, the Germans failed to exploit the tactical surprise of the gas attack, mainly because of their lack of reserve troops to follow up and consolidate the break-through. They had not anticipated or planned for such a success. The next day they twice attacked Canadian positions with chlorine, but the wind was not favourable and the defences grimly held on in furious fighting, despite heavy losses to the defenders – 5,975 casualties, 1,000 of them killed in action.

Ypres was not the first time the Germans had experimented with chemical warfare. (That is all it was in the minds of the High Command – purely an experiment.) On October 27, 1914 the Germans fired 3,000 105mm artillery 'T- shells' containing the lung irritant dianisidine chlorosulfate at the British lines near Neuve Chapelle, between Béthune, Fleurbaix and Armentières, in north-west France. There was no discernable effect, probably because the shells' explosives destroyed the chemical agent. Three months later, on January 30, 1915 their 9th Army used a liquid irritant or tear gas – xylyl bromide – in a barrage of 18,000 150mm artillery shells fired at the Russian lines along the Rawka and Bzura rivers during the battle of Bolimov in present-day Poland. The weapon also proved a failure because an errant wind blew the fumes back towards the German lines and the extreme cold also prevented the gas vaporising. (Later, bromo-acetone was added to counteract the freezing temperatures.)*

The First World War German army may later have congratulated itself on discovering a new type of weapon to break the hideous, bloody stalemate of trench warfare – and later be internationally vilified for their first use of this weapon of mass destruction – but such plaudits, or indeed recriminations, may not be totally justified.

There is nothing new under the sun, and chemical warfare is no different from any other innovation. Thucydides records the use of an arsenic smoke by Spartan forces against the defenders of Delium, an Athenian city in 423 BC, during the 25-year Peloponnesian War. Its effectiveness is not recorded. During China's Sung Dynasty (AD 960–1279) similar smoke was used by Imperial Chinese forces. Two hundred years later, invading Turks were defeated near Belgrade, reportedly by the use of rags dipped in some kind of poison, that were then set ablaze to create toxic fumes. In 1591, Germans burned a mixture of shredded cattle horns, and hooves with a gum resin to create a foul stench to disrupt advancing enemy formations. But in the moralistic 19th century, objections to the use of poison in war were

* The Germans used 263 tons of chlorine against Russian forces at Bolimov in May 1915, causing well over 1,000 casualties.

already emerging. On April 24, 1863 the US President, Abraham Lincoln, signed the US War Department's General Orders 100 stating that the 'use of poison in any manner, be it to poison wells, or food, or arms, is wholly excluded from modern warfare. He that uses it puts himself out of the pale of the law and usages of law.'

Even in the First World War, the Germans could point to earlier (but low-key) Allied use of chemical agents in their munitions. The French introduced rifle grenades, called *cartouches suffocantes*, filled with liquid ethyl bromo-acetate, another tear gas that affected the nose, eyes and throat, used in the first battles of the conflict in the autumn of 1914. In February 1915, the French had produced a variant, the *grenades suffocantes*. Both weapons were less than effective. The Germans subsequently cited these weapons to justify their deployment of chlorine.

The British too had tinkered with chemical munitions, although they had not used them in combat. Official British Army documents record experiments in 1903–1913 with a range of lachrymators, or tear gases – methyl-idoacetate and benzyl bromide (later used by the Germans in 1915) – which caused temporary blindness and inflammation to the nose and throat. These chemical compounds are the ancestors of today's riot gases used by police and security forces the world over to quell troublesome crowds.

British experiments were restarted in March–August 1914 with other lachrymators, such as mono-chloroacetone and methyl-idoacetate (again) but the results were officially reported to be 'unfavourable'. The Army and Navy, in their own self-satisfied demonstration of moral righteousness, rejected the use of shells containing tear gases at the end of September and on October 16, the War Office formally decided that international convention barred the use of chemical munitions. Their deployment was somehow not gentlemanly, certainly not *British*.

There were already several agreements in force covering the use of poison gases that could be cited by a smart government lawyer. Indeed, as far back as 1675, a Franco-German bilateral accord, signed in Strasbourg, banned the use of poisoned bullets. Two centuries later, fifteen European states met in Brussels on July 27, 1874 on the initiative of Czar Alexander II of Russia, to discuss, in a chivalrous way, the future conduct and regulation of war by their armies. The subsequent declaration's article 13 not only forbade the 'employment of poison or poisoned weapons' but also 'arms, projectiles or material *calculated to cause unnecessary suffering*.' Later, the First Hague Convention of July 29 1899 on the Laws and Customs of War had, in Article 23, prohibited the use of projectiles that disseminated 'asphyxiating or deleterious gases'. (Deleterious? No doubt a carefully chosen, polite, diplomatic word that hides the abominable effects of gas warfare.) The agreement especially included a declaration by the contracting powers to abstain from use of poison. A second Hague Convention, in 1907, reaffirmed the prohibition.   But such agreements were unenforceable, were couched in imprecise language and therefore open to different inter-pretations. The Germans claimed, for example, that their use of cylinders to disseminate chlorine was *not* covered by the terms of the 1899 Convention, because this only mentioned projectiles.

After the commencement of European hostilities in August 1914, the issue of chemical warfare would not go away for the British. On December 3, 1914 General Fowke, the Engineer-in-Charge to the British Armies in France, inquired whether 'stink bombs' (which sound more like a schoolboy prank than a weapon of war) could be employed against the Germans on the Western Front, already trapped in the attrition of trench warfare. Work finally started in England, with the patriotic assistance of the chemical sub-committee of the Royal Society, the country's premier scientific organisation, on providing 'offensive (lachrymatory or irritant) *but non-poisonous* compounds for use in stink pots'.   During January–March 1915, various chemicals were investigated in field trials and ethyl-idoacetate, called SK, selected. Production began at the Cassel Cyanide works, 'though no decision as to its use had been made either at the Front or at the War Office', according to army documents preserved in the Public Record Office in Kew, south London.

The first 24 hours of the second battle of Ypres changed all that. The following day, April 23, Sir John French, commander-in-chief of the British Armies in France, signalled Lord Kitchener, the British War Minister in Whitehall, requesting an 'effective means of retaliation'. Twenty-four hours later, Kitchener condemned the German use of chlorine in a speech in the House of Commons and, it transpired, 'the employment of similar weapons by our troops was thereupon decided.'

Deciding something and implementing that decision are two very different actions. The British were clearly caught wrong-footed by the

German use of a poison gas in war. The secret report on the activities of the British 'Special Brigade' – the army's rather prissy euphemism for gas offensive troops – written after hostilities ended, said:

> Owing to the backward state of the chemical industry in the United Kingdom before the war, chlorine was the only gas available when it was decided to resort to gas reprisals on the enemy. Although it is easy to extemporise protection against it, chlorine is by no means ineffective as a battle gas: the output in June, 1915 was, however, very limited and the existing plant had to be expanded and suitable receptacles, discharge pipes, etc. designed and manufactured.
>
> Moreover, the subject of gas warfare had not been previously studied [*sic*] nothing was known of the enemy's system of discharge, and no experimental ground was available; nor was there time for experimental work to be undertaken before the machinery of the new department had to be put in motion.

The British war machine kicked into top gear to find the elusive reprisal weapons. There is a sense, gleaned from surviving army documents of the time, of an official desperation to find effective noxious substances, *any* noxious substances, which could be used against the enemy. Moral righteousness had given way to practicality through *force majeure* on the battlefield.

The first British experiment with chlorine in cylinders was speedily arranged on May 13 near Runcorn, Lancashire, with successful large-scale trials following on June 4. On May 4, a naval committee was formed to consider both offensive and defensive gas warfare and a Lieutenant Brock suggested 'Jellite' – a hideous cocktail of prussic acid, chloroform and five per cent triacetyl cellulose, a chemical agent subsequently recommended by the group. (A factory was to be built at Stratford, in east London, by the Admiralty to produce this chemical agent.) Six days later, as a temporary measure, grenades containing sulphur dioxide and carbon bisulphide with a small quantity of capsicine were produced and several thousand despatched to the Western Front. However, the 'grenades were found to be unsatisfactory and manufacture was stopped in the beginning of June at the request of the commander-in-chief.'

The first 12 gallons of SK were produced by May 21 and used to fill glass bulbs held inside tin-cased grenades. These were rushed to

France. At the same time, the use of hydrogen sulphide, with its characteristic bad egg stench, was first suggested and 'the necessary preliminary experiments put in hand' at Hednesford, Staffordshire, with 'satisfactory results'.

In France, as an emergency protective measure, British troops were issued with pads of cotton or flannel and instructed to urinate upon them. (One wonders how the government chemists discovered this stopgap solution.) The soldiers were told the impregnated fabric should be held to the mouth and nose during chlorine attacks to neutralise the effects of the gas. The improvised masks were only partially successful as concentrations of gas soon overwhelmed them and there was no protection provided for the eyes.

But the soldiers' commanders were more interested in aggressive, attacking warfare. On June 16, the War Office in London received

> further urgent demands from Sir John French for offensive gas appliances in the form of cylinders, grenades, shell and trench mortar bombs. Sir John was insistent that adequate means of retaliation should be available as soon as possible.

Three days later a conference was held at Boulogne, on the French coast, between General Ivor Phillips, from the British Ministry of Munitions, and Colonel. Charles Foulkes and a Colonel Cummins from the War Office's newly set-up offensive and defensive gas departments respectively. They decided to investigate phosgene, or carbonyl chloride, an asphyxiate gas, twice as toxic as chlorine, with frequently fatal consequences for its victims. On August 30 the decision to produce phosgene in the UK was taken. Any remaining British scruples over the use of lethal gases on the battlefield were disappearing fast.

Meanwhile, the Special Brigade, hastily made up of civilian technical experts and men drawn from the infantry battalions in the line to provide vital experience of war in the trenches, was undergoing intensive training. Just seven weeks after the unit's formation, the first British offensive use of chlorine gas, released from 5,500 cylinders, came on September 25, 1915, at the battle of Loos. The result was less than satisfactory, triggering a persistent belief among British troops on the Western Front that their gas, as a weapon, was ineffective.

On the day, a sudden shift in the wind direction blew the chlorine across the British trenches. The dry, reassuring words of officialdom later described the botched attack by the hapless four companies of the Special Brigade:

> The number of discharge pipes was insufficient, only two being available for each emplacement, so that they had to be connected to one cylinder after another during the discharge, a procedure which resulted in a certain amount of leakage.
>
> Further escapes of gas were caused by the intense hostile artillery retaliation provoked, while in the northern part ... the direction of the wind was unfavourable and although cylinders were turned off a few seconds after they had been opened, some of the bays [of the British trenches] were flooded with gas.
>
> In the medical return of gas casualties no distinction was made at that period between casualties caused by our own and hostile gas.
>
> [A total of] 2,911 total gas casualties among 13 divisions were reported for the period September 25–October 14 1915, during which three gas attacks were made on wide fronts; of these about 550 were definitely attributed to the enemy's gas shells and it is certain that this figure is an underestimate ... The accidental casualties probably totalled about 2,000, of which 10 died from gas poisoning (including three of the gas personnel). It is clear from the reports that the great bulk of the cases were extremely mild and only 55 were definitely described as severe ...I have taken the opportunity of reproducing these figures in some detail because an erroneous impression existed at the time as to our own gas losses.

After Loos, the 'method of releasing the gas was considerably improved by the introduction of rubber piping' and a number of smaller attacks were mounted by the British during the autumn and winter of 1915 and the early months of the following year.

In January 1916, the General Staff abandoned chemical grenades 'as the fillings so far supplied were not considered sufficiently effective to be of military value.' In plain language, they were not lethal enough – or failed even to disable the adversary. Phosgene was now adopted as Britain's prime battle gas but there were continual and intransigent problems in its production at the United Alkali Company, the main manufacturer.

In stark contrast to the unseemly British scramble for chemical weapons, Germany, with a more extensive and developed chemical industry, continued   calmly to experiment with different chemical munitions to find the most effective. They maintained a clear techno-logical lead in gas warfare over the Allies throughout the remainder of hostilities. The so-called 'father' of German gas warfare was Fritz Haber, (1868–1934), of the then Kaiser Wilhelm Institute, who was to receive the Nobel chemistry prize in 1918 for his work on the complex fixation of nitrogen from the air. It was this 'approachable and courteous' man (in the words of the Nobel Foundation), doubtless a patriot, who convinced a sceptical German High Command of the potential military value of chemical weapons.

Haber also evaluated phosgene as a weapon. This is a high-density gas with a smell that resembles wet and decaying hay or grain cereals, which insidiously attacks the target's lungs. In concentrated form, it creates a sense of shock and a feeling of tightening in the chest for the victim, but these sensations happily quickly pass off. The relief is short-lived, however. It is only later that the true appalling damage to the lungs becomes apparent and, like chlorine, the resultant fluid finally chokes or asphyxiates the tortured casualty. On May 31, 1915 Haber supervised the first phosgene gas attack, totalling 220 tons, on the Eastern Front against massed Russian conscripts, causing heavy casu-alties in the frontline trenches. But some resistance continued and the attackers were forced to retreat to their own lines.

The French, as well as the British, continued to suffer casualties from German gas attacks and sought to blunt the sharpness of this new weapon of war by interdicting its source – the manufacturing plants. During 1915, a squadron of French open-cockpit Voisin 8 light bombers made a daring daylight attack on a gas-making factory just over the border at Ludwigshafen am Rhein, each dropping its load of 368lb bombs on the plant.

The Germans deployed phosgene against the British on December 9, 1915, again at Ypres, in conjunction with chlorine. By this time, however, the newly created secret chemical warfare station at Porton Down in Wiltshire had developed the 'gas helmet', a crude and claus-trophobic sack-like mask of heavy flannel, chemically impregnated with glycerin and sodium thiosulfate to neutralise chlorine, that was pulled over the entire head. Vision was through two dim celluloid disks serving as eyepieces. As well as badly impaired vision and uncomfortable heat, the hoods induced a feeling of isolation among soldiers. More than 2,000,000 of these had been quickly manufactured and sent to France. Later that year, the 'PH Helmet', with more enduring chemical protection and a spoon-like rubber tube as a mouthpiece with an expiratory valve, was developed which provided some protection against phosgene.

The British had to wait until July 1, 1916 before they had enough supplies of this latest war gas to retaliate in kind. Again there were self-inflicted casualties, amounting to around 14% of total personnel deployed, among the Special Brigade releasing the gas:

> ... largely owing to the danger of the new gas (the full effects of which were not then known) and disregard of precautions other than those which had been found sufficient when handling chlorine.

Poison gas came into its own during the almost suicidal German attacks on the double ring of 20 large French fortresses surrounding the garrison town of Verdun. The main attack began on February 21 1916 with a nine-hour artillery bombardment by 850 guns using phosgene shells. The bitter fighting continued day after day and included the use of the even more lethal diophosgene (tri-chlormethylchloroformate, or superpalite) on June 22, wiping out many of the defending French artillery and the horses that pulled the gun carriages. In planning the offensive, the German High Command had deliberately sought to make their French enemy *weissbuten* ('bleed to death') and the total casualties (dead, missing and wounded) of more than 750,000 for both sides during the 10-month battle reflected the appalling intensity of the struggle. Certainly, the use of gas placed intolerable strains on the already over-burdened French military medical system.

Poison gas and other chemical munitions by now formed a common component of artillery barrages to suppress enemy opposition. By the end of hostilities in 1918, one in every four shells fired contained a filling of a chemical warfare agent. In addition, the British sought a better method of releasing gas from trenches rather than the risky and, as we have seen, sometimes unreliable cylinders that sometimes totalled 20,000, massed along the frontline trenches,* causing huge logistic problems. This methodology was particularly susceptible to unpredictable changes in wind direction – with dire consequences. Official Army documents detail one of these 'serious accidents', on

---

* The British used a total of 87,968 cylinders of gas in attacks in the First World War.

September 1, 1916, opposite Messines:

> The cloud blew over part of the front of discharge for a few minutes. Although precautions to prevent crowding of the trenches had been taken, about 200 casualties resulted among the infantry, of whom 19 died.

One way to overcome this problem was to ensure the gas was discharged only *over* enemy trenches. The gung-ho Captain William Livens developed the first trench projector, proposing it to the War Office in the autumn of 1916. This was merely a metal smoothbore pipe, less than 4ft long and 8in in diameter, the bottom end buried in the mud and pointed at the enemy lines at an angle of 45°. They were normally positioned in banks of 200 to 800 and to fire them, propellant charges in each pipe's base were ignited electrically. The 30lb drums were fitted with small explosive charges to burst the container when they hit their target. The projector was rushed into production and first used to lob 2,268 drums of gas during the battle of Arras, on April 4, 1917 creating, at range of less than a mile, a dense concentration of liquid phosgene in a very localised area. Throughout the war, the British 'Special Brigade' fired a total of 196,940 projector drums, with the largest single discharge occurring on March 21, 1918 when 3,728 were fired into the French town of Lens and its outskirts. The War Office believed that overall, the Germans lost one man from every five drums fired compared to one from every cylinder discharged. They estimated enemy mortality at 25% of total gas casualties.*

In operations, even the cheap but impressive Livens projector had its problems, either from the drums falling wide as they tumbled slowly through the air, or from them prematurely bursting in the trench before being fired. The latter type of incident occurred about 30 times, causing 29 fatalities amongst friendly troops.

As the war progressed, both sides developed new and yet more horrific war gases.

France and Britain produced so-called blood agents, intended to inhibit or block the victim's vital, life-supporting absorption of

---

*An optimistic estimate. The true figure was 4.7%. The British Army, in reviewing its own gas casualties estimated an average 24% death rate from cloud gas attacks in 1915–16; 6% from gas shell bombardments in 1916–17 and 3.5% from the same method of attack in 1917–18, indicating the increasing effectiveness of protective measures.

oxygen through the blood. These gases were deadly in enclosed spaces such as field fortifications but were less effective in the open air. French forces used shells filled with hydrogen cyanide, or 'Vincennite' and cyanogen chloride in 1916, the latter gas much more dense, enabling it to maintain persistent lethal concentrations over its target. The British also sought to penetrate enemy soldiers' gas masks through the use of arsenic smokes, called DA, which was cleared for use as an offensive weapon, on June 28, 1914.

In humane terms, perhaps the worst was mustard gas, or dichlorethylsulphide (sulphur mustard) so-called because of its smell, like mustard or garlic, used by Germany against British forces for the first time on the night of July 12–13, 1917, at Ypres. This oily, yellow-to-brown fluid is a vesicant or blistering agent, producing large painful burn-like blisters wherever and whenever it comes into contact with skin, even seeping through the thick cloth of uniforms. Gas masks could provide protection only to the eyes and lungs. As a slowly vapor-ising liquid, mustard gas persisted in puddles, on the ground or on foliage for several days and could be easily transferred to the bodies of the unwary days after an attack. It was toxic in concentrations that could not be detected by smell. It could freeze and still be effective, once thawed out. It remained potent, mixed in concrete, even after 25–30 years. As we shall see, it remains harmful even after more than half a century on the seabed.

Major Harry Gilchrist, medical director of the Gas Service for the American Expeditionary Force after the USA's entry into the war in April 1917, wrote of its symptoms:

> At first the troops didn't notice the gas and were not uncomfortable but in the course of an hour or so, there was marked inflammation of the eyes. They vomited and there was erythema [reddening] of the skin. Actually the first cases were diagnosed as scarlet fever. Later there was severe blister-ing ... especially where the uniform had been contaminated and by the time the gassed cases reached the casualty clearing stations, the men were virtually blind and had to be led about, each man holding on to the man in front with an orderly in the lead.

Although its effects were not immediate, it was a militarily useful weapon for three reasons. Firstly its use could create 'gas barriers' - areas of ground denied to an enemy because of the effects of mustard

gas on unprotected troops, useful to prevent the use of road communications, billeting areas, artillery positions, or to halt an advance.
Secondly, the horrific blisters could incapacitate large numbers of
enemy forces and saturate their medical services very quickly, each
casualty having to be evacuated by the able-bodied. One mustard
casualty could contaminate an ambulance or a dugout shelter. Finally,
the war gas had a powerful psychological impact on the morale of
enemy forces because of the agony of the afflicted and the horror,
amongst comrades, of the sight of wounds it caused. Soldiers began to
endure the psychological problems of 'gas fright'.

In the six weeks following its first use by the Germans, the British
army alone suffered more than 9,000 casualties from mustard gas. In a
'very secret' report on British casualties after the conclusion of hostilities, a British Army medical officer was clinical in his assessment of
mustard gas:

> Mustard gas has proved by far the most effective as a means of producing
> material casualties, i.e. casualties who remain unfit for duty for a consider-
> able time, though the mortality among these casualties is low. Any failure
> in anti-gas discipline resulted, however, not only in an undue number of
> casualties but also in a great increase in the severity of the cases and in the
> mortality.
>
> It has proved possible by careful measures to get 75% of the mustard gas
> cases fit for duty within two months, but, in practice, this period has been
> nearly always exceeded and the invaliding power of mustard gas was there-
> fore very considerable.

Inevitably, both sides came to use this blistering agent by the end of
the conflict. On July 27, two weeks after the German attack, the
British Chemical Warfare Committee held its first discussion on
mustard-gas production in the UK. On August 2, a Professor Irvine
reported a successful method of making mustard gas from glycol-
chlorohydrin and 12 days later, commanders in France urged the War
Office to adopt this war gas for the British Army.

On October 13, 1918 the British fired mustard-gas shells into the
German lines, defended by the 16th. Bavarian Reserve Regiment, straddling the small Belgian village of Werwick. One of many casualties
suffering from skin burns and temporary blindness was a headquarters
messenger or runner, an infantry corporal called Adolf Hitler:

> I stumbled back with burning eyes, taking with me my last report of the
> war. A few hours later, my eyes had turned into glowing coals. It had
> grown dark around me,

he wrote after the war. Still in great pain, he was evacuated to
Germany two days later.

A similar but faster-acting war gas, lewisite (dichloro-2-chlorovinyl
arsine), was developed by the Americans, named after the chemist who
first produced it, Captain Winford Lee Lewis, (1878–1943) of the US
Army Chemical Warfare Service. This is a colourless volatile liquid,
with a faint smell of the geranium flower. It can penetrate most clothing, even rubber, and just 30 drops on the skin is fatal to the average
man. If the eyes are affected, total blindness occurs within one minute.
The US began production of lewisite at the Ben Hur automobile
factory in Willoughby, Ohio in the last months of the war but sufficient quantities came too late to be deployed on the Western Front
and the only shipment was dumped in the Atlantic Ocean after the
Armistice.

The US Army quickly jumped on the chemical warfare band-
wagon, forming its Chemical Warfare Service on June 26, 1918 and
launching production at the newly constructed Edgewood Arsenal in
Maryland, which had manufactured 935 tons of phosgene and 711
tons of mustard by the end of hostilities.

A number of methods were used to detect gas, with the British developing a number of indicator dyes that changed colour when in contact
with battlefield gases. At one point, the US Army enthusiastically
pursued scientific reports that ordinary garden snails waved their horns
in the air and withdrew into their shells when contaminated by mustard
gas. A French army doctor pointed out, rather wryly, that *his* troops were
more likely to eat the snails than use them to detect gas attacks.

Because of its dreadful attributes, mustard gas remains a potent military weapon today, although outlawed by international convention.

Enormous quantities of poison gas were used on the battlefields of
the First World War. Germany is reported to have used 68,000 tons
alone: Britain, 25,000 tons and France 36,000. Assessments of the
number of casualties caused by the use of chemical weapons in this
'war to end all wars' are difficult to evaluate accurately. What looks a
reasonable, if possibly conservative, estimate is a total of 1,296,000
casualties from poison gas, of which 91,000 were fatalities. Of this

total, Russian forces suffered by far the worst numerically, with 56,000 deaths out of a total of 420,000 casualties – just under a 12% mortality rate, mainly because they were slow in developing an effective gas mask. Germany lost around 9,000 men out of 191,000 affected by poison gas (4.7%); France 8,000 out of 182,000 casualties (4.4%); the USA 1,462 from 69,975 (2.1%). Troops from the (then) British Empire sustained 8,109 deaths from 180,597 casualties (4.5%). Of this last total, 4,086 British soldiers died from the effects of mustard gas and 1,976 from chlorine alone. The choking agents – chlorine and phosgene and the associated gases – caused the vast majority of casualties, although the US Expeditionary Force suffered 27,711 from mustard (the prevalent chemical agent after its troops arrived in France) or over 39% of all those GIs who received chemical wounds.

Poison gas had become a weapon of mass destruction.

For many, the enduring image of the First World War is the line of blinded soldiers, their hands gripping each other's shoulders, being guided to their battalion casualty clearing station amid the mud and destruction of a battlefield. It encapsulates the agony and horror of this new facet of war.

But for many thousands on both sides, the agony of the after-effects of a gas attack did not abruptly end with the long-awaited ceasefire bugles on Armistice Day, November 11, 1918. Around 12% of all casualties suffered various types of permanent injury or medical condition. The heroes of all the combatant nations were faced with years of suffering to come.

The horrors of gas warfare made a deep impact on the public psyche, and this in turned influenced the politicians, always nervous of public opinion and the result of the next election. (Meanwhile, the military, in considering future threats, inevitably planned for conflict using chemical weapons.) At the peace conference at Versailles, the victorious allies insisted that Germany should be strictly prohibited from manufacturing, importing, or ever using chemical agents again. The 1919 Treaty reaffirmed the banning of poisonous gas in war, as did the Geneva Protocol signed on June 17, 1925 by 41 states, which added (with a laudable premonition of the technologies to come) a similar measure against the use of bacteriological warfare. The USA and Japan refused to ratify the Protocol,* and among the Great Power signato-

---

* They did in 1975 and 1970, respectively.

ries, all reserved the right to retaliate in kind if confronted by chemical warfare attacks in the future. Thus the Protocol's intended total ban on the deployment of 'asphyxiating, poisonous or other gases and analogous liquids, materials or devices ... [use of which] has been justly condemned by the general opinion of the civilised world,' became, in practice, merely a prohibition on their first use against an enemy.

Again, whilst the protocol became embodied into international law, there were no sanctions included for any infringement, no facility for verification and most significantly, no ban on the research and development, production, weaponising or stockpiling of war gases. The Protocol's authority had become based on morality rather than legality. The nations' well-intentioned desire to eradicate the scourge of poison gas had been disastrously diluted and the spectre of chemical warfare was not to disappear from the battlefield.

Britain used the non-persistent incapacitating gas, adamsite (which induces severe vomiting and blinding headaches) against Bolshevik troops in the Russian civil war in 1919, and the following year, RAF bi-plane aircraft dropped mustard on insurgent tribesmen north of the Khyber Pass, a main route into Afghanistan, west of Peshawar. Spain also deployed mustard in bombs and shells against Rif rebel tribesmen in the mountains of Spanish Morocco in 1925.

Japan, formerly an ally of Britain, France and the USA in the First World War, launched an ambitious research programme into poison gas in 1921, with production beginning six years later. Large-scale output began in 1929 on the island of Okunoshima in Japan's Inland Sea, producing lewisite and mustard gas and the blood agent hydrogen cyanide. They also developed new ways to deliver the chemical weapons: aircraft spray tanks, anti-tank grenades and artillery rockets. The Japanese believed firmly in the concept of 'total war' and this meant being able to fight effectively in a chemically hostile battlefield: hence protective clothing and masks were developed not only for soldiers but for horses and camels, used for transport, and also dogs. Russia began its own war-gas production, with help from Weimar Germany, in the 1920s and another former ally, Italy, also began research at the Centro Chemico Militare and initiated production of mustard gas, again, as we shall see, for very carefully considered reasons.

In 1927, there were growing fears that the nationalist armies sweeping through China were planning to use chemical weapons in their offensive, then moving towards Shanghai. This prosperous city, on China's east coast, was then a major centre for trade with the West, and had foreign troops to defend Western interests in the city. The British had intelligence that the nationalists had received shipments of chemical sufficient to make 20 tons of mustard gas from Russia and that these were stored in Canton. British agents reported a 'Professor Avalov, a Russian chemical warfare expert,' in the area. It was also known that the northern armies were negotiating for the purchase of gas from Germany as well as quantities of respirators, or gas masks, from Japan, and there were reports that '50 gas cylinders, said to contain chlorine' had been seen at Hang Chow railway station.

The British Army sent a 'special section' of Royal Engineers to Shanghai to organise the defences against chemical attack in March 1927. With the grim humour that frequently accompanies such serious events, two experts in chemical warfare were despatched by ship to Shanghai to bring expertise to the defending forces. On the ship's passenger list, they were described as 'gas officers' and on arrival, they were surprised to be sent to No. 12 Field Ambulance, the local disembarkation authorities believing the description meant 'anaesthetists'.

In the event, all the precautions were unnecessary, as no chemical attacks were mounted. It is known, however, that the Chinese may have had a chemical capability. There are unconfirmed reports that gas was used against insurgents in Manchuria in the early 1930s, and British intelligence reports of the time report the construction, by an American company, of a mustard-gas plant in Kunghsien; in 1938 it was said to be within reach of advancing Japanese forces and may have still been in production during the subsequent occupation.

Gas warfare still loomed large in the public consciousness and coupled with increasing popular and political fears of the power of bomber aircraft, there were frequent apocalyptic predictions in the early 1930s of the carnage that would be wrought on civilians from aerial gas attacks, either by bombs or aircraft spraying swathes of chemical agents on densely populated cities and towns. A secret British government report evaluating the threat to the population and the measures necessary to defend civilians against gas attack prepared by the Committee of Imperial Defence in 1933 remains closed to public view to this day, 70 years after it was written. If Britain's national security still risks damage by the report's release, the findings must still be regarded as chilling.

Another deployment of battlefield gas after the First World War came from an ostensibly unlikely source in an equally improbable theatre of war. The Italians, a signatory to the Geneva Protocol (they ratified it in 1928), deployed mustard gas in January 1935 against the unsophisticated and unprotected army of the Emperor Haile Selassie during their invasion of his country, Abyssinia (now Ethiopia) in north-east Africa. Despite the primitive weaponry equipping their adversaries, during an action at Warieu Pass, the Italians were forced to resort to using mustard-gas shells to avoid a humiliating defeat. During the following two months, Italian aircraft bombed or sprayed the retreating barefoot Abyssinian forces with chemical agents. The Rome government attempted to justify the use of chemical agents as merely a reprisal for the alleged illegal killing and torture of Italian prisoners of war. In vain did the dignified and courteous Selassie complain to the League of Nations in Geneva about the use of mustard gas against his soldiers being in contravention of international law.

Japan also deployed poison gas in their invasion of Manchuria in 1937, using mustard gas against both troops and civilians, a fact until recently denied by Japan. There seems little doubt that phosgene, lewisite and incapacitating agents were also used against Chinese guerrilla forces, with some reports claiming up to 2,000 separate attacks involving artillery shells and aerial spraying, although the figure may be substantially lower. Soviet sources maintain that 25% of Japanese shells had chemical fillings and 30% of bombs contained poison or incapacitating gas during this campaign. Again, the League of Nations in Geneva was ineffective in policing the use of chemical agents. (Since the 1990s, Japan and China have been involved in negotiations over the disposal of Japanese chemical weapon stocks still located in China and a number of munitions have been removed from Chuzhou, Nanjing and several other sites and safely disposed of by the Japanese Self-Defence Forces.)

The US Army firmly opposed any new restrictions on research into battlefield gases or their production. General Douglas MacArthur, Army Chief of Staff, wrote to Secretary of State Henry Stimson in 1932:

No provision that would require the disposal of destruction of any existing installation of our Chemical Warfare Service or of any stocks of chemical warfare material should be incorporated in … [any new] agreement. Furthermore, the existence of a War Department agency engaged in experimentation and manufacture of chemical warfare materials and in training for unforeseen contingencies is deemed essential to our national defense.

Science was not standing still. In Germany, scientists working on organo-phosphorous insecticides accidentally discovered a powerful new type of chemical weapon – nerve gases. These compounds were found to efficiently attack the body's nervous system and respiratory functions, resulting in almost immediate fatality. They work by neu-tralising the natural enzyme *cholinesterase* that controls the transmission of nerve impulses in the human body, to and from the brain. Only a tiny amount is lethal. A new, deadly generation of chemical agents had been born.

Dr Gerhart Schrader of Germany's giant chemical company I. G. Farben, discovered tabun (GA), a colourless liquid in 1936. He quickly began to suffer shortness of breath and contraction of the pupils in the eyes from the effects of the chemical vapour in the laboratory. The war-fighting potential of this new gas was reported to the German War Ministry and after further experiments, a pilot produc-tion plant was established at Münster, south of Hamburg. After a number of accidents to civilian workers, full-scale production was eventually set up at a large purpose-built plant, employing 3,000 people, at Dyernfürth-am-Order (Brzeg in present-day Poland), south-east of Wroclaw (then Breslau) from 1942. All the workforce had to wear respirators and special rubberised clothing to protect them against the effects of the gas. Shells and bombs were also filled with tabun, called 'Trilon-83' by the German Army, at Dyernfürth in an underground facility. By the end of the Second World War, the plant had produced about 12,000 tons of tabun, with 2,000 tons weaponised into 105 and 150mm artillery shells, 150mm Nebelwerfer rockets and 10,000 tons in airdropped munitions, such as the 250kg bomb and spray tanks.

Tabun poisoning, absorbed by inhalation or through the skin, has thoroughly devastating symptoms. The victim suffers a runny nose at the onset, then tightness in the chest, a dimming of vision, and then progressive and swift loss of the nervous system's control of the body's functions; drooling, copious perspiration, vomiting, involuntary defe-cation and urination. The final stages are massive convulsions and muscle tremors, before the victim goes into a coma and dies. There is no shred of dignity in this death. The cycle is frighteningly rapid and distressing to witness.

The second nerve agent, the colourless and odourless sarin (GB), with similar effects to tabun, was discovered in 1938 in Germany and joined the production processes at Dyernfürth, with a second facility built at Falkenhagen, south of Berlin, but remaining uncompleted at the end of the Second World War. Sarin, or Trilon-46, is five times more toxic than tabun and 25 times more lethal than cyanide gas. A droplet of liquid sarin, merely the size of a pinprick, is enough to quickly and horribly kill a human. The third of the trio of nerve gas, soman, was created by the German army chemist Richard Kuhn in early 1944.

Although both sides in the Second World War were armed with chemical weapons, none were used, although Britain was prepared to deploy mustard gas on the landing beaches along the English Channel if the Germans had invaded in 1940. The British government issued 30 million gas masks to the UK civilian population before the outset of hostilities, in the firm belief that the Luftwaffe would deploy chemical munitions or aerial sprays against towns and cities. (These would have provided some protection against lachrymator and asphyxiate gases but would have proved useless against mustard or other blistering agent.) Civil defence workers and the police were trained in the treatment of mass gas casualties.

Considerable production runs of chemical weapons were achieved during the war. Germany produced 78,000 tons, including 13,000 tons of nerve agents, but concentrated on the output of mustard. The USA built production facilities at Huntsville, Alabama, Pine Bluff, Arkansas and the Rocky Mountain Arsenal at Denver, Colorado, manufacturing a total of 146,000 tons, 87,000 of which were mustard.

Happily, the official fears of the use of war gases were not realised. Here was an example of deterrence working in conflict. Even though stockpiles of chemical munitions, amounting to more than 600,000 tons, were held by Germany and the Allies, there *were* no gas attacks, primarily because of fears of retaliation, like for like, by the opposing forces, a pattern followed in the subsequent Korean War and in the Middle Eastern conflicts in the two decades after the 1940s.

In the Second World War, however, there were some close calls. We have already seen how Churchill wanted to deploy gas against German cities in response to the V-1 attacks on London, but was dissuaded from this escalatory course of action. Later, after the invasion of Europe and towards the end of hostilities, the Allies, particularly the Americans, became increasingly worried that Germany would use chemical weapons in a last-ditch defence of the tottering Third Reich. On January 4, 1945 this coded signal was sent by General Dwight Eisenhower's command, SHAEF, (Supreme HQs, Allied Expeditionary Forces):

> Instructions have been issued by 12th and 60th Army Groups that all personnel, including visitors, forward of division and corps rear boundaries respectively, will [now] carry gas masks.
>
> This HQs is NOT in possession of any definite information indicating possible early initiation of gas warfare by the enemy. Action taken by 12th and 60th Army Groups is purely precautionary.

The genie was out of the bottle, despite SHAEF's calming words. What followed provides us with a graphic illustration of what the Allies planned if the final stages of the War saw Germany deploying poison or nerve gases and how ready they were to retaliate. Signals, still extant, also indicate how the Allies' firm policies on chemical munitions began to unravel as commanders grew ever more nervous about possible German use of chemical agents, much of it on the basis of unfounded rumour, but also stemming from the growing belief that Hitler had something very unpleasant up his sleeve, if total and humiliating defeat stared him in the face.

Four days after the reassuring SHAEF service message, the USAAF's 9th Air Force, which at that time had no retaliatory capability, submitted a Top Secret plan for approval to mount chemical warfare operations if required. It also sought authorisation to stockpile chemical agent munitions at its air bases and depots. The plan describes how it would employ gas bombs and medium- and high-level spraying with these objectives and missions:

- Neutralisation of terrain, areas, vehicles, installations.
- Contamination of vital support.
- Creating of chemical barriers.
- Anti-personnel attacks, 'particularly against inclosed installations'.
- Hampering the rehabilitation of areas.
- 'Coverage' of vital areas out of reach of ground weapons.

The report adds: 'Medium and heavy bombardment airplanes and their support components will be used as carriers. The gases will be persistent and non-persistent casualty agents.'   The 9th Air Force then describes the inventory of immediately available chemical munitions (i.e. stockpiled in Britain) for the planned 'first retaliatory measures':

M78 500lb. Phosgene	3,600 bombs
M79 1,000lb Phosgene	5,850 bombs
M79 1,000lb Hydrogen Cyanide	3,225 bombs
M79 1,000lb Cyanogen Chloride	280 bombs
British 400lb 'Flying Cow' H-filled*	20,000 bombs
M10 spray tanks complete	Approx. 9,000
Bulk Mustard in 55-gallon drums	500,000 gallons
Bulk Mustard in 1 ton containers	250,000 gallons

Helpfully, the Air Force explains the effectiveness of the munitions: 'Mustard is a typical persistent agent and areas attacked with this gas are likely to remain dangerous for a considerable length of time, depending on the concentration achieved, temperature, humidity and general weather conditions. Extreme casualties can be inflicted on enemy personnel and lasting contamination of enemy aircraft, installations and fortifications can be accomplished. This gas can be dropped by bombs and sprayed by spray tanks. The use of both types ... is generally more effective when used in conjunction with HE and incendiaries.' The chemical bombs would arm the Air Force's B-26 aircraft, four to eight each, and P-47 Mustangs would be fitted with spray tanks.

Various USAAF command levels approved the plan on January 22.

Early the previous September, SHAEF, in pursuance of Eisenhower's firm 'no first use' policy, had decided that all chemical munitions would remain in the UK 'in case and until gas warfare begins.' Now that policy would be swiftly changed, on the basis of fear of the unknown rather than hard intelligence. On January 10, at 13.03, before he went into lunch, General Omar Bradley of the 12th Army Group signalled SHAEF that:

---

* H-fill was mustard gas.

Proportionate share of offensive chemical agents to be brought to the Continent [of Europe] as it becomes possible, without interference with other essential supplies.

In the event the enemy resorts to chemical warfare, effective retaliation can be had approximately 3 weeks sooner than under present conditions.

SHAEF responded, no doubt after some debate, by signalling all commands at 22.28 that night:

Restrictions on movement of offensive gas ammunition to the Continent are lifted.

Munitions immediately began to be shipped to Cherbourg for use by the American 9th Air Force and the 1st Tactical Air Force.

There was an immediate scurrying within Allied intelligence circles, checking and re-checking agent reports, signal intercepts, prisoner interrogation statements and other information that could positively confirm or deny the Germans were about to use chemical agents. On January 31, the British Joint Intelligence Committee (JIC) told SHAEF:

There is no recent evidence to show more than an increased German interest in gas warfare. Items of evidence indicated that this interest may be operational and not purely precautionary.

Routine anti-gas preparedness is being energetically maintained and even slightly stepped up, which conforms with either offensive or defensive intention.

General strategic factors do not show an immediate likelihood of an initiation of gas warfare by enemy but turn of events on land decisively in favour of Allies would produce a situation in which use of gas by Germans would have to be regarded as possible ...There might be little warning. The possibility always remains of Hitler's resort to gas warfare if he felt that it was Germany's last resort.

The JIC were somewhat hedging their bets – and their message did nothing to assuage the doubts of jumpy American commanders in the field. Their other concern was that Allied troops faced a 'severe shortage of gas masks in the theatre of war' in north-west Europe – a potentially catastrophic limitation on the effectiveness of their forces if the Germans did resort to poison gas.

There continued to be straws in the wind that might indicate a German use of chemical agents. The French reported on February 4 on a report 'received one month ago that gas shells [had been] moved forward to the Siegfried Line' – the massive line of concrete forts and defences along the southern border of Germany. On March 2, JIC reported that 'chemical warfare stocks and personnel [have been] dispersed from areas threatened by Russian advance to depots generally further west and south west.' A week later, Allied intelligence said 'an increasing number of prisoners of war taken by Northern Armies mention possible employment of chemical warfare [agents].' Another, unconfirmed, report spoke of 'airfields in north central Germany [have] aircraft held in reserve for use in chemical warfare.' It is now known that some tabun munitions had been moved to Bavaria in anticipation of the feared German apocalyptic defence.

But all those fears and anxieties came to nothing, despite mounting pressure on the cornered German war leader by some of his Nazi acolytes, including Goebbels and Bormann, to use chemical weapons against the Allies as a last gamble. The Third Reich disappeared with the suicide of Hitler and his immediate circle in the closed world of the bunker beneath the smoke and rubble of the Reichschancery in Berlin, battered by the artillery of the advancing Russian troops, only a block or so away.

After the war, the German Armaments Minister, Albert Speer, told the Nuremberg war crimes tribunal, where he was arraigned:

> All sensible [German] army people turned gas warfare down as being utterly insane, in view of your [the Allies'] superiority in the air ... it would bring about the most terrible catastrophe upon German cities.

There was no Wagnerian last stand in a 'national redoubt' in the mountains of southern Germany. There was no use of chemical agents, sowing poison across the ravaged countryside, as a final, desperate throw of the Nazi dice.

(There is one remaining mention of chemical agents in the SHAEF files. In June 1945, with the end of hostilities was just days away, Eisenhower banned the 'use of non-lethal, non-asphyxiating gases' by Allied troops 'for the suppression of disturbances in Germany' without prior consent of the Supreme Commander.)

Chemical agents *were* released in the European theatre of war in one notorious incident. A 20-minute attack by 105 Luftwaffe twin-engined Ju-88 bombers early on the evening of December 2 1943 on the Italian port of Bari, sunk or damaged 17 Allied ships in the harbour, including the SS *John Harvey*, a 10,000 ton Liberty ship carrying 2,000 M47A1 100lb mustard gas bombs as well as conventional HE munitions, awaiting unloading at pier 29. A fire and the subsequent explosion on board sent a mustard-laden cloud mushrooming over the town, creating burns, blisters and breathing problems among many of its inhabitants. A total of 617 Allied troops and seamen died from mustard poisoning and 534 were wounded – with a 14% mortality rate, higher than experienced in the First World War, because many swallowed the agent or were burned after they were thrown into the harbour waters by the explosion. The population was evacuated. Decontaminating the harbour area took three weeks.

In the Far East, there were reports that the Japanese used chemical agents against Chinese forces. Intelligence reports received by the British GHQ India from an American source describe what happened in one battle:

In the Ichang action of October 1941, a heavy attack was launched by the Chinese to take the city and carry the heights ... [Japanese] artillery and mortar fire increased in intensity and considerable lachrymatory and sneeze gas was reported mixed in with the HE ... Chinese soldiers reported eye trouble and stomach sickness from the gas but no deaths were reported prior to October 8.

[The Chinese attack was launched that day and the Japanese retired to new positions.]

When the Chinese pressed the attack to take the ridges necessary to hold the city proper, Japanese launched counter attacks from both flanks and great quantities of lethal gas were placed on the attacking Chinese and in the low areas behind them. On October 10–12, planes ... dropped lethal gas bombs all over the area.

The Chinese were either barefoot or wearing straw sandals and no gas masks or protective clothing were available. In the attack they were severely gassed and burned.

Chinese in reserve were heavily gassed and received many casualties, most of which proved fatal. Retiring from the attack, the Chinese had to proceed through very low areas to avoid machine-gun fire and thus passed through very heavily concentrated gas barriers.

It is very difficult to obtain accurate strength figures from the Chinese but it appears there were over 2,000 casualties due to gas and gunfire. Of the casualties who came out of the area, 29 were gas cases, 12 of whom died *en route* to hospital. Later six were located in hospitals and were able to give an account of the action. Only two of the six lived to return to their units.

The Chinese claimed the Japanese mounted two major gas attacks on the Chekiang front during May 1942. Chinese positions on the Sinan river near Kienteh were bombed and shells with chemical munitions and after an unsuccessful assault on the railway town of Tangki, 'a large volume of gas' was released on the Chinese defenders as a curtain-raiser to a Japanese attack. The Chinese were forced to evacuate the town. In 1937–8, the Japanese used mostly tear- and sneeze-producing irritants to disable the enemy. 'Since the Chinese victory at Taierhchwanh, toxic gases have been used with greater intensity,' said the British report. 'Gas units were attached to each Japanese regiment and storm unit and gas tactics were resorted to with much greater frequency. Lethal and blistering gases are the main agents employed ... in recent years.'

Strange then that an Allied report after the end of hostilities found no evidence of Japanese chemical munitions in South-East Asia outside Burma – nor of special gas warfare troops. In fact, the Japanese had stopped development and production of war gases in 1941. The only reports uncovered were of chemical shells existing in 1943 but these were sent on to Rangoon, the Burmese capital. Chloropicrin was found at Petchar Boon, in Thailand 'but these were Siamese property, bought before the war.' A Dutch laboratory making mustard gas in Banojijahru, Bandon, with a monthly production capacity of 15 tons, was left untouched by the Japanese.

In contrast to the Allied campaign in north-west Europe, American military leaders at one stage apparently considered deploying chemical weapons in Operation DOWNFALL, the planned invasion of the Japanese islands. Part of the campaign, OLYMPIC, was aimed at capturing the southernmost island of Kyushu, and a US Army secret plan, produced in June 1945, called for the dropping of 55,000 tons of phosgene on Tokyo and other Japanese cities in the two weeks before the landings. 'Gas attacks of the size and intensity recommended on 250 square miles of urban population might easily kill 5,000,000 people and injure that many more,' according to a US Chemical Warfare Service draft report, only released in July 1991.

The motivation behind the report was the US Army's strong fears of suffering unacceptably high casualty rates during the invasion — American forces had already lost 46,000 killed in action in the previous year of the Pacific war, plus another 200,000 wounded. In addition, there were reports that the Japanese were threatening to kill Allied prisoners of war and interned civilians in retaliation for an invasion. In the face of what was predicted to be a fierce Japanese defence of their homeland, American estimates of the expected casualty rate from the Kyushu campaign alone totalled 100,000 with a further 150,000, rising to one million, in CORONET, the invasion of Honshu, planned for March, 1946.

The report's proposals stressed:

> Our plan of campaign against the Japanese is one which we think will bring the war against Japan to the quickest conclusion and cut our cost in men and resources to the minimum. Japan's complete defeat is assured, providing we persevere in this plan... Gas is the one single weapon hitherto unused which we can have readily available and which assuredly can greatly decrease the cost in American lives and should materially shorten the war.

It urged President Truman to change the policy of no first use against the Japanese. In the event, the 30-page plan was not approved. The B-29 bombing campaign continued, with horrific firestorms over Tokyo, killing about 300,000 people and making eight million homeless. And the Allies had an even more potent weapon that eventually was to force the Japanese government into surrender — the atomic bomb.

After the end of the Second World War, the victorious Allies were confronted with the problem of disposal of 296,000 tons of captured German chemical munitions alone. Sea-dumping was the favourite and cheapest method adopted. Ecology and environmental concerns were less fashionable in the 1940s.

The USA's Operation DAVY JONES LOCKER, from June 1946 to August 1948, involved five separate dumps, totalling around 40,000 tons of munitions, held in nine ships, which were scuttled in the Skagerrak Strait, between Norway and north Denmark, and two further vessels in the North Sea; all at depths of between 2,100–3,800ft. The US Navy also dumped phosgene, mustard, hydrogen cyanide, lewisite and cyanogen chloride munitions in the Adriatic Sea, off Italy's east coast, in November 1945–April 1946. Russia and Britain together disposed of a further 46,000 tons of tabun, adamsite, mustard and phosgene, dumped in three deep-water sites in the Baltic Sea, the Gotland Deep, Little Belt and the Bornholm Deep, the latter 15 miles north-east of the Danish island of the same name. The British also dumped 34 loads totalling 127,000 tons in the 2,300ft deep waters of the Skagerrak, 25 miles south-east of the Norwegian town of Arendal, as well as utilising another site in the Atlantic, 65 miles off the Irish Republic's western coast. Similar disposal operations were mounted in the Pacific and off Japan's southern and south-eastern coasts, with another 14,000 tons of mustard dumped off three Australian states: Cape Moreton, Queensland, Victoria, and off Sydney, New South Wales. In addition, in Operation GERANIUM, the US Army disposed of its stocks of lewisite in the sea in 1948.

The sea-dumping continued in the 1950s and 1960s. In this period, the US dumped more than 21,000 tons of nerve agents, mustard and other chemical munitions, some of it still vintage German, in a series of operations off the coasts of Alaska, Louisiana, California, and North and South Carolina. Around the time the British Government officially pulled out of offensive chemical warfare, at least three ships, named as the SS *Vogtland, Clare Tee* and *Kokta*, containing 76,000 tons of chemical bombs and 3,500 tons of 23lb artillery shells were secretly scuttled in Operation SANDCASTLE in 1955–6, in the North Atlantic deeps about 80 miles north-east of Ireland's Malin Head. Some of the shells were reportedly leaking and had to be resealed before the ocean dumping. About 17,000 tons were captured German munitions and 8,000 tons from redundant Second World War stocks of mustard and phosgene. After inquiries by the Irish government in 1995, the UK Defence Ministry acknowledged that the ships held tabun, mustard and phosgene. Britain stopped sea dumping of chemical munitions in 1957.

In 1966, the US Army discovered that its stockpile of 400,000 M55 artillery rockets, with sarin nerve gas warheads, were increasingly in poor condition, with some leakage occurring because the aluminium casing proved unsuitable for long-term storage. It was decided to scrap the entire arsenal, and in Operation CHASE (rather inaptly named from 'Cut Holes and Sink 'Em'; in every sense, a throwaway phase), 51,180 of the rockets were dumped in the Atlantic in waters 6,500ft deep, 150 miles off the coast of New York state. The last mission in this operation was the sea disposal of concrete blocks sealing M55 rounds off Florida in 1970, after a long rail journey to the dockside. US sea-dumping ended two years afterwards, following a public outcry over Army plans to dispose of a further 27,000 tons of chemicals and other munitions.

In the last two decades there have been increasing concerns about the environmental hazards posed by these dumped poison gases. Nerve agents break down and dissolve in seawater, but mustard is insoluble, oxidises and forms a thick outer crust still containing an active liquid core. There had been many reports of such nodules unwittingly being brought to the surface in fishing nets. During the period 1946–97, more than 230 cases of mustard contamination have been recorded among Adriatic fishermen, trawling in the region of the Second World War sea-dump there. Other incidents have occurred regularly in Japan and Denmark where 45 samples of chemical munitions were dredged up in 1985 alone. The ecological damage of sea-dumping is more difficult to define. In the Baltic, in the Bornholm Deep, research has revealed bacteria that have developed resistance to mustard; indeed, a new kind has emerged that actively aids the disintegration of the vesicant. Some argue that the sunken war-gas ships are an environmental time bomb ticking away on the floors of the world's seas and oceans. Other experts maintain that the scuttled ships are more secure, as the munitions are sealed in their holds behind bulkhead doors. Underwater examination in the last decade indicates little evidence of seepage or damage to the local ecosystem at some of the shallower sites, but the slow process of decay continues and it's difficult to predict the likelihood or timescale of any major escape. What is certain is that there are approaching 500,000 tons of abandoned chemical munitions on the seabed and the chances of a disaster increase, slowly, inexorably every year as the process of decay continues.

Not all the German poison gases were disposed of in the seas around Europe. Nor did the secret of the new nerve gases' manufacture drown with the tons of munitions sinking beneath the waves.

During 1945–7, American forces shipped more than 40,000 250kg tabun bombs back to the USA, together with 21,000 mustard bombs, 2,700 nitrogen mustard and 750 tabun artillery shells for examination and research. Another 8,000 tons were despatched to Britain. The Russians did not need to scavenge for German chemical munitions: they captured the tabun and sarin nerve gas plants at Dyenfürth and Falkenhagen intact, despite the best efforts of the Wehrmacht and Luftwaffe to destroy the former. Soviet production of tabun and sarin began a year after the end of the Second World War, later transferring to a purpose-built plant at Stalingrad (now Volgograd) where soman was also produced. A new agent, 'GF' was developed (and later produced in Iraq). The secret of German nerve gas technology had been revealed, and with production replicated in the USA and Britain, this new chemical weapon proliferated.

After the Second World War various antidotes were developed to counter the battlefield threat of nerve gas. The primary military treatment for tabun and sarin is atrophine sulfate, carried in doses of around 1–2 mgs, in a dangerous-looking ready-use hypodermic, called an 'autojector'. Because of the speed and intensity of the effects of the agents, it is standard army practice for a comrade to press the autojector into a fleshy party of the affected soldier, normally the thigh, and activate the powerful spring-loaded needle. This is the so-called buddy system: everyone looks after one another. Often, many doses of atrophine are necessary to neutralise the effects of the gas. Pralidoxime chloride, or 3-PAMC1, is also employed but is not so effective against soman.

Combatants may also be issued special pink prophylactic pills to swallow if a nerve-agent attack is imminent. These are pyridostigmine bromide, effective against soman and physostigmine. The former was reported in trials to cause increased flatulence, loose stools and additional urinary urgency and frequency, a particularly personal and distressing problem for a soldier wearing the all-encompassing 'Noddy suit' – nuclear, biological and chemical protective clothing. In the aftermath of DESERT STORM, the Coalition war against Iraq, some prophylactics have been at the heart of the continuing controversy over so-called 'Gulf War Syndrome', a wide range of symptoms affecting some of the veterans of the conflict.

Research into the military uses of organophosphates moved on, creating new, still more terrible chemical weapons. British scientists at the Porton Down Chemical Defence Establishment's outstation at Nancekuke in Cornwall developed the new V-class of nerve agents in the 1950s, able to defeat the protection provided by gas masks. (V in the terminology, was derived, simply, from the unimaginative adjective venomous). The chemistry was passed on to Washington. V-agents are very persistent, enabling an area to be denied to an unprotected enemy for days, if not weeks. In 1957, the US army selected VX as a prime agent, with the Chemical Corps, in its *Summary of Major Events and Problems,* for Fiscal Year 1958, predicting:

> The reign of mustard gas, which has been called the King of Battle gases since it was first used in July 1917, will probably come to an end.

Production of VX began in 1961 at the Newport Chemical Plant in Indiana and continued until 1968. The Russians also began production of their version of the V-agents to add to their G-agent nerve gases inherited from the Germans and the vesicants, mustard and phosgene.

Deployment of battlefield gases, like the use of tactical nuclear warheads, formed an integral part of the Soviet ground and air force war plans. In Moscow's General Staff during the Communist era, there would have been no scruples, indeed, little hesitation, to use these weapons in a general offensive against the NATO forces across the northern plains of Europe in time of war.

The US Army Chief Chemical Officer, Major General Marshall Stubbs, reported this assessment of the Soviet chemical warfare programme in 1959:

> Soviet chemical weapons are modern and effective and probably include all types of chemical munitions known to the West, in addition to several dissemination devices peculiar to the Russians. Their ground forces are equipped with a variety of protective chemical equipment and they are prepared to participate in largescale gas warfare. They have a complete list of protective clothing which will provide protection in any gas situation and a large variety of decontaminating equipment.

Others shared the Soviet doctrine about the use of battlefield gases. Egypt, a signatory to the 1925 Geneva Protocol that banned first use of chemical agents, began production of war gases at Military Plant No.

801 located at Abu Za'abal, six miles north-east of Cairo in 1963, under a project codenamed IZLIS, that focused on mustard and phosgene. These weapons were to be quickly used in anger.

In the Yemen, a civil war between royalists and republicans broke out in 1962 as each struggled for power in the Islamic state. Egypt intervened on the side of the republicans by sending forces into the country. Soon after, there were reports of a chemical attack on the village of Al Kawma, in July 1963, in which seven civilians were killed, but subsequent United Nations investigations could not find any hard evidence of agents being used. There were a number of press reports of similar attacks, again all unsubstantiated, until January 1967, when Soviet-built Ilyushin-28 aircraft of the Egyptian air force bombed the village of Kitaf, creating a greyish cloud that spread over the village. Press reports said 95% of the occupants died within 50 minutes of the air raid, with a total death toll amounting to more than 200. Other air attacks were mounted on the town of Gahar and on the villages of Gabas, Gadr, Gadafa and Hofal in May 1967, killing altogether more than 320 civilians.

In Geneva, the International Red Cross decided to send a team of investigators to the Yemen to discover whether chemical weapons had been deployed against the population. After thorough analysis of soil samples, bomb fragments, and interviewing some of the victims, the conclusion was that, yes, mustard gas and possibly nerve agents had been used in munitions dropped by the Egyptian air force. (We now know the Egyptians used Soviet-made KHAB-200 R5 mustard and AOKh-25 phosgene bombs – their nerve gas production did not begin until the 1970s.) Cairo firmly denied the claims at the time, although a senior officer subsequently confirmed the use of poison gas in 1990.

The USA meanwhile was studying the use of incapacitating gas in war, beginning with mescaline, and later moving on to non-military drugs like the hippie favourite, lysergic acid (LSD) and tetrahydrocannabinol, similar to cannabis. The programme, designated 'K-agents', soon discovered that these off-the-shelf candidates to confuse and immobilise a potential enemy were ineffective militarily. A specific agent had to be developed to fulfil the US Army's requirement for what is now known colloquially as a 'non-lethal weapon'.

In 1958, experiments began with an agent called BZ, capable of slowing mental and physical activity in an adversary, and creating confusion through hallucinations and spatial disorientation. Trials on more than 360 human volunteers proved encouraging and the Army began production in 1962 for use in airdropped cluster bombs, each containing either 57 separate bomblets or 126 canisters and, for close-quarter combat, the M9A1 gas grenade. The agent was used in Vietnam from 1964 against the Viet Cong insurgents, but its effects were regarded as too slow. After concerns arose over its lethality and unpredictability, production was ended in the late 1960s and it was withdrawn from the Army's inventory. BZ is still around, however; NATO intelligence believes it was used by Serbian forces in Bosnia in the mid-1990s and later against the Kosovo Liberation Army in 1999. There are reports that it has been exported to Iraq, arming multi-launch artillery rocket systems.

The US Army also used a new riot-control tear gas, CS, earlier developed by British scientists at Porton Down, to drive Viet Cong and North Vietnamese troops out of their deep underground bunkers or to neutralise potential ambushes in dense jungle. Defoliants, such as 'Agent-Orange', were also used to kill off vegetation to deny the enemy the use of cover near strategically important locations or to destroy crops they could live off.

In the early 1970s, there were persistent reports that chemical agents were being used against the pro-American Hmong tribesmen in the South-East Asian country of Laos. Although victims spoke of aircraft spraying multi-coloured 'smoke' – the so-called 'yellow rain' – and despite repeated efforts to verify the information, no definitive evidence of deployment of chemicals was found. These allegations were followed by others concerning the use of agents against Afghans by Soviet forces, following Moscow's invasion of Afghanistan in the late 1970s, including the use of 'Blue-X,' an incapacitator said to cause instant immobilisation of a victim, lasting several hours. Again, no definite evidence was confirmed.

In the US, concerns amongst military planners grew in the early 1980s that an increasing number of countries were arming themselves with chemical weapons – many of them distinctly unfriendly to Washington. More sophisticated methods of delivery were required, and in 1988, the US Congress approved production of binary weapons. These contained nerve gases in a number of delivery vehicles and only became lethal when, for example, an artillery shell was fired, the shock of the gun's discharge rupturing a seal between two normally harmless materials. While the projectile is in flight, these chemicals were automatically mixed to create the nerve agent.

Deployment of binary weapons, with their inherently safer storage was, in part, a military reaction to mounting public opposition in the Western democracies to the use, transportation, or stockpiling of chemical weapons. In the decades after the 1960s, this resistance grew, galvanised by the use of riot gases and defoliants by US forces in Vietnam, and reports of poison gas being used in a number of conflicts. In the USA, three particular incidents or events hastened the tide of opposition to these weapons. The first was Operation CHASE, but the other two were accidents involving nerve agents. On March 17, 1968, 3,000 sheep were killed by an accidental drift of nerve agents away from the US Army's Dugway Proving Ground in Utah. The sheep were held in the unfortunately named Skull Valley, which ran alongside part of the open-air trials area. The final incident was in the US Army base in Okinawa, Japan. On July 8, 1969 soldiers were cleaning bombs filled with sarin when a leak occurred. Twenty-three military personnel and one American civilian were exposed, and fortunately, none died. But the accidental release highlighted the dangers of storing chemical weapons near large centres of population, and the Pentagon was forced to accelerate the removal of chemical agents from the base.

That public revulsion in the West against war gases was strangely muted when confronted with evidence, in the 1980s, of the largest deployment in conflict of chemical agents since the First World War. During the Iran–Iraq war of 1980–8, Teheran made continual claims that Baghdad used chemical weapons against its ground forces. Iraq, which ratified the Geneva Protocol in 1931, certainly used mustard and the nerve agent tabun in artillery barrages against Iranian human-wave assaults (reminiscent of some of the Western Front actions), in battles in the Talayeh area, Shatt e-lai, Hur ul-Hoveyzeh, Majnoon Islands, Kawther and Jofeyr-Al Ba'iza in February and March 1984 and later. Up to 100,000 chemical munitions were used by Iraq during the war. Although Iran claimed 8,500 casualties from chemical weapons, reports suggest that the mortality rate of those treated was less than 5%, possibly indicating that the effectiveness of the war gases was blunted by terrain and weather conditions. Later, Iran may have retaliated in kind.

Iraq also used mustard and hydrogen cyanide in bombs dropped on

the town of Halabja on March 19, 1988 during its campaign against
the Kurds rebelling against Saddam Hussein's regime. Reports suggest
that between 3,200 and 5,000 Kurdish civilians were killed and 10,000
injured in that one attack. Sarin was also used in a wave of air attacks
on Kurdish targets up to August 1988.

Despite the deployment of chemical weapons in a number of wars,
there was progress in diplomatic attempts to sharpen international law
banning their use. In September 1961, the US and Soviet governments
declared they would consider chemical disarmament through a
'sequential and verifiable process' administered by some form of international agency. What eventually emerged from a plethora of
interminable negotiations was the Chemical Weapons Convention
(CWC), which opened for signature by the world's nations in 1993
and became binding on April 27 1997. It now has 147 countries
bound by its measures, with a further 27 as signatories. The treaty pro-
hibits the use, manufacture or stockpiling of all chemical weapons
(save riot gases), and includes a number of verification measures. These
amount to declarations concerning the 'environmentally friendly'
destruction of holdings and production facilities, and on-site inspections by 200 trained staff from the Organisation for the Prohibition of
Chemical Weapons (OPCW), based in the Dutch capital, The Hague.
Non-compliance involves the suspension of rights and privileges of
the errant state and 'in cases of particular gravity', the country is
reported to the UN General Assembly and Security Council.

As of December 31, 2000, 69,505,085 tons of agents, held in 8.6
million munitions, were declared, of which 5,327,678 tons had been
destroyed, most of them nerve agents. Verification by OPCW inspectors has covered 522 locations in 51 states. The signatories have up to
April 29, 2007 to destroy all stocks, but despite substantial financial
assistance from the West, the Russian Federation is making only very
slow progress with the disposal of its holdings and has extended the
deadline to 2012. The huge number of sites and stockpiles to be
destroyed is one of the problems for Moscow: in the obsolete
weapons category alone, Russia has 350 sites to clear. Its main storage
facility is said by the media to hold enough nerve agents to destroy the
world's population 100 times over. But progress *is* being made to rid
the world of chemical weapons. Globally, the number of chemical
agent production facilities declared under the CWC totalled 61, of
which 27 have now been destroyed and nine converted to other

approved peaceful uses.

Although the CWC has sharper teeth than the old Geneva Convention, there remain weaknesses in the verification process. The first covers the issue of so-called 'dual use' chemicals. A wide range of substances are employed for entirely laudable purposes – the manufacture of pesticides or agricultural fertiliser, for example – but also can be used to produce potent chemical weapons. This poses a real problem for the verification inspectors. Whilst simplified, this could mean that a plant would be producing organo-phosphate insecticides in the morning, entirely legally, but by throwing a switch, could be producing illegal nerve gas in the afternoon. Then, as we have seen in Iraq, the inspectors are largely reliant on the host nations being open about their facilities. The UN weapons inspectors checking Iraqi compliance with the Gulf War armistice discovered sarin, tabun and mustard munitions hidden in caves, in railway tunnels and buried in the desert, during 272 separate inspections at 1,015 sites alleged to be linked with Baghdad's programme to develop and deploy weapons of mass destruction. They were unable to account for 4,000 tons of 'precursor chemicals' used in the production of vesicant gases, 610 tons used in the manufacture of nerve agents, 1.5 tons of VX, 260 tons of other war gas and 31,000 chemical weapons munitions. Dr John Yurechko, a senior analyst at the Pentagon's Defense Intelligence Agency, accuses Iraq of having a 'deliberate, methodical, extensive and well-organised national-level strategic effort' for 'denial and deception'.

Verification activity costs money and straitened finances meant that 30% of the OPCW chemical weapons inspection programme could not be undertaken in 2001. The shortfall was more in 2002, given the agency's continuing budget deficits.

Around 22 nations still retain an offensive chemical capability. Western intelligence sources, for example, maintain that Iran, a signatory to the CWC, is involved in a major chemical weapons programme, despite repeated and angry denials from Tehran, insisting, in the words of Foreign Minister Kamal Kharrazi, on February 3, 2002:

As the only victim of weapons of mass destruction in the last generation, the Iranian people have felt the horror of these weapons and are determined to ensure that no other people will have to go through the same agony ...

Unlike the United States, weapons of mass destruction have no place in Iran's defence doctrine ... Its compliance has been repeatedly verified by the relevant international organisations ...

At the same time, Iran insists and vigorously pursues its inalienable right to develop its nuclear, chemical and biological industries for peaceful purposes.

Then there is the problem of the 20 non-signatory states to the CWC, which include Iraq, Egypt, North Korea, Syria and Libya, all of whom are known to hold substantial stockpiles of battlefield gases. Most, if not all, have ballistic missiles with chemical warheads, like Syria, which has probably armed its Scud B and C missiles with sarin. US intelligence also believes Syria is investigating VX gas: 'If they haven't weaponised a VX warhead, they're pretty close,' according to one official.

North Korea, which set up its first chemical warfare units in 1954, is believed to be currently armed with between 2,500 and 5,000 tons of chemical weapons, including VX, sarin, blister (phosgene and mustard) and blood agents. These are produced at eight plants, including Hamhung, Manpo, Sinuiju and Chongjin, and stored at seven locations near the border with South Korea. Western intelligence sources estimate that around 55% of North Korea's ballistic missiles have chemical warheads, as do 10% of its artillery shells. South Korea has launched a 10-year programme to supply every household with gas masks – 25 million of them – as a precautionary measure.

US sources maintain the Libyans have built a chemical weapon facility beneath a mountain at Rabta, producing 30 tons of mustard a month. Libya was previously accused of using poison gas in Chad.

The CWC bans the use of riot gases in war, but permits them to be used for law enforcement. There was much speculation as to the nature of the gas used by Russian special forces in their assault on the Chechen rebels holding hostages inside a Moscow theatre in October 2002. Was it a nerve gas and thus illegal or was it an irritant? German investigators later identified the agent as halothane, an anaesthetic used in the West until the mid-1980s. At least 155 hostages were killed by respiratory problems, caused by dense concentrations of the gas, pumped into the theatre, through air vents, to knock out the rebels and prevent them detonating explosives inside the building.

Terrorism is another major stumbling block to ridding the world of chemical weapons. No international convention can cover their activities. With increasing sophistication of terrorist organisations, the threat of unorthodox chemical attack has grown only too real in the 21st century.

Indeed, the nightmare has already happened. Home-made sarin was used twice in terrorist attacks in Japan by followers of the Aum Shinrikyo cult. The first, at Matsumoto in June 1994, killed seven and injured 193 more. The second, on March 20, 1995, was more serious. The sarin was released within the Tokyo subway system, killing 12 and affecting 5,510 others. In February 2002, Rome police arrested four Moroccans for alleged involvement in a plot to mount a chemical weapons attack on the US embassy there, using potassium ferrocyanide in the water supply. Cyanide was found in drums in a complex of al-Qa'eda tunnels near Kandahar airport in Afghanistan and video tapes used by the group show pet dogs being gassed to death in chemical weapons tests, possibly at Darunta. In March 2001, the Ethiopian terrorist group, the Oromo Liberation Front, were said to have used bombs filled with a blister agent against the Kenyan army near Wajir, in northern Kenya, with the official death toll put at 142.

The potential 'leakage' of chemical weapons from nations such as Iraq to terrorist groups is one of the motivations in the Bush Administration's preoccupation with dismantling the Baghdad regime; yet there is little publicly expressed concern in Washington about the equally possible terrorist acquisition of poison gases from the plethora of poorly maintained Russian chemical weapons stores.

Although some gases require little more than senior school-level knowledge of chemistry to manufacture, terrorists do not even have to go to these lengths to make chemicals a weapon of mass destruction.

An attack, using mere high explosive, to damage or destroy a chemical plant could achieve their evil aim by releasing toxic compounds into the atmosphere. An unpublished report by the US Surgeon-General in 2002 suggests that as many as 2.4 million could be killed or injured in a terrorist attack on a toxic chemical plant in a densely populated area. In October of that year, Russia and NATO mounted their first joint crisis response exercise, tackling a simulated terrorist attack on a chemical plant at Noginsk, about 100 miles from Moscow. The European Union staged a similar exercise two weeks later in the south of France. Although much has been done to enhance protection of civilian populations, such as setting up the 22 American weapons of mass destruction quick-reaction teams, more is necessary. In the USA, 80% of mayors have confirmed their emergency services lack adequate protective clothing for use in a chemical attack.

Nothing then is certain. For all the conventions and verification procedures, allegations of the use of chemical weapons continue. We have already looked at the probable use of BZ in the Bosnia and Kosovo conflicts in the 1990s, but there are also claims of deployment in Angola, against and by UNITA rebels at the start of the decade, against government forces in Mozambique in 1992 and in Azerbaijan in 1992, when Armenian forces allegedly used cyanide and phosgene during the Nagorno–Karabakh conflict. In 1990, the Liberation Tigers of Tamil Elam, fighting for independence in northern Sri Lanka, reportedly used chlorine against government forces. As usual, no hard evidence has been discovered.

The world has come a long way since the siege of Delium in 423 BC. The 20th century, particularly, saw the development year by year of ever more terrible chemical weapons and the suffering of the ever-growing number of victims of poison gas. The threat of use has not gone, nor, sadly, is it ever likely to completely fade away. No one has the power to wave a magic wand and make the knowledge of how to make chemical weapons disappear from the mind of man.

One ray of good shines out from the inhumanity of chemical warfare. During the First World War doctors discovered that casualties exposed to mustard-gas attacks suffered a fall in their white blood-cell count. In 1942, it was proved that nitrogen mustard agents could treat leukaemia and lymphonia –a discovery that marked the beginning of today's use of chemotherapy in the treatment of cancer.

CHAPTER 10
UNLOCKING PANDORA'S BOX –
BIOLOGICAL WARFARE

WHOEVER DECIDES TO DEPLOY biological weapons must verge on the insane. In many respects, the use of bacteria, viruses or toxins as a weapon of war must render them the most terrifying of all the weapons of mass destruction. Their deployment truly unlocks Pandora's Box. Nothing then is certain. Who can predict the eventual outcome, once biological weapons are released? Once disseminated, there may be little control over the containment of a disease or infection – or its longevity as an epidemic. Wind, temperature, or the uncontrolled movement of infected people or animals may all play a part in determining the spread of a man-made disease. The bacteria or virus may also mutate, perhaps rendering medical science, or natural immunities, less effective in combating its effects. There may be unimaginable damage to local or regional ecologies, with unpredictable results. Yet, biological weapons formed part of the military arsenal of nations in the past, still do in the case of around a dozen countries, and may yet be used by terrorists in attacks on water supplies or the food chain.

Unlike nuclear weapons, the deployment of biological agents is normally silent and unseen, but certainly just as apocalyptic, in terms of casualties.

But *like* the use of chemical weapons, 'germ warfare' is not a 20th century weapon of war. Its concept and deployment once again goes back into the mists of time.

In the 6th century BC, the Assyrians are said to have poisoned enemy wells with the pathogen, rye ergot. In 1346, invading Tartars catapulted lifeless victims of bubonic plague into the Genoese-held

city of Kaffa in the Crimea (modern-day Feodosiya in the Ukraine) in
a successful attempt to spread the disease to the defenders. And in
1710, the Russian Czar Peter I's forces hurled the bodies of plague
dead over the walls of the city of Reval, in Estonia, to infect the
besieged Swedish troops — although one suspects it's more likely they
were just as anxious to get rid of the diseased corpses, such is the fear
of plague. Just over 50 years later, the British in an ostensibly generous
gesture to Indian supporters of the French army in the Ohio Valley,
provided them with blankets infected with smallpox from British
victims of an epidemic in Fort Pitt. Beware British generals bearing
gifts!

So what exactly are biological weapons? They fall into five main
groups: *viruses* (such as Ebola, Marburg, smallpox, Rift Valley and
yellow fevers); *bacteria,* (anthrax, cholera, plague); the micro-organisms
rickettsiae (typhus, Q fever, Rocky Mountain spotted fever); *fungi*
(poisons derived from fungi) and *toxins* (ricin, botulinum toxins
staphylococcus enterotoxin, tetrodotoxin). They are also categorised
by their method of delivery. Firstly, there are the airborne infections
such as influenza, lassa fever, anthrax and Q fever; then water or food-
borne diseases, covering dysentery, E-coli, Salmonella, cholera and
typhoid. Finally, there are the infections spread by insects and ticks,
such as bubonic plague, typhus and yellow fever.

Viral agents have been researched and developed as agents by a
number of countries during and since the Cold War. The best known
is *smallpox* or variola, the naturally recurring strain of which was
declared eradicated in 1980, after the last cases were recorded in a
Somalian village in north-east Africa in 1977. This was a triumph of
medical science, as the disease had killed an estimated 500 million
throughout the world during the 20th century. The World Health
Organisation (WHO) subsequently recommended that all laboratory
stocks should be destroyed, primarily because of the robustness of the
virus, once released. These can be produced in large quantities, freeze-
dried and remain virulent for many years, and this makes the disease
an ideal candidate for biological weapons.

Symptoms of the disease include an initial intense fever, headaches
and vomiting followed by a rash, two to four days later, developing
into skin pustules. The Soviet biological weapons programme produced 100 different strains of the virus, some of them DNA-modified
to be resistant to medical treatment. Judging from the huge stocks of

vaccine now being assembled by Western nations, this seems one of the most likely biological weapons that could be used by terrorist groups because of its ability to infect in aerosol form. WHO maintains vaccine sufficient for 200 to 300 million separate inoculations. In Britain, the Government announced in October 2002 that every member of the population could be vaccinated against smallpox in the event of terrorists using this disease in an attack on the UK, but this would only be 'a last resort', with the main thrust of countermeasures focused on the containment of outbreaks, using vaccine held in 'pods' at strategic locations around Britain which also contain supplies of ready-printed public information sheets. Cost of the 59 million doses was estimated at £100 million.

In July 2001, the USA staged an exercise codenamed DARK WINTER simulating an attack on America using the smallpox virus. It is reported that by the end of the simulation, the disease had spread to 25 states in the USA and 15 other countries. A biological warfare expert from the Centre for Strategic and International Studies told a Congressional hearing afterwards: 'No city, no state is capable of dealing with an incident like this.'

The *Ebola* virus is virulent and is passed on through direct contact with a victim's blood or other bodily fluids, so health-care workers are particularly at risk. Symptoms are a sudden fever, severe headache and sore throat, general weakness and muscle pain. Internal and external bleeding follows after about five days, after vomiting, diarrhoea, and damage to kidney and liver functions. Mortality occurs in more than 50% of cases.

The *Marburg* virus is another member of the family of African haemorrhagic fevers, but is less virulent. It produces headaches, fever, vomiting, diarrhoea, muscle pain, leading to light sensitivity, skin rashes, conjunctivitis and jaundice. Around 25% of victims die.

Dengue fever, normally passed by mosquito, is naturally endemic in Africa, central and South America, South-East Asia and the eastern Mediterranean. Symptoms are a blinding headache, fever, chills, joint and muscle pain, skin rashes, bleeding in the gums, skin and internally, prostration, reduced blood pressure and finally a state of critical shock.

Yellow fever affects the bloodstream and the infection arrives via mosquito bites. It produces headaches, fever, chills, prostration, nasal and chest congestion, with jaundice and internal bleeding in the stomach in severe cases. It is not normally lethal.

Venezuelan equine encephalitis is another insect- or tick-borne disease and causes vomiting, sore throats, coughs and stomach upsets that incapacitates sufferers. A small number of victims in naturally occurring epidemics suffer damage to the central nervous system, followed by paralysis and coma.

The last viral infection to appear in the arsenal of biological weapons is *Rift Valley fever*, again spread by mosquito. The weaponised version may be spread by aerosol spray. Symptoms include bodily weakness and fever, but severe cases may suffer hepatitis, blood in the mucus and failure to urinate. This latter group of victims may suffer a 50% mortality rate.

Of the modern bacterial weapons, *bubonic plague*, caused by the bacillus *Yersinia pestis*, has been a scourge of the human race for several millennia. In the Bible, the First Book of Samuel describes how the plague devastated the Philistines after they captured the Israelites' Ark of the Covenant:

> ... the hand of the Lord was against the city [of Ashdod] with a very great destruction and He smote the men of the city, both small and great, and they had emerods [tumours] in their secret parts ...

The first pandemic of bubonic plague occurred in the eastern Mediterranean in AD 541–2, killing around 100 million. The second, popularly known as the Black Death, killed 24 million Europeans during the 14th and 15th centuries in Europe, sweeping across from Asia, through Italy, France and England and into Scandinavia. The third originated in China in 1894 and killed 13 million Indians in the next half-century.

Bubonic plague is spread by the bite of an infected flea that normally lives on the black rat. The more virulent version, *pneumonic plague*, is spread by airborne infection through victims' exhalations. Symptoms of the bubonic plague begin with high fever, glandular swelling, including the creation of enlarged lymph nodes or buboes in the area of the groin — hence the name of the disease. Pneumonic plague produces severe bleeding in the infected lungs. It is normally fatal and, as we shall see, has been weaponised in the past.

Anthrax, spread by the *Bacillus anthracis*, is a disease that can afflict those working with infected animal hides, wool or bones and is still prevalent in 82 countries in Africa, Asia and the Middle East. One version affects the skin, forming dry scabs and ulcerated sores. The more deadly pulmonary anthrax induces initial symptoms similar to influenza, followed by breathing difficulties and terminal shock with death coming a day later. The mortality rate for this version can be more than 90%. Pulmonary anthrax is contracted through inhalation of the spores that are easy to propagate. It formed part of the Soviet biological weapons armoury and more recently has been weaponised by Iraq, according to Western intelligence sources. The US has tried to acquire a sample of one genetically modified strain of anthrax, developed under the old Soviet research and development programme and now held in a laboratory at Serpukhov, near Moscow. This Russian strain is said to be resistant to vaccine.

In November 1969, a team of WHO consultants, in a report on chemical and biological weapons, calculated that if an aerosol spray containing 150lbs of anthrax was disseminated by an aircraft over a city with a 500,000 population, around 250,000 cases of anthrax could occur, of whom 94,000 would be fatal.

Military Compound 19, within the Soviet Institute of Microbiology and Virology, in Sverdlovsk (now Yekaterinburg), 850 miles east of Moscow, suffered a mysterious explosion on April 3, 1979 which released a cloud of anthrax spores to the outside world. The narrow plume extended 35 miles downwind from the city, and at least 66 people died from pulmonary, or inhalation, anthrax and a further 77 cases were identified. Livestock also died. Moscow maintained, rather feebly, at the time that the casualties were caused by eating contaminated meat, producing intestinal anthrax, but in February 1992, the then Russian President, Boris Yeltsin, acknowledged there had been an accidental release of airborne spores.

Anthrax was infamously used in a campaign of terror in the USA, beginning just 24 days after the September 11 attacks in 2001. Four letters, containing the spores of the disease held in a fine white powder, were sent in the US mails: two to the Senate building in Washington and two to media organisations in New York, affecting postal workers and administrative staff along the way. Five people died from pulmonary anthrax after inhaling the fine spores, including a journalist in Florida. That fifth letter addressed to him has never been found. Thirteen more victims recovered from the infection. Around 300 postal and other facilities were tested for anthrax and around 32,000 Americans took medication to prevent infection. The concentrated version used is called the 'Ames' strain, first isolated from a cow in Iowa in the 1950s and this, together with the fact that the spores were unmilled, strongly suggests a US military or government laboratory source for the bacteria. Motivation behind the attack remains unclear.

Cholera, passed on by contaminated water or contact with infected faeces, produced widespread and deadly epidemics in the unhealthy, overcrowded slums of Europe in the 19th century. It is a gastrointestinal disease, manifested by vomiting, liquid diarrhoea, loss of body fluids and collapse.

Typhoid, or *Salmonella typhi,* can be present naturally in some foods such as shellfish or milk and was again the cause of huge epidemics in Europe in the 19th century, killing off several of the British Royal Family, including Victoria's consort, Prince Albert. It causes high fever, spleen enlargement, spots on the skin and ulceration of the intestines.

Glanders, or *Malleomyces mallei,* normally affects horses, sheep, mules, goats and dogs but infected animals can pass on the disease to humans by inhalation or by contact with skin abrasions, producing large skin lesions and ulcers in the mucous membrane but in the inhaled form, damages the respiratory tracts. Untreated cases are frequently fatal.

In the First World War, undercover German agents were accused in 1915 of using anthrax and glanders to infect livestock and animal feed destined for export to Allied countries. These alleged attacks included the infection of Romanian sheep that were to be shipped to Russia; American horses and feed due to be exported to France, and mules in Argentina. A German was arrested in 1917 in Mesopotamia (in present-day Iraq) and accused of infecting 4,500 mules with glanders. Germany firmly denied these allegations and post-war League of Nations inquiries failed to find any substantive evidence. The Japanese are also reported to have used glanders as a biological weapon in China in the Second World War.

Diphtheria, another disease once common in European children before the Second World War, is a local infection of the respiratory passages in the nose and chest and can be passed on via airborne infection or contact with the mucous discharge. Symptoms include sore throats and blockages to the air passages and the disease can damage the body's vital organs if left untreated.

Brucellosis, a disease more associated with the dairy industry, could be spread by aerosol or contaminating food supplies. It causes fever, chills, body aches and headaches but is rarely fatal.

Tularaemia, or rabbit fever (*Francisella tularensis*), is a highly infective disease with just one bacterium capable of infecting a human. It is normally contracted through the bites of infected insects, sometimes by inhalation of contaminated dust or by eating or drinking infected food and water, the latter called typhoidal tularaemia. Symptoms include chills, headache and fever and sometimes skin ulcers. The typhoidal version causes fever, weight loss and prostration. The Soviet Union produced a new strain of this disease in 1983 in a laboratory at Obolensk, 60 miles south of Moscow.

Of diseases caused by micro-organisms, or rickettsia, the best-known is *typhus,* either endemic or epidemic. The former is passed on via flea or rat bites and is the milder version, causing high temperatures, skin rashes and bodily pain. Epidemic typhus is contracted through contact with infected larvae and has similar symptoms.

Rocky Mountain spotted fever, or *Rickettsia rickettsi,* is naturally contracted through the bite of an infected tick, inducing pains in the muscles and fever and later a skin rash spreading from the wrists and ankles.

The incapacitating diseases, *Q fever,* or *Coxiella burnetti,* first described in 1937 amongst abattoir workers in Brisbane, Australia, is contracted through inhalation of contaminated particles held by infected farm animals. Symptoms include chest pains, chills, fever, headache and appetite loss. It is rarely fatal but very infective. The US Army reports that 100lbs of dried powdered *Coxiella burnetti* could produce similar casualty levels as the same amount of anthrax or tularaemia organisms.

The most viable biological agent in the toxin group is *ricin,* easily made from the residue of castor oil beans after industrial processing. An average lethal dose is 15,000th of a gram. Symptoms include a tightness of the chest, coughing fits, breathing difficulties and failure of the respiratory and circulation systems. In September 1978, Georgi Markov, a Bulgarian journalist who worked in the West, was stabbed in the right thigh with an umbrella tip as he waited for a bus on London's Waterloo Bridge. Seventy-two hours later he was dead, a victim of assassination by the then Bulgarian Intelligence Service. The umbrella was a form of gun that fired a small pellet into his body, later recovered in a post-mortem. The pellet held a tiny quantity of ricin, wrapped in a waxy paste that was dissolved by Markov's body heat, thus releasing the agent into his tissues. The technology was said to have been supplied by the Soviet Union. Ten days before, a similar operation had been mounted against another Bulgarian exile, Vladimir Kostov, in Paris, but he was wearing a thick overcoat and this prevented the pellet entering his body very deeply. The wax fortunately failed to melt, preserving Kostov's life.

Other toxins include *botulinum,* found naturally in undercooked or badly stored food (and one of the most toxic of substances known to man), which causes paralysis leading to death by suffocation; and *Staphylococcus enterotoxin B,* again occurring as a result of poor food hygiene and *saxitoxin.*

Biological weapons have distinct advantages. They are easily disseminated, perhaps by aerosol or spray, or by contaminating water supplies. No high-technology delivery means are necessary for an effective attack — basic crop-spraying equipment on aircraft can be an efficient method. The agents are difficult to detect. The enemy may be totally unaware of the attack and, indeed in some environments, may initially confuse it with a natural epidemic. The effects may not be apparent for some days as the incubation period runs its deadly course. Once deployed, some agents can multiply, further spreading the infection, and saturating the adversary's medical facilities as well as triggering panic within his population. Their use involves no physical destruction of buildings or infrastructure. For the military, biological weapons are also *cheap* to produce and to deploy. A United Nations report in 1969 estimated the cost of such an offensive against a civilian population at $1 per square kilometre for biological agents; $600 to cover the same area for chemical weapons; $800 for nuclear warheads and $2,000 for conventional armaments.

The military disadvantages in the use of biological weapons are grave. The eventual outcome will always have an element of uncertainty. Weather can influence the way an agent is dispersed in an unpredictable way — and sunlight can kill some organisms. Conversely, some agents like anthrax may contaminate an area for generations. Biological agents may infect friendly forces as well as the enemy. At the very least, at the military tactical level, vital precautionary and protective measures would slow down advances or inhibit defensive actions. Finally, a biological weapons release may trigger overwhelming retaliation and thus escalate the conflict. In this context, recent statements by British politicians seem to imply that the UK would consider using nuclear weapons to respond to an attack on its civilian population by biological or chemical weapons. The British Defence Secretary Geoff Hoon said in March 2002 that there are 'some states who would be deterred by the fact that the United Kingdom possesses nuclear weapons and has the willingness to use them in the appropriate circumstances'.

But to other 'states of concern' such as Saddam Hussein's Iraq, who may be 'willing to sacrifice their own people in order to make that kind of gesture,' Mr Hoon repeated that they should be 'absolutely confident we would be willing to use our nuclear weapons.'

For the terrorist, few of the disadvantages of biological weapons apply. Their objective, after all, is to create alarm among their target's population, now increasingly without fear of the outcome to themselves. Such weapons meet all the requirements of an ideal terrorist strike: maximum terror, caused particularly by fear of the unknown, maximum publicity, and maximum disruption to an adversary's infrastructure, as thousands may seek medical attention whether infected or not. Some pathogens and toxins do not require sophisticated equipment to replicate. And biological weapons can represent a low-risk method of attacking a powerful state. Not for nothing are they known as the 'Poor Man's Atomic Bomb'. On a lower level, injecting an agent through packaging could affect processed food. Imported food products could also be sabotaged, such as the cyanide contamination of Chilean grapes in the USA in March 1989. The terrorist with a hypodermic needle loaded with a deadly agent could be thousands of miles away, even in another country.

As we have seen, the 1925 Geneva Protocol, prohibiting the use of poison or asphyxiating gases, also created a new ban on the use of bacteriological agents in war. In Germany, in the mid-1930s and in the early part of the Second World War, military scientists investigated anthrax, plague and cholera as potential weapons, but these were never weaponised. Japan was more enthusiastic, and in 1932, established the Epidemic Research Laboratory in the army military medicine school.

In the run-up to the Second World War and in its early years, Japan deployed biological agents against China and the Soviet Union. In 1936, the now notorious Unit 731 of the Imperial Japanese Army, operating under the cover of a water purification unit, created a base at Ping Fan, 20 miles south of the provincial capital of Harbin, in north-east China, to investigate the effects of various bacteriological weapons. The facility included 150 buildings, occupying nearly four square miles, with five satellite camps, and a total of 3,000 Japanese scientists and technicians at work there. A second unit, designated 100, operated south of Chang-Chun in Manchuria, and was officially called the Army Military Horse Epidemic Prevention Department. Its main role was to adapt the agents into weapons: bombs, artillery shells and spray tanks for aircraft.

In May 1939, fighting broke out along the border with Mongolia between Japanese forces occupying Manchuria and Soviet troops, in a skirmish now called the 'Nomonhan Incident'. The initial encounter rapidly escalated into full-scale conflict with tank battles, supported by ground attack and interceptor aircraft and by early September, the Japanese army was in full retreat, after losing around 61,000 men in combat. It was in these dire circumstances that the Japanese resorted to the first use of biological weapons in modern times. A special detachment from Unit 731, comprising two officers and 20 men, formed a 'suicide squad' to infiltrate the advancing Russian forces and to contaminate Soviet water supplies from the Khalkin-Gol river with typhus, para-typhoid and cholera. The army's list of their names was signed by each volunteer in his own blood.

Unit 731 investigated plague, anthrax, dysentery, typhoid, para-typhoid, typhus and cholera as potential weapons of war, as well as biological crop and livestock destroyers, and were capable of mass-producing a number of strains of bacteria and viruses. The experiments used prisoners – Chinese, Russians, Mongolians and Koreans, all contemptuously known as *marutas* or 'logs' – as human guinea pigs to test the efficacy of the pathogens, sometimes practising surgery without anaesthetic to evaluate the medical effects. An estimated 3,000 Allied prisoners of war – including Americans, British, French and Australians – were also almost certainly used in these trials. Victims were tied to stakes on a test site and sprayed with disease cultures to test range and spread of various delivery methods. Some 3,000 died in these experiments, which later included research into gas gangrene, botulism, brucellosis and meningococcal infections. Around 1,000 post-mortems alone were carried out on those exposed to anthrax spores spread by aerosol. No prisoner was known to leave Ping Fan alive.

The Unit also undertook field trials, attacking at least 11 Chinese cities with air-sprayed diseases. These began on October 4, 1940 when a Japanese aircraft dropped plague-contaminated rice, wheat and fleas over Chuhsien in Chekiang province. An outbreak of bubonic plague, a disease hitherto unknown in the area, followed a month later in which 21 died in just over three weeks. On October 29, a similar operation was mounted over the city of Ningpo in the same province, and again, plague appeared, killing 99. The trials continued throughout 1941–2 in Suiyan and Ninghsia provinces, with aircraft dropping a variety of substances, including grain and granules, all impregnated with plague bacilli. Although detailed evidence is lacking, it is believed that thousands of civilians were treated in hospitals and at least 700 were victims of plague. Another trial over the business district of Changteh in Hunan province in 1941 infected more than 1,000 civilians and led to the reported death of 1,700 Japanese soldiers, the latter unplanned victims of the experiments.

There are unconfirmed reports that the Japanese army loaded some form of biological weapon on a submarine and despatched it to the defenders of the island of Saipan, in the north Marianas in the Pacific in 1944, but the boat was sunk before it could reach its destination. Certainly, by early 1945, the Japanese had 900lbs of anthrax stockpiled for use in airdropped fragmentation bombs.

With the tide of war turning against it, Japan also worked on plans for a biological weapons attack on continental USA. The first idea was to use the so-called 'balloon bomb' – huge dirigibles that could be carried by prevailing high-altitude westerly winds across the Pacific to targets on the western seaboard of America, armed with plague or anthrax. This idea was rejected in July 1944 because of fears of American retaliation with chemical weapons against the Japanese homeland, although balloons *were* launched, armed with high-explosive charges and around 200 landed in the western states of the USA, one killing six people in Oregon and another in Montana.

The next idea was even more bizarre: to use the two giant *Sen Toku* seaplane transport submarines to launch *kamikaze* air attacks on San Diego, California. Each had three Aichi M6A1 Seiran aircraft in cylindrical hangars below the conning tower. Each seaplane would carry a cargo of plague-infected fleas and would crash into its objective. The mission was planned for September 22, 1945 but was overtaken by the Japanese surrender on August 15.

At the end of the war, Ping Fan was destroyed and thousands of infected animals were released into the Chinese countryside. These were probably responsible for the plague epidemic that swept Harbin afterwards.

No member of Unit 731 was arraigned by the Western Allies to stand trial for war crimes at the end of the Second World War (although 12 Japanese prisoners of war were tried by a military tribunal at Khabarovsk, in the Soviet Union, in 1949 for the use of biological weapons). A memorial tower to the unit stands in Tokyo. Its commander, Lieutenant General Shiro Ishii, died in his bed from throat cancer in 1959.

Successive Japanese governments initially denied the existence of Unit 731 but continued to firmly discount Japan's use of biological warfare against Chinese civilians by claiming lack of evidence. In August 2002, the Tokyo district court acknowledged for the first time that the Imperial Japanese Army *had* used biological weapons in China but rejected individual claims for £55,000 compensation and demands for official apologies by 180 Chinese plaintiffs who testified that their relatives had been killed by Unit 731. All claims for compensation, said the court, had been settled by the 1951 San Francisco Treaty that ended the Pacific War and agreements.

Although the Japanese dynamited much of the Ping Fan facility at the end of the war, the Chinese government has converted the former headquarters building into a museum at the site and visitors can see some of the ruined structures.

Britain began research into biological agents in 1940 when the War Cabinet set up a highly secret group – the 'Biology Department' - at the Chemical Weapons facility at Porton Down, Wiltshire, to examine new weapons and potential defences against the threat of 'germ warfare'. In size, the team never exceeded 50 doctors, scientists and technicians, but included two American bacteriologists, specially commissioned as army and navy officers in the British forces.

It was quickly discovered that anthrax could become a viable weapon against the Third Reich. The remote west Scottish island of Gruinard, just a few hundred yards from the mainland coast and the small village of Mungasdale, in Ross and Cromarty, was requisitioned as a test site in 1942. Its 522 acres, covered in bracken, peat and heather, was declared a 'prohibited place' and secret trials with two types of bombs filled with anthrax spores were undertaken in the summers of 1942 and 1943 employing flocks of sheep, tethered in measured concentric circles around the points of impact. A film of the trials remained classified until 1997. The sheep died within three days, the island became contaminated with anthrax and jubilant scientists confirmed that this was a potent biological weapon. As a result, Operation VEGETATION was launched, which involved the manufacture of five million linseed oil cattle-cakes, each one injected with a lethal dose of the disease. The plan was to drop these infected cakes onto German pastureland as an anti-livestock weapon: a number of RAF Lancaster four-engined bombers were specially modified for the mission. But the order to use the anthrax weapon was never given, and the stockpile of deadly cattle-cakes, stored behind the closely guarded barbed wire perimeter of Porton Down, was destroyed after the end of the war.

Regular tests demonstrated that Gruinard's contamination showed no signs of reduction and the British government was forced to acquire the island in 1946 and impose a strict quarantine. So it remained for almost three decades, with grim warning signs posted on its rocky shores to warn off the curious. Tests in the early 1980s showed the area of contamination was then limited to about three acres around the immediate test site and a microbiological survey demonstrated the anthrax spores could be destroyed. In August 1986, work began on the long-awaited decontamination of Gruinard by government contractors, clad in bulky protective clothing. The area was first sprayed with an herbicide and the dead vegetation burnt off. A total of 280 tons of a 5% solution of formaldehyde in seawater was then applied to the spore-affected zone. Soil samples from 130 separate spots were tested and the very few spores remaining were re-treated in July 1987. Cost of the cleaning-up operation was in excess of £500,000. The island was given the all-clear and returned to its civilian owner on May 1, 1990, with the then junior Defence Minister, Michael Neubert, symbolically removing one of the red warning signs on Gruinard.

The Soviets mirrored the Gruinard experiments with their own, likewise with anthrax, on Vozrozhdeniye ('renaissance') island in Central Asia's inland Aral Sea, one of Moscow's test sites for biological weapons in the 1970s. They also hastily buried hundreds of metal barrels containing anthrax spores there around 1990. This followed the defection of two Russian microbiologists, Drs Kanatjan Alibekov and Vladimir Pasechnik, who worked on the biological weapons programme, to Britain and the United States in the late 1980s. Their disclosures led to the US president George Bush senior and British prime minister Margaret Thatcher confronting the Soviet government with firm evidence that they were breaching international law by continuing biological weapons development under the organisational cover name of Biopreparat.   The island is said now to hold enough spores of the disease to kill the population of the world several times over.

After the break-up of the Soviet Union, neighbouring Uzbekistan and Kazakhstan refused to accept responsibility for the dump on Vozrozhdeniye island. Russian guards were withdrawn in 1992, thus removing all security at the site and to make matters worse, ecological damage in the area is shrinking the waters of the Aral Sea. Shortly, the island will be one no longer — raising fears of the spread of the disease by animals becoming contaminated when visiting the site. The US Department of Defense now plans to provide funding to assist Russia to clean up Vozrozhdeniye and to destroy the remaining facilities there.

The British continued their experiments with anthrax in 1949, together with the brucella bacteria, off the island of Antigua in the Caribbean. In Operation HARNESS, 600 sheep and guinea pigs were held in containers on rafts and sprayed with the bacteria. Documents now released into the public domain indicate the trials proved inconclusive because of the heat and sea conditions. Five hundred of the sheep had to be shot because it was found they were 'unsuitable' for the tests. One member of the research team became infected by the spores being tested. All had to undergo acclimatisation in preparation for wearing the heavy protective suits; even so, some collapsed from heat exhaustion. The Porton Down report said: 'Operation HARNESS has shown above all else that the keynote to success in field trials is simplicity. The technique was overcomplicated and impracticable.'

The USA launched its programme to create biological weapons in 1943 after Secretary of War Henry Stimson asked the National Academy of Sciences to assess the feasibility of such weapons. There were fears that Berlin had developed an offensive biological weapon capability. Ironically, Germany had not gone down that road, but Japan very definitely had. After some work at American universities, the US Army's biological research got under way, focusing on anthrax, botulism, tularaemia, glanders and brucellosis for use only in retaliation: a policy of limitation declared the year before by President Roosevelt and Churchill, in line with the Geneva Protocol. Using British expertise, there were also American plans to destroy the Japanese rice crop with the fungus *Helminthosporium oryzae van brede de haan* in 1994–5 but these were abandoned in favour of the faster-acting conventional incendiary bomb. The army programme set up its headquarters at a National Guard airfield at Camp Detrick in Frederick, Maryland and a 2,000-acre test site was established at Horn Island, Pascagoula, Mississippi, the latter replaced in 1944 by the Dugway Proving Ground in Utah. A production facility was also built near Terre Haute in Indiana.

As with the German rocket programmes, the US was keen at the end of the Second World War to capture enemy expertise and information, but this time regarding biological weapons. Twenty-two Japanese scientists engaged in this research were granted immunity from war crimes prosecution by the US in return for full and frank information being handed over to the Camp Detrick team. From documents now in the Public Record Office, it seems clear the British also acquired some of this information.

A Pentagon review in 1948 suggested that the USA was particularly vulnerable to a covert biological weapons attack and the American biological warfare programme continued at Fort Detrick, protected by the highest level of classification. The programme was reaffirmed in October 1950, based on intelligence assessments that the Soviet Union now had an offensive capability and that biological weapons would be used by the Chinese and North Koreans. A ten-storey production facility was built at the Pine Bluff Arsenal, Arkansas, in 1951, manufacturing *Brucella suis* (brucellosis) and *Francisella tularensis* (tularaemia). These pathogens were later deployed in Air Force anti-personnel cluster bombs. In 1959, the US Army chose yellow fever as another of its biological weapons, the virus having been isolated from an individual infected in a 1954 epidemic in Trinidad in the West Indies. The chosen vehicle for spreading the biological weapon was the mosquito (see below) and army laboratories were said to be capable of breeding half a million of the insects each month.

Western governments mounted a series of secret trials in the 1950–60s on their unknowing civilian populations to evaluate the scale of the threat from biological weapons. A British report by the Microbiological Research Establishment (MRE) at Porton Down, released to the Public Record Office in London in February 2002, details one such experiment in a series, codenamed SABOTAGE, in the London underground system, undertaken (of course!) with ministers' permission from 1963–4.

Spray-dried spores of harmless *Bacillus globigii*, which mimics the physical properties of anthrax, were secretly released in packages (one was a face powder carton) from the windows of a Northern Line tube train travelling in the tunnel system across south London from Colliers Wood to Tooting Broadway stations. London Transport staff monitored air samples at the two stations to measure the movement of air. Dust swabs were then taken at other stations along the Northern Line.

The trial showed that bacterial spores could be carried for several miles underground and locally could persist as a high-concentration aerosol 'for a considerable period'. The inhaled dose at Tooting Broadway, the station closest to the release, would have been about five million spores in the first half an hour after the arrival of the aerosol and about 100 times less at the neighbouring stations, Tooting Bec, or Collier's Wood. 'Only a few hundred' people were exposed to the highest doses and, 'given the non-pathogenic nature of this bacterium, it is unlikely that these releases caused any disease', according to a later Defence Ministry inquiry report. Similar experiments were staged in the tunnels beneath government departments in Whitehall.

There were other trials in Britain, which recently have triggered public anxiety about the possible health hazards involved, including reports of a high level of miscarriages among women in the Dorset coastal village of East Lulworth.

These secret experiments were staged because of growing official fears in the 1950s that an aircraft flying 'along the British coastline, outside of territorial waters, might be able to cover much of the country with a lethal dose of a germ warfare agent' and were designed to indicate the concentrations, speed and spread of such bacteria. Others were aimed at investigating the protection of warships and armoured vehicles against biological attack in 1968–76. About 100 trials were staged by Porton Down.

The Ministry of Defence commissioned an eminent scientist, Professor Brian G. Spratt, to investigate these concerns. During his inquiry he examined a still classified internal review of all biological warfare experiments carried out in Britain between 1940 and 1979.

His report, published in June 2002, reveals the surprising scale of these covert trials along or off the Dorset coast, using four species of bacteria or viruses – *Bacillus globigii* (which we last met on the London Underground), *Bacterium aerogenes* (now called *Klebsiella aerogenes*), *Esherichia coli* and *Serratia marcescens.*

Both the *aerogenes* and *Serratia marcescens* were first killed either by adding formaldehyde to the final concentration and then heating, or using phenol. Although both are now known to present health risks while alive, the inquiry found no reason to believe that any survived the sterilisation process and were safe to use in the trials.

Other bacteria were live, including *Esherichia coli,* more familiarly known as E-coli – something of a bogeyman in popular perception because of the publicity over food-poisoning cases. In fact, there are between 10 million and one billion E-coli bacteria in every gram of human faeces and the great majority of strains, such as MRE162, the one used off Dorset, are almost totally harmless. That used in the environmental trials was, in the stark words of Professor Spratt's report 'isolated in 1949 by a microbiologist at MRE Porton Down from a lavatory seat and will have been derived from faeces.' One can't help wondering how the scientist thought of looking for a handy bacterium there. The report acknowledges, however, that it is 'considered possible that a strain of E-coli such as MRE162, which is unlikely to cause diarrhoea on ingestion, may on inhalation be able to initiate a blood or chest infection in a small number of highly susceptible people,' although this should be placed in the context of everyday exposure to the bacteria such as using the lavatory or changing a baby's nappies.

Thirty six releases, some 'massive', of live bacteria were carried out at night from a ship, the *Icewhale,* moored between one and 20 miles off the Dorset coast, with the bacteria drifting inland between April 1963 and January 1968.

Another series in 1955–63, called the 'Fluorescent Particle Trials', involved the dropping of zinc cadmium sulphide, again mimicking the characteristics of bacteria, by a Canberra bomber aircraft, flying from north-east England and along the south and west coasts.

Overall, Professor Spratt clears the trials of causing problems such as miscarriages, learning difficulties in children or birth defects, or indeed chronic ill health. 'The release of bacteria ... were very unlikely to have had health consequences for the overwhelming majority of individuals that were exposed,' he stresses.

The US trials in populated areas were another matter, however. The first large-scale field trial testing vulnerabilities to bacterium-charged aerosols was conducted from a ship in San Francisco Bay in 1950, using *Bacillus globigii*, which mimics anthrax, and live *Serratia marcescens*. Over the next few years, the incidence of pneumonia-like serratia infections in the area increased by between five to ten times the normal rate, with one man dying and ten others treated in hospital. *Serratia marcescens* was later used in tests involving the public water supply.

Two years later, the US used the same chemical as the British, zinc cadmium sulphide, in trials over S. Louis, Missouri, and Minneapolis, Minnesota.

Even more controversial was the US Army test in 1951 designed to discover whether African Americans were more susceptible to the fungus infection *Aspergillus fumigatus*, with a number of black citizens deliberately exposed. In 1955, there was a sharp increase in whooping cough cases, including 12 deaths, in Tampa, Florida after a covert trial by the CIA involving bacteria. Details of the test remain classified.

The US conducted trials to establish the mosquito as a method of disseminating yellow fever in the late 1950s with uninfected insects released by helicopter or aircraft above Savannah, Georgia and at the Avon Park bombing range in Florida. In just 24 hours hundreds of people had been bitten, demonstrating their spread over a wide area. The use of the insect as a purveyor of the weapon had been proven.

The London Underground trials were mirrored in New York in 1966, when US Army tests were mounted to gauge the vulnerability of the subway system to biological attack with harmless *Bacillus subtilis*. The experiment demonstrated that the release of organisms in just one station could infect the whole system because of the draught through the tunnels caused by the passage of subway trains.

Happily, however, the international political tide was turning against biological weapons. In July 1969, the UK submitted a statement to the Conference of the UN Committee on Disarmament, suggesting a prohibition on 'the development, production and stockpiling of bacteriological and toxin weapons.' Two months later, the Soviet Union urged the UN General Assembly to set up a disarmament convention. The moves were given added impetus by an analysis by WHO specialists published in November of that year, which stressed that biological weapons posed a special threat against civilians:

> This is because of the often indiscriminate nature of such weapons and
> because the high concentrations in which they would be used in military
> operations could lead to significant unintended involvement of the civil-
> ian population within the target area and for considerable distances
> downwind.

Large-scale use could cause medical illness that would overwhelm
existing health resources and facilities and cause 'lasting changes of an
unpredictable nature in man's environment', said the report. As we
have seen, it suggested that a single bomber disseminating just over
100lbs of dried anthrax in aerosol form over a city with a population
of half to five million people would cause tens of thousands of deaths
over an area of 15 square miles. There were worse predictions to come:

> Sabotage-induced or open attacks, causing the secondary spread of epi-
> demics of yellow fever, pneumonic plague, smallpox or influenza, might
> under certain conditions ultimately result in many millions of illnesses and
> deaths.

After ten years of research, US President Richard Nixon stopped all
American offensive biological and toxin weapon research and production in November 1969 and February 1970 and Washington's
stockpiles were destroyed between May 1971 and May 1972. These
included anthrax, botulism, Venezuelan equine encephalitis, brucellosis and staphylococcal enterotoxin B.

In 1972, the USA, Soviet Union and the UK signed the long-
awaited Convention on the Prohibition of the Development,
Production and Stockpiling of Bacteriological (Biological) and Toxin
Weapons (BWC) and the transfer of such technologies to other states.
It has been signed by more than 180 nations but has proved inadequate
to tackle the proliferation of biological weapons throughout the
world or indeed, adequate verification.

The issue here is similar to that posed by policing research and production of chemical weapons. Facilities that could produce biological
weapons may quite legally manufacture vitamins, antibiotics, vaccines
or even the innocent breakfast yoghurt. The equipment is essentially
the same.

Indeed, some of the toxins that can be used as biological agents have entirely peaceful uses as well, such as the employment of botulinum toxin to treat disorders of the muscles of the eye, or in the cosmetics and beauty industry. The US Army's *Textbook of Military Medical Aspects of Chemical and Biological Warfare*, stresses:

> We must acknowledge that potential biological warfare agents are currently found worldwide in laboratories and medical centers.

Inspectors can investigate production facilities but who can judge the *intentions* of a government? So detection of offensive biological weapons development is extremely difficult, as indeed, is detection of their deployment on the battlefield. A great deal of research into the latter is continuing. In 2002, the US Army began trialling a new biological detector, based on DNA-test kits. The analysis is done in one cartridge, held in the hand, and can produce a definitive result in just 30 minutes. Kits for detecting anthrax, plague, tularaemia and botulism were delivered for the trials.

The US Department of Defense (DoD) has continued to express 'serious concerns' about Russia's biological warfare activities and the status of the offensive agents programme inherited from the Soviet Union. 'Some key components of the program remain largely intact and may support a possible future mobilisation capability ... Despite Russian ratification of the BWC, work outside the scope of legitimate biological defense may be occurring now at selected facilities and the United States continues to receive unconfirmed reports of some ongoing offensive biological warfare activities,' the DoD told Congress in April 2002.

Some 50 sites in Russia were involved in the Soviet-era biological weapons programme, which covered anthrax, smallpox, plague, tularaemia, glanders, Ebola and Marburg. These were all described by the catch-all 'Weapons of Special Designation'. One of these locations, the Vektor Institute, in Koltsovo, Novosibirsk in western Siberia, is said to maintain more than 15,000 viral strains, as well as being an official repository for smallpox samples. Another, the State Research Centre for Applied Microbiology at Obolensk, holds a 2,000-strong collection of bacteria and viruses, including genetically modified anthrax. A laboratory at Pokrov, outside Moscow, developed agricultural weapons, including foot and mouth disease, targeted on poultry, livestock and crops. US officials maintain that today, many viruses are housed at Pokrov in a 'dilapidated compound' with a patched-up alarm system and inadequately guarded.

Worries in the West about Russian inability or unwillingness to dismantle its offensive biological weapons programme led to the 1992 Trilateral Agreement signed by Russia, the USA and Britain. It committed Moscow to ending biological warfare development; approving inspections of suspect installations and conversion of facilities into civilian uses. Conversely, Russia is able to inspect sites in the UK and USA. Despite this, the doubts remain ...

China is another candidate of concern. The DoD said in 2002 that China 'possesses an advanced biotechnology infrastructure as well as the munitions production facilities necessary to develop, produce and weaponise biological agents. China has consistently claimed that it never researched, produced or possessed any biological weapons and would never do so. Nevertheless, China's declarations under the voluntary BWC ... are believed to be inaccurate and incomplete and there are reports that China may retain elements of its biological warfare program.'

Lisa Bronson, US Deputy Undersecretary for Defense (Technology Security Policy and Proliferation) believes that at least a dozen nations have or are actively seeking anthrax as a biological weapon. 'Countries like Iraq, Iran, North Korea, Libya [and] Syria have consciously over the last seven to ten years gone ahead and been developing' biological weapons, she says. The USA's non-proliferation efforts 'have not resulted in preventing them from getting the capability ... They have it and we can't turn a blind eye to the fact that they have it.'

As far as Iraq is concerned, Baghdad told the UN weapons inspectors that before the second Gulf War, DESERT STORM, it had manufactured 100 botulinum freefall bombs, 50 anthrax bombs and seven aflatoxin bombs. Anthrax had been weaponised into five missile warheads and 16 were filled with botulinum, four with aflatoxin. Then, the Iraqis had ten Scud missiles remaining. In January 1991, these were deployed to four separate locations.

Iraq had begun research into biological weapons in the mid-1970s with a research and development facility established at al-Salam, also known as Salman Pak, 20 miles south of Baghdad. After switching funding briefly away from biological agents to focus on chemical weapons, the programme restarted after the outbreak of the Iran–Iraq war. The regime set up biological agent production plants at Taji, Baghdad, a single-cell protein plant converted to manufacture botulinum toxin in the late 1980s; al-Dawrah, (botulinum toxin) al-Hakam, (Project 324) al-Muthanna, Samarra, al-Fudhaliyah, Mosul, (aflatoxin production and genetic engineering) al-Salam, Fallujah 1 (Habanniyah).

In 1995, Iraq declared the production of 19,000 litres of botulinum toxin, 8,500 litres of concentrated anthrax and 2,200 litres of aflatoxins (the poisons produced by fungi and moulds, with the capacity to cause liver failure). The Iraqi biological warfare arsenal probably still includes these agents and British intelligence believes that some, together with chemical weapons, could be deployed offensively within 45 minutes of the release order being given. The Iraqis are also believed to hold stocks of ricin as well as the bacterium, *Clostridium perfringens*, which causes gangrene.

The US Department of Defense told Congress in April 2002 that North Korea's resources 'presently include a rudimentary biotechnology infrastructure that is sufficient to support the production of limited quantities of toxins, as well as viral and bacterial biological warfare agents such as anthrax, cholera and plague' as well as accomplishing weaponisation. 'It may have biological agents available for use.'

Confirmation of the North Korean biological weapons programme has come from the unlikely source of the Russian Foreign Intelligence Service, the successor to the KGB. In 1993, it disclosed that it had knowledge that North Korea

is performing applied military-biological research in a whole number of universities, medical institutes and specialised research institutes. Work is being performed in these research centres with inducers of malignant anthrax, cholera, bubonic plague and smallpox. Biological weapons are being tested on the island territories belonging to the DPRK [Democratic Peoples' Republic of Korea].

Libya is said to have a small-scale biological warfare programme at a complex near Tripoli, disguised as a medical facility. It is believed this has not progressed much further than the research and development stage, although the North African country is also believed to be seeking to equip itself with artillery shells and short- and medium-range missiles fitted with botulism and anthrax-filled warheads, assisted by Iraqi scientists The same is said of Syria, with only pilot quantities of usable agents produced.

The US DoD says Iran's programme began during the war with Iraq in the 1980s and that Tehran continues 'to pursue offensive biological warfare capabilities and its effort may have evolved beyond agent research and development to the capability to produce small quantities of agent. In fact, it may hold some stocks of BW agents and weapons.'

Israel and Egypt are understood to be included in the DoD's 'watch list' although they are not publicly named. The Egyptian biological warfare project began in the 1960s and in the early 1970s, President Sadat announced the presence of a stockpile of agents held in refrigerated conditions. Research continues and it may be far more than coincidence that in 1991, a major outbreak of botulism occurred in Cairo, infecting 91 people, of whom 20% died. Botulism was previously unknown in Egypt.

Of equal concern in the 21st century, is the grim prospect that terrorists will get their hands on biological warfare agents. The Japanese group Aum Shinrikyo, who, as we have seen, used sarin nerve gas in two attacks, also dispersed small-scale aerosol sprays containing botulism and anthrax on at least ten occasions, apparently without any ill-effects. They had sent members to what was then the African state of Zaire in 1992 to acquire samples of the Ebola virus. CIA Director George Tenet said in 2002 that 'terrorist groups are actively searching the Internet to acquire information and capabilities for chemical, biological, radiological and even nuclear attacks.'

In the USA, a previously secret programme, Project BACCHUS, in 1999–2000 helped the intelligence agencies estimate how easy it would be for a terrorist group to create a biological warfare agent. Officials assembled a production plant at a remote location in the Nevada desert and using commercially available substances, produced simulated agents.

Like nuclear materials, there is continuing concern that biological agents held in former Soviet facilities could fall into the hands of terrorists. Several examples of pathogens, including smallpox, plague and anthrax, have been stolen or diverted from research laboratories in Russia, Kazakhstan and Georgia in recent years. Expertise may also be acquired. In November 2001, Dr Lev Sandakhchiyev, director of

Russia's Vektor Institute, said his scientists earned just £75 a month and could be tempted to sell the smallpox virus and work on it for a well-funded terrorist group. 'Everything is possible in today's world,' he added. The CIA in 1997 replicated a Soviet biological warfare bomblet, which they feared could be used by third-party states that had acquired the technology, to assess its effectiveness.

There were reports in late 2002 that Iraqi scientists had migrated to Syria, Libya and Sudan taking their biological and chemical weapons knowledge with them under a number of government-to-government contracts, raising new fears of this expertise falling into the hands of a wider pool of terrorism.

If fears of terrorist acquisition of biological weapons seem alarmist, consider recent history. In 1972, a group of so-called 'eco-terrorists' in the USA planned to kill civilian populations in five states surrounding Chicago 'to prevent the destruction of nature.' They somehow got hold of eight pathogens, including typhoid, diphtheria, dysentery and meningitis, which they planned to disseminate by aircraft spray or by contamination of urban water supplies. The plot was foiled only when the cultures were discovered and the two leaders fled to Cuba. Twelve years later, the Rajneeshee, an Indian religious cult in Oregon, con-taminated food in salad bars with *Salmonella typhimurium* in an attempt to incapacitate voters in local elections and win political office in both the town of The Dalles and Wasco County, causing 751 cases of food poisoning, happily none fatal.

In 1991, a right-wing anti-government organisation, the Minnesota Patriots Council, planned to attack local tax and law enforcement offi-cials with the toxin ricin, extracted from castor oil beans, obtained by mail order. Members were arrested before the attacks could be mounted (by smearing ricin on door knobs or handles), and two were later convicted.

We are only too aware that al-Qa'eda, with its substantial financial resources and worldwide network of operatives, is interested in acquiring biological warfare agents and US intelligence sources grimly believe it is not a matter of 'if' an attack of this kind will be mounted on the USA, but 'when'.

Matters may be even more serious than that. The eminent British microbiologist Sir William Stewart, chief scientist to the UK govern-ment until 1995, warned in 2001 that:

There are those who say the First World War was chemical; the Second World War was nuclear and that the Third World War – God forbid – will be biological. Information on the potential use of biological agents is widely available. The offensive use of biological weapons is forbidden by international convention. Yet, published literature lists around 30 conventional microbes as potential biological warfare agents.

For the sake of the human race, let us fervently hope Sir William's forebodings are wrong.

GLOSSARY

ABM – Anti-Ballistic Missile.

AC – hydrogen cyanide. A blood agent war gas.

ADM – Atomic Demolition Munitions, nuclear land-mines, planned by NATO to destroy strategic transport hubs or large areas of buildings to hinder any invasion by Soviet conventional forces in Europe. Now in the Israeli, Chinese and possibly Iraqi nuclear inventories.

ALCM – Air Launched Cruise Missile.

ALERT – Attack and Launch Early Reporting to Theatre.

ANTELOPE – an abandoned US project to fit agile warheads and advanced penetration aids to the US Navy's Polaris A3 SLBMs.

API – Ascent Phase Intercept – knocking out an attacking missile as it climbs out of the Earth's atmosphere.

ASAT – Anti-Satellite weapon.

ASMP – *Air-Sol Moyenne Portée*. French air-launched missile armed with a single 300 kT warhead, equipping three squadrons of Mirage 2000N bombers and naval Super Etendard aircraft. A new version, the ASMP-A will enter service in 2007, arming the Mirage 2000N and the new Rafale fighter.

BACCHUS – codename for a US Defense Threat Reduction Agency project in 1999–2000 to establish the ease with which terrorists could make a biological warfare agent.

BACKFIRE – British War Office test-firing of German V-2 missile at conclusion of World War Two.

BALTAP – NATO military sub-command covering the Baltic Approaches.

BENT SPEAR – US military codeword describing a 'significant' incident involving a nuclear weapon that does not present risk of detonation or contamination.

BIG BEN – British codename for German V-2 ballistic missile attacks.

BLUE BUNNY – formerly **BROWN BUNNY** and later **BLUE PEACOCK**, a British 20 kT ADM, later cancelled.

BLUE DANUBE – First British atomic weapon, designed to be delivered by RAF V-bombers.

BLUE STEEL – UK stand-off air-launched guided bomb of 1960s that armed RAF V-bomber force.

BLUE STREAK – abortive plan for a UK silo-based medium-range ballistic missile in 1950s.

BLUE YEOMAN – codename for an early warning radar planned for a planned British ballistic missile defence system of the 1950s–60s. It was never deployed.

BMD – Ballistic Missile Defence (system).

BMDO – US Ballistic Missile Defense Organisation.

BMEWS – Ballistic Missile Early Warning System

BROKEN ARROW – US military codeword for an accident involving accidental damage to a nuclear weapon, involving non-nuclear detonation, radiation contamination, loss or theft of the device; all involving potential danger to the public.

BUMPER – US Army ordnance project to develop a two-stage rocket (with a V-2 as the launch vehicle), first tested on May 13, 1948.

BURLINGTON – codename for British Government nuclear bunker or redoubt in the Cotswolds.

BW – Biological Warfare.

BWC – (1972) Biological Weapons Convention.

BZ – 3-Quinuclidinyl benzilate. A battlefield gas inducing hallucinations and mental confusion.

CA – bromobenzylcyanide riot control agent, or tear gas.

CANOPUS – First French thermonuclear test on August 24, 1968, with a yield of 2.6 MT. This was also France's largest atmospheric test.

CBM – Confidence Building Measures. Actions taken by a nation to instil confidence that it is adhering to an arms reduction treaty or to reduce potential military tension.

CBW – Chemical and Biological Warfare (USA).

CDE/CBDE – [British] Chemical Defence Establishment, later Chemical and Biological Defence Establishment, at Porton Down, Wiltshire. Now called DSTL, Porton Down.

CEP – Circular Error Probability. A calculation to determine a missile's accuracy in delivering warheads to hit a target.

CG – phosgene. A choking battlefield gas.

CHASE – US Army operation in 1966–70 to dispose of 400,000 M55 sarin-armed artillery rockets, dumped off the coast of New York state and Florida.

CHEVALINE – The British designed and built system, improving Polaris A3 warhead penetration aids, with the specific objective of defeating Soviet ABM defences around Moscow.

CIS – Commonwealth of Independent States, the very loose confederation of former republics in the Soviet Union, formed after the superpower's collapse in 1991.

CK – cyanogen chloride. A blood agent war gas.

CN – chloroacetophenone riot control agent, or tear gas.

COELACANTHE – French project to develop a ballistic missile-firing submarine squadron, formed in June 1962.

CORONET – US codename for the planned American invasion of the main Japanese island of Honshu in March 1946.

CROSSBOW – codename for Allied intelligence gathering and countermeasures against World War Two German V cruise and ballistic missiles.

CS – O-chlorobenzylidene malonontrile. A riot control agent or tear gas.

CTBT – Comprehensive Test Ban Treaty signed in 1963 banning nuclear tests in the atmosphere, underwater and in outer space.

CW – Chemical Warfare.

CWC – Chemical Weapons Convention. The current treaty banning the use, stockpiling and production of battlefield gases, including the destruction of inventories and production facilities, which came into force in April, 1997, supported by verification procedures.

CX – Phosgene oxime. A vesicant or blistering gas.

DA – First World War British arsenic smoke, designed to penetrate enemy soldiers' gas masks.

DA – diphenylchloroarsine riot control gas, inducing vomiting.

DARK WINTER – US exercise in July 2001, simulating an attack on the USA using the smallpox virus.

Davy Crockett – US Army infantry low-yield nuclear weapon with a range of between 1,000–13,000ft, deployed between 1960 and 1971.

DAVY JONES LOCKER – US codename for the sea-dumping of 40,000 tons of chemical munitions in the Skagerrak Strait and North Sea in June 1946–August 1948.

DC – diphenylcyanoarsine riot control gas, inducing vomiting.

DEFCON – or Defense Readiness Condition, the US military alert system. DEFCON 5 is peace: DEFCON 1 is maximum war readiness.

DESERT STORM – codename for the expulsion of Iraqi occupation forces in Kuwait by a Western-led coalition of forces in the second Gulf War, 1991.

DEW – Directed Energy Weapons.

DF – Dong Feng ('East Wind'). Beijing's designation for its land-based intercontinental ballistic missiles.

DISINFECTION – German codeword for the release of chlorine gas in the Ypres salient on the Western Front on April 22, 1915.

DIVER – British codeword for German V-1 cruise missile.

DM – adamsite riot control gas, inducing vomiting. Also briefly used as a battlefield incapacitator by the British immediately after the First World War.

DoD – US Department of Defense (the Pentagon).

DOWNFALL – Overall US codename for the planned American invasion of the Japanese homeland islands at the end of World War Two.

DP – diphosgene. A choking battlefield gas.

DSP – Defense Support Program, the US early warning satellite system.

DSTL – [British] Defence Science and Technology Laboratory, Porton Down, formerly the Chemical Defence Establishment and latterly, the Chemical and Biological Defence Establishment.

DULL SWORD – US military codeword describing an incident involving a nuclear weapon that is not 'significant'.

ED – ethyldichloroarsine vesicant or blistering gas.

EKV – Exo-atmospheric kill vehicle. A system of destroying warheads in flight outside the Earth's atmosphere.

ELDO – European Launcher Development Organisation – former European programme for civilian satellite development.

EMP – Electro-Magnetic Pulse, the huge blast of energy released in a nuclear explosion that can destroy communications and other electronic/electrical devices. A similar phenomenon occurs in electrical storms.

ER – Enhanced Radiation.

EWR – Early Warning Radar.

FADED GIANT – US military codeword covering incidents involving nuclear reactors.

FALSTAFF – codename for British Chevaline penetration aids carrier mounted atop the Polaris A3 TK missile.

FFA – *Flygtekniska Försöksanstalken,* Swedish defence and aeronautical research institute.

FIRST LIGHTNING – Soviet codename for the test of its first atomic weapon on August 29, 1949. In the West, it was called 'Joe-1' after the Soviet leader, Marshal Josef Stalin.

FOST – *Force Oceanique Stratégique,* the French ballistic missile submarine squadron.

FROG – Free Rocket Over Ground, an early Soviet short-range surface-to-surface ballistic missile.

GA – Tabun nerve agent.

GB – Sarin nerve agent.

GBI – Ground-Based Interceptor.

GD – Soman nerve agent.

GE – nerve agent battlefield gas.

GERANIUM – US Army operation in 1948 to dump, at sea, its entire holdings of the lewisite chemical agent.

GERBOISE BLEUE – first French test of a nuclear weapon on February 13 1960.

GF – nerve agent battlefield vapour, abandoned by the USA but later produced by Iraq.

GHQ – General Head Quarters.

GLCM – Ground Launched Cruise Missile.

GMT – Greenwich Mean Time.

GPS – Global Positioning System.

GRABLE – codename for the first test-firing of a nuclear artillery round, fired by the US Army's giant 280mm 'atomic cannon' at a target area seven miles away at Frenchman Flat, Nevada Test site, on May 25, 1953.

GREEN GRANITE – Early British 1–3 MT thermonuclear freefall bomb.

GRU – *Glavnoye Razvedyvatelnoye Upravlenie*, the Russian Defence Ministry main intelligence administration or agency, responsible for collecting overseas military intelligence.

GTO – Geostationery Transfer Orbit.

H – First World War British code letter for mustard gas (dichlorethyl-sulphide), the battlefield vesicant or blistering gas.

HARNESS – codeword for British trials with anthrax off the island of Antigua in the Caribbean in 1949.

HD – Sulphur mustard vesicant or blistering gas.

HE – High Explosive.

HENDO – High Endo-Atmospheric ABM interceptor.

HEO – High Earth Orbit.

HN – Nitrogen mustard vesicant or blistering gas.

HOB – Height of [nuclear] burst above a target.

Hochdruckpumpe – 'high pressure pump', German term for their Second World War V-3 supergun.

HOE – Homing Overlay Experiment, part of the US ballistic missile defence research and development programme.

HTK – Hit to Kill. ABM warheads that use kinetic energy to destroy attacking warheads.

HURRICANE – First British atomic weapon test, exploded on board the war-surplus frigate *Plym*, in Monte Bello islands, off north-west coast of Australia on October 3, 1952.

HYDRA – RAF Bomber Command raid on Peenemünde on August 17–18, 1943.

IAEA – International Atomic Energy Authority, based in Vienna.

ICBM – Inter-Continental Ballistic Missile (normally land-based).

INDIGO HAMMER – 6kT lightweight British nuclear warhead planned to arm Bloodhound SAMs in an abortive British ballistic missile defence system in the 1950s. Formerly codenamed BLUE FOX.

INF – Intermediate Nuclear Force treaty, or 'Treaty between the USA and the USSR on the Elimination of their Intermediate Range and Shorter Range Missiles' in Europe, (1987).

IRBM – Intermediate Range Ballistic Missile.

ITTISALAT – Libyan codename in the early 1980s for its programme to develop or acquire ballistic missiles.

IVY – Codename for US first test of a hydrogen bomb in shot 'Mike' on the island of Elugelab in the Pacific on October 31, 1952.

IZLIS – codename for the Egyptian project for production and weaponisation of chemical weapons in the 1960s.

JCS – (US) Joint Chiefs of Staff.

KEW – Kinetic Energy Weapon.

KIRSHKERN – 'Cherrystone'. German codename for prototype V-1 cruise missiles.

KRAFTWERKE NORDWEST – 'power station north west'. The German codename to disguise a V-2 launch site in Pas de Calais, France.

kT – Kiloton. The explosive power of a nuclear weapon, equivalent to a thousand tons of TNT.

KW – Kilowatt, a measurement of electrical power.

L – lewisite vesicant or blistering gas.

LAA – Launch (missiles) on Attack Assessment. Launching a retaliatory strike after working out the size and scale of the enemy strike.

LEAP – Lightweight Exo-Atmospheric Projectile. An anti-ballistic missile weapon.

LENDO – Low endo-atmospheric ABM interceptor. An anti-ballistic missile weapon.

LEO – Low Earth Orbit.

LGM – US designation for a silo-launched Inter-Continental Ballistic Missile.

LITTLE FELLAH – test firings of the Davy Crockett atomic anti-tank weapon on July 7 and 17, 1962 at the USA's Nevada test site.

LoADS – Low Altitude Defense System, the US Army planned successor to the Sprint high speed BMD system.

LOI – Launch (missiles) on or after Impact by enemy missiles and the resultant nuclear explosions.

LOOKING GLASS – USAF's Strategic Command's airborne command post that was airborne 24 hours a day during the period 1961–90.

LOW – Launch (missiles) on Warning, generated by radar indications of an incoming attack by enemy missiles.

LOX – Liquid oxygen.

LTA – Launch (missiles) Through Attack. This is adopted if the attack is mounted in salvoes of incoming missiles and allows an accurate assessment of the scale of the attack. Some damage to one's own missile capability is assumed before launching a counterstrike.

LUA – Launch (missiles) Under Attack. Retaliatory response after determining that an attack by enemy missiles in under way. In US parlance, this would be a 'massive attack'.

MAD – Mutual Assured Destruction.

MADM – Medium Atomic Demolition Munition, weighing less than 400lbs, deployed by the US Army in 1965, with a variable 1–15 kT yield W-45 warhead.

MAP – Multiple Aim Point.

MARV – Manoeuvrable Re-entry Vehicle.

MELBA – codename for first South African fission device.

MHz – Megahertz, measurement of radio frequency.

MIRV – Multiple Independently targetable Re-entry Vehicle(s).

MITTELWERKE – German underground factory in the Harz Mountains producing V-2 and V-1 missiles.

MRBM – Medium Range Ballistic Missile.

MRE – [British] Microbiological Research Establishment at Porton Down operating between 1957–1979.

MRV – Multiple Re-entry Vehicle.

MT – Megaton – explosive power of a nuclear weapon, equivalent to a million tons of TNT.

MTBF – Mean Time Between Failures, a measurement of a weapons system's reliability.

MW – Megawatt – unit of power generation used in nuclear reactors.

NAOC – National Airborne Operations Center, the E4-B aircraft used by the US President and Secretary of Defense in national emergencies.

NATO – North Atlantic Treaty Organisation, the military alliance of Western European and North American nations, founded on April 4, 1949 to oppose the Soviet Union and her satellite states in Eastern Europe.

NBC – Nuclear, biological, chemical (warfare).

NCA – National Command Authority, (USA).

NDB – Nuclear Depth Bomb.

NMD – National Missile Defense, the late 1990s' reincarnation of a US anti-ballistic missile system, designed to protect against attacks against the US homeland by 'rogue nations' ballistic missiles.

NORAD – North American Air Defence.

NPT – Non-Proliferation Treaty, 1970, covering the transfer of nuclear weapons technology.

NRRC – Nuclear Risk Reduction Centres, set up in 1987 in Washington and Moscow.

NUCFLASH – US military code for the accidental or unauthorised detonation, or possible detonation, of a nuclear or thermonuclear weapon.

NWE – Nuclear Weapons Effects – blast, thermal and ionising radiation, residual radiation and electro-magnetic pulse.

OKB – Russian missile design bureau.

OLYMPIC – US codename for the invasion of the southernmost Japanese island of Kyushu at the end of the Second World War.

OPCW – Organisation for the Prohibition of Chemical Weapons, the agency, based in The Hague, that oversees the implementation of the Chemical Weapons Convention.

ORANGE HERALD – British 0.72MT nuclear warhead planned for the abortive Blue Streak medium-range silo-launched ballistic missile.

OTH – Over the horizon (long-range radars).

OVERCAST – Secret Anglo-American deal at the end of World War Two about the fate of the German Peenemünde V-2 scientists.

PAC – Penetration Aids Carrier, the British version of a warhead 'bus' that would sow Polaris A3-TK CHEVALINE warheads and decoys during flight in space.

PAL – Permissive Action Link, code system that arms a nuclear weapon, normally by punching in a code number or combination word.

PAPERCLIP – US operation at the end of World War Two to collect and transport German Peenemünde V-2 scientists to Washington DC.

PBV – Post Boost phase Vehicle.

PD – phenyldichloroarsine vesicant or blistering gas.

PENGUIN – German codeword for V-2 campaign against England.

PING-PONG – codename for Polish resistance sources who provided London with information about the German rocket research station at Peenemünde.

PLA (N) – People's Liberation Army (Navy), China's naval force.

PS – chloropicrin riot control agent or tear gas.

psi – pounds per square inch, the measurement of static overpressures or dynamic pressure caused by a nuclear explosion.

RAF – Royal Air Force. The UK's air force.

R&D – Research and Development.

RED BEARD – early British freefall bomb with a yields of 15–20kT carried by Royal Navy Scimitar and Buccaneer aircraft.

REDUT – codename of a series of Russian exercises of nuclear command and control system in 1996–7.

REICHENBERG – codename for German project for a manned V-1 cruise missile.

RIVET CAP – USAF codeword for operation to deactivate Titan 2 ICBM force from US silos, ending in June 1987.

ROA – Ride Out Attack. Postponing a nuclear retaliatory response until the enemy's pre-emptive strike is over,

RUMPELKAMMER – German codename for V-1 cruise missile offensive against England.

RV – Re-entry Vehicle. A missile warhead.

RVF – Rift Valley Fever.

SA – arsine blood agent war gas.

SABOTAGE – codename for trials in the 1960s on London Underground system to monitor spread of bacteria.

SACEUR – Supreme Allied Commander Europe – one of the top NATO military commands.

SADM – Special Atomic Demolition Munition, weighing just 163lbs, with a yield of 0.01 kTs and contained in a metal suitcase, deployed by the US Army.

SAFEGUARD – the US ballistic missile defence system providing protection for ICBM bases in the mid-West of the USA.

SALT – Strategic Arms Limitation Treaty.

SAM – Surface-to-air missile (anti-aircraft or anti-missile missile).

SAMSON Option – The Israeli plan for an all-out nuclear attack on its enemies if its population centres are placed in jeopardy by an enemy offensive.

SANDY – US plan to launch a V-2 from the flight deck of the brand new US aircraft carrier *Midway* in the Atlantic, almost miraculously achieved on September 6, 1947 without loss of life or injury.

SAR – Synthetic Aperture Radar.

SAS – Sealed Authenticator System. A method of validating missile launch codes.

SCHOTTERWERKE NORDWEST – 'rubbleworks north west', German codename and cover for a V-2 launch site hidden in a quarry at St-Omer, France.

SDI – Strategic Defense Initiative (former USA ballistic missile defence programme).

SENTINEL – the US ballistic missile defence system planned to provide area defence and protection for 25 and later 52 US cities.

SH – NATO designator for Russian Sary Shagan anti-ballistic missile system.

SHAEF – Supreme HQs, Allied Expeditionary Forces, controlling Allied forces in the Second World War invasion of Europe.

SHAPE – Supreme HQs, Allied Powers in Europe. Major NATO command, controlling the Alliance's forces in Europe.

SIGINT – Signals intelligence – eavesdropping on an adversary's radio communications.

SIOP – Single Integrated Operational Plan, the US nuclear war plan.

SLAM – Stand-off Land Attack Missile.

SLBM – Submarine Launched Ballistic Missile.

SLCM – Submarine Launched Cruise Missile.

SK – Ethyl- idoacetate, an early British irritant battlefield gas.

SMILING BUDDHA – First Indian nuclear test, of a 15 kT fission device on May 18 1974 at the Pokhara range in the Rajasthan desert.

SNDV – Strategic Nuclear Delivery Vehicle.

SNLE – *Sous-Marines Nucléaire Lanceur d'engines balistique*. French designation for a nuclear-powered submarine armed with strategic ballistic missiles

SOLIMOES – reported secret Brazilian military project to build air-dropped nuclear weapons in 1964–85.

SOW – Stand Off Weapon. A missile or self-propelled bomb launched or dropped by an aircraft some distance from the intended target to avoid enemy SAM defences.

SPRN – *Sistema preduprezhdeniya o raketnom napademii,* the Russian missile attack warning system.

SRAM – (USAF) Short Range Attack Missile.

SRHIT – Short Range Hit-to-Kill missile.

SS – NATO designator for Russian surface-to-surface missiles.

SSBN – Nuclear-powered submarine armed with strategic ballistic missiles.

SSBS – *Sol-Sol-Balistique-Stratégique* (French strategic silo-launched ballistic missile).

SSN – Nuclear-powered hunter-killer submarine, designed to destroy enemy SSBNs, submarines or surface shipping.

START – Strategic Arms Reduction Treaty. START 1 was signed on July 31, 1991 and the successor START 2 on January 3, 1993. The latter was ratified by the Russian Federation in May 2000.

SUBROC – [Anti] Submarine Rocket (USA).

SUPER ANTELOPE – original codename for British KH 793 Chevaline warheads.

TACAMO – Former US Navy 'take charge and move out' EC-130Q airborne command aircraft used to transmit missile launch orders to ballistic missile submarines.

TBM – Theatre Ballistic Missile.

TBMD – Theatre Ballistic Missile Defence.

TEL – Transport/Erector/Launcher vehicle, a mobile launcher for ballistic missiles.

TELAR – Transport/Erector/Launcher and Radar vehicle, a mobile launcher for ballistic missiles equipped with radar.

TERCOM – Terrain Comparison or Terrain Contour matching, an accurate guidance system for missiles that follows a satellite-map of land overflown *en route* to the target.

TGM – Terminally Guided Missile.

TIR – Terminal Imaging Radar or Tracking and Illuminating Radar.

TLAM-C – Tomahawk Land Attack Missile – Conventional (armed with an HE warhead) (USA).

TLAM-D – Tomahawk Land Attack Missile – Submunitions warhead (USA).

TLAM-N – Tomahawk Land Attack Missile – Nuclear.

TNF – Theatre Nuclear Forces.

TRINITY – codename for first above-ground test of an atomic weapon in New Mexico on July 16, 1945.

TSAR BOMBA – 'King of Bombs'. The largest nuclear device yet exploded, equally more than 50 MTs. Detonated by the Soviet Union at Novaya Zemlya on October 30 1961.

TUBE ALLOYS – Early British codename for atomic weapons.

UDMH – Unsymmetrical dimethyl hydrazine, Russian liquid pro-pellent fuel for missiles.

UHF – Ultra High Frequency radio

UKWMO – UK Warning and Monitoring Organisation, the British Cold War system to inform the population of impending nuclear attack and subsequent spread of radioactive fallout.

UMSPANNWERKE C – transformer station C. German codename to disguise a V-2 radio guidance site at Roquetoire, France.

UN – United Nations.

UNIVERSAL – Russian codename for a project to develop two new ICBMs in the 1980s to rationalise Moscow's land-based missile deter-rent force.

UNSCOM – United Nations Special Commission, the inspection of Iraq's weapons of mass destruction facilities after DESERT STORM.

USAAF – US Army Air Force – the World War Two US air arm.

USSR – Union of Soviet Socialist Republics.

V-series – family of highly persistent toxic nerve agents: **VE, VM** and **VX,** discovered in the 1950s.

VVS – *Voyenno-Vozdushyye Sily.* The Soviet air forces.

WASSERWERKE 2 – 'waterworks 2'. German codename and cover for a V-2 and V-2 launch site at Brécourt on France's Cherbourg Peninsula.

VEGETATION – British codeword for a plan to drop five million anthrax-infected linseed cattle-cakes onto German pasture-land as an anti-livestock weapon.

WFZ – Weapons Free Zone.

VIOLET CLUB – hybrid hydrogen bomb, briefly in RAF service from late 1958.

VIOLET FRIEND – codename for abortive British ballistic missile defence system of the mid-1950s.

VIOLET MIST – codename for a British 1.5 MT ADM abandoned in 1961.

WHITEBAIT – RAF Bomber Command diversionary raid to facilitate the attack on Peenemünde during the night of August 17–18, 1943.

WHO – World Health Organisation, an UN agency.

WIESE – 'meadow', German codename for the HDPV-3 super gun.

WMD –Weapons of Mass Destruction.

YELLOW RIVER – codename for a target illuminating radar planned for an abortive British ballistic missile defence system in the 1950s–60s.

YELLOW SUN – British freefall nuclear bomb, with yields of 750 kT–1MT, that armed RAF V-bombers.

BIBLIOGRAPHY

Adams, James: 'The untold story of Russia's secret biological weapons', *Sunday Times,* London, March 27 1994.

Albright, David: 'South Africa and the affordable bomb', *Bulletin of the Atomic Scientists,* Vol. 50, July/August 1990.

Ali, Javed, Rodrigues, Leslie and Moodie, Michael: *Jane's Chemical Biological Defense Guidebook,* Alexandria, (Virginia), 1998.

Anon: 'London's 80 days' (V-1 attacks) *Evening Standard,* (London) September 7 1944.

Anon: 'Saudi missiles now operational', *Flight International*, June 6 1990.

Anon: 'Saudi Arabia takes steps to acquire nuclear weapons', *Defense and Foreign Affairs,* October 30, 2002.

Arnold, Lorna: *Britain and the H-Bomb,* London, 2001.

Bermudez, Joseph: 'Ballistic missile development in Libya', *Jane's Intelligence Review,* January 2003.

Bernstein, B. J.: 'The Birth of the US Biological Warfare Program', *Scientific American,* Vol. 256, 1987.

Brankowitz, W. R.: *Chemical Weapons Movement. History Compilation.* Office of the Program Manager for Chemical Munitions, Aberdeen Proving Ground, Maryland (SAPEO-CDE-IS-87001) June 1987.

Carle, Christopher, 'Fighting fire with fire: missiles against missiles', in 'NMD Jumps the Gun', *Disarmament Forum,* United Nations, 2001.

Carus, Seth: 'Iranian Nuclear, Biological and Chemical Weapons: Implications and Responses,' *Middle East Review of International*

Affairs, March 1998.

Cohen, Avner: *Israel and the Bomb,* Columbia, 1998.

Collier, Basil: *Battle of the V Weapons,* London, 1964.

Compton, J. A. F.: *Military Chemical and Biological Agents. Chemical and Toxicological Properties,* Caldewell (New Jersey), 1988.

Cordesman, Anthony J: *The Iran–Iraq War and Western Security, 1984–87,* London, 1987.

Dàil Éireann *Official Report,* Vol. 451, March 23 1995. (Chemical weapon dumping off Irish waters.)

Defense Intelligence Agency: *Soviet Biological Warfare Threat,* Washington, 1986.

Derbes, V. J.: 'De Mussis and the Great Plague of 1348 – a Forgotten Episode of Bacteriological Warfare', *Journal of the American Medical Association,* Vol. 196, 1966.

Eitzen, Edward and Takafuji, Ernest: *Historical Overview of Biological Warfare,* in Zajtchuk, 1997.

Ekeus, R.: *Iraq's Biological Weapons Programme: UNSCOM's Experience,* Memorandum report to the UN Security Council, New York, 1996.

Fialka, J: 'CIA says North Korea Appears Active in Biological, Nuclear Arms', *Wall Street Journal,* February 25, 1993.

Franz, David, Parrott, Cheryl and Takafuji, Ernest: *The US Biological Warfare and Biological Defense Programs* in Zajtchuk, 1997.

Freedman, Prof. Lawrence: *Britain and Nuclear Weapons,* London, 1981.

Gertz, Bill: 'Saudis withheld missile to spare civilians', *Washington Times,* June 10, 1991.

— 'US secrets aboard latest Chinese sub', *Washington Times,* December 6 1999.

— 'Moscow tests new missile', *Washington Times,* July 30, 2001.

Gilchrist, H L.: *Residual Effects of Wartime Gases,* Washington, 1933.

Gott, Richard: 'The Evolution of the Independent British Deterrent', *International Affairs,* Vol. 39, April 1964.

Hackett, James T: 'Moscow's overlooked missile defenses', *Washington Times,* May 17, 2000.

Hansard (Official House of Commons Report) March 31, 1995. (British chemical munitions dumping policy.) December 16 1994. (Gruinard Island).

Hansen, Chuck: *US Nuclear Weapons: The Secret History.* New York, 1988.

Henderson, Prof. D. A.: *Bioterrorism as a Public Health Threat,* www.cdc.gov. 1998.

Hennessy, Peter: *The Secret State: Whitehall and the Cold War,* London, 2002.

– *Muddling Through, Power, Politics and the Quality of Government in Postwar Britain,* London, 1996.

– *The Prime Minister: The Office and its Holders since 1945,* London, 2000.

Hoon, Shim Jae: 'Seoul concern over North's [Korea] biochemical stockpile', *Jane's Defence Weekly,* December 5, 2001.

Hutchinson, Robert: 'Chevaline: UK's response to Soviet ABM system', *Jane's Defence Weekly,* December 15, 1984.

Hylton, A. R.: *History of Chemical Warfare Plants and Facilities in the United States,* US Arms Control and Disarmament Agency, Washington, 1972.

Infield, Glen: *Disaster at Bari,* New York, 1971.

Iraq's Weapons of Mass Destruction: The Assessment of the British Government, London, September 2002.

Isby, David: 'Syrian Scud carried a simulated chemical warhead', *Jane's Missiles and Rockets,* September 2001.

Jeffery, K.: *History of Chemical and Biological Warfare: An American Perspective.* See Zajtchuk, 1997.

Joy, Robert: *Historical Aspects of Medical Defense against Chemical Warfare.* See Zajtchuk, 1997.

Koch, Andrew: 'US exposes previously secret work on biological warfare threat', *Jane's Defence Weekly,* September 12, 2001.

Kunz, R. & Muller, R-D.: *Giftgas gegen Abdel Krim. Deutschland, Spanien under der Gaskrieg in Spanisch-Marokko 1922–27,* Freiburg, 1990.

Lake, Darren & Burger, Kim: 'US breakthrough in detecting bio agents', *Jane's Defence Weekly,* January 23 2002.

Lennox, Duncan: *Jane's Strategic Weapons Systems,* issue 37, London 2002.

Levine, Alan J.: *The Strategic Bombing of Germany 1940–45,* Westport, 1992.

Livingstone, N. C. & Douglass, J. D .J.: *CBW – the Poor Man's Atomic Bomb,* Institute for Foreign Policy Analysis, Cambridge, Massachusetts, 1984.

Malone, Peter: *The British Nuclear Deterrent,* London, 1984.

McNamara, Robert: 'American ABM Deployment', *Survival,* November 1967. (Extracted from his speech of September 18, 1967.)

  Blundering into Disaster: Surviving the First Century of the Nuclear Age, London, 1987.

McWilliams, James & Steel, James: *Gas! The Battle for Ypres, 1915,* Ontario, 1985.

Menaul, Stewart: *Countdown, Britain's Strategic Nuclear Forces,* London, 1980.

Meselson, M., Guillemin J., Hugh-Jones M., *et al:* 'The Sverdlovsk Anthrax Outbreak of 1979', *Science,* Vol. 266, 1994.

Novichkov, Nikolai: 'Russia to retain MIRVs beyond START II deadline'. *Jane's Defence Weekly,* August 28, 2002.

Office of Technology Assessment, US Congress: *The Effects of Nuclear War,* Montclair (New Jersey), 1980.

Oppenheimer, Andy: 'Russian Biological Weapons Materials: the Price of Non- Proliferation', *Jane's Defence Weekly,* September 23, 2002.

Paxman J. & Harris R.: *A Higher Form of Killing: The Secret Story of Chemical and Biological Warfare,* New York, 1992.

Plunkett, Geoff: *Chemical Warfare Agent Sea Dumping off Australia,* Royal Australian Navy Hydrographic Office website, www.hydro.gov.au. January 2000.

Polmar, N. & Allen, T.: 'Poisonous invasion prelude', *Pittsburgh Post-Gazette,* August 4, 1995.

 —*Codename Downfall: The Secret World War II Plan to Invade Japan,* New York, 1995.

Prentice, A. M: *Chemicals in War: A Treatise on Chemical Warfare,* New York, 1937.

Public Record Office, London –

AIR 2/13720 – Blue Steel stand-off missile proposal 1957–9.

AIR 2/13748 –Warhead for Blue Steel. 1953–64.

AIR 8/2145 – Development and production of Blue Steel guided bomb. 1956–61.

AIR 14/4350 – Aircraft safety in delivery of YELLOW SUN and Blue Steel nuclear weapons.

AIR 19/833 – British replacement of nuclear weapons if Skybolt fails to be available.

AIR 20/10620 – Deployment of Thor missiles in UK.

AIR 20/10668 – Design study of anti-ballistic missile defence system, 1959.

AIR 40/1773 – Press statement on September 7, 1944, on V-1 attacks.

AVIA 9225 – History of Blue Streak.

CAB 21/4979 – Skybolt missile.

CAB 121/214 – British Cabinet papers relating to 'V' weapons: CROSSBOW committee.

CAB 121/215 – British Cabinet papers relating to the V-2 and Operation BACKFIRE.

CAB 130/2 – Cabinet sub-committee GEN 75 discussions on need for a British atomic bomb.

CAB 130/16 – Cabinet sub-committee GEN 163 decision to build a British atomic bomb.

DEFE 4/224 – Nuclear Targets in the UK. Assumptions for Planning.

DEFE 7/1392 – Blueprints for silos for abortive British medium range ballistic missile, Blue Streak.

DEFE 19/115 – Nuclear tests and ballistic missile defence system. Correspondence. January 1, 1962–December 31, 1962.

DEFE 25/49 – British Cabinet papers on nuclear retaliation.

FO 371/149664 – French military interest in Blue Streak. 1960.

HO 186/2352 – Home Office papers on V-1 attacks on London.

WO 33/1443 – Chemical Defence Research Department Report, 1936.

WO 33.1634 – Chemical Defence Research Department Report, 1938.

WO 142/243 – Report on German Chemical Warfare organisation and policy 1914–18, c. 1921.

WO 142/240 – Offensive chemical warfare prior to formation of Scientific Advisory Committee, 1915.

WO 158/123 – War diary of 'Special Section, Royal Engineers, Shanghai'.

WO 158/434 – World War I British Army gas casualties. Report on activity of British Army 'Special Brigade' during World War I.

WO 188/211 – League of Nations Preparatory Commission for Disarmament Conference: chemical warfare, 1926–30.

WO 188/357 – Development of British offensive gas in World War I.

WO 188/653 – War Cabinet Bacteriological Warfare Committee minutes 1939–42.

WO188/658 – Operational Panel of Bacteriological Warfare Committee minutes, 1943–44.

WO 188/829 – H (mustard gas) tactical uses. 1942–3.

WO 188/841 – MI 10 (Military Intelligence 10) chemical warfare bulletins 1943–5.

WO 208/406 – Japanese use of chemical agents.

WO 208/3991 – Translation of Japanese documents on bacteriological warfare, May 1945.

WO 208/3992 – Japanese bacteriological warfare activities in Rangoon, June 1945.

WO 208/3993 – 'Concerning bacteriological warfare' a paper by Dr Enyro Hojo, Chief Army Medical Officer, 9 Army Medical School, July 1945.

WO 208/3995 – Japanese use of chemical agents in Second World War.

WO 208/4279 – Correspondence in German official files on organisation of bacteriological research, 1943–4.

WO 219/1248 – German preparations for chemical warfare in World War II.

WO 219/4962 – Civilian casualties caused by V-1 and V-2 weapon stocks in Belgium.

Rhodes, Richard: *The Making of the Atomic Bomb*, London, 1980.

Richardson, Doug: 'Israel's triad could deter TBM attacks', *Jane's Missiles and Rockets,* June 2001.

Rodan, Steve, & Hughes, Robin: 'Israel starts assembly of second Arrow 2 battery', *Jane's Defence Weekly,* October 10, 2002.

Robinson, Julian: *The Problem of Chemical and Biological Warfare,* in 'The Rise of CB Weapons', Stockholm International Peace Research Institute, Stockholm, 1980.

Sharad, Joshi: 'Israel's Nuclear Policy: A Cost Benefit Analysis' *Strategic Analysis,* Vol. 23, March 2000.

Shoham, Dany: 'Chemical and Biological Weapons in Egypt', *Nonproliferation Review*, Spring–Summer, 1998.

Sirak, Michael: 'Nuclear weapons treaty leaves key issues unaddressed', *Jane's Defence Weekly,* May 22, 2002.

Spratt, Prof. Brian: *Independent Review of the Possible Health Hazards of Largescale Release of Bacteria during the Dorset Defence Trials,* London, June 2002.

Stubbs, M.: 'CBR – A power for peace' [US] *Armed Forces Chemical Journal*, Vol. 13, No. 3. 1959.

Terraine, John: *The Right of the Line: The Royal Air Force in the European War 1939–45*, London, 1985.

Tucker, Dr. Jonathan B: *Historical Trends Related to Bio-terrorism: An Empirical Analysis.* www.cdc.gov. 1999.

US Army: *US Army Activity in the US Biological Warfare Programs 1942–77.* Special Report to Congress, Washington, 1977.

US Chemical Corps: *Summary of Major Events and Problems FY58.* Army Chemical Center, Maryland, March 1959.

US Chemical Warfare Service: *US Chemical Warfare Policy* (draft) June 14, 1945.

US Department of Defense: *FY 73 SAFEGUARD Rationale,* February 27, 1972. US National Archives, Records of the Office of Undersecretary of State 1969–73. Box 4. George Washington University.

—*Soviet Military Power, 1985,* Washington 1985.

—*Soviet Military Power: Prospects for Change 1989,* Washington, 1989.

—*Chemical and Biological Defense Program Annual Report 2001,* Washington, 2002.

Williams P. & Wallace D.: *Unit 731: Secret Biological Warfare in World War II,* New York, 1989.

Warthin, Arthur & Weller, Carl: *The Medical Aspects of Mustard Gas Poisoning,* St Louis, 1919.

Weisse, A. B.: 'From Trench Warfare to War on Cancer', *Hospital Practitioner,* Vol. 27, 1992.

WHO consultants: *Health Aspects of Chemical and Biological Weapons,* World Health Organisation, Geneva, 1969.

Woolven, Robin: 'London and the V-Weapons, 1943–45', *Royal United Services Institute for Defence Studies Journal,* London, February 2002.

www.v2rocket.com. V2 rocket resource site.

Yost, David: *Soviet Ballistic Missile Defence and the Western Alliance,* Cambridge (Mass.) 1988.

Zajtchuk, Brig. Gen. Russ (general editor): *Textbook of Military Medical Aspects of Chemical and Biological Warfare,* US Army Medical Research Institute of Chemical Defense, Washington DC, 1997.

Zaloga, Steven: 'Moscow's ABM shield continues to crumble', *Jane's Intelligence Review,* February 1999.

Zaloga, Steven: 'Red Star Wars', *Jane's Intelligence Review,* May 1997.